LIBRARY OF RELIGIOUS BIOGRAPHY

Edited by Mark A. Noll, Nathan O. Hatch,
and Allen C. Guelzo

The LIBRARY OF RELIGIOUS BIOGRAPHY is a series of original biographies on important religious figures throughout American and British history.

The authors are well-known historians, each a recognized authority in the period of religious history in which his or her subject lived and worked. Grounded in solid research of both published and archival sources, these volumes link the lives of their subjects — not always thought of as "religious" persons — to the broader cultural contexts and religious issues that surrounded them. Each volume includes a bibliographical essay and an index to serve the needs of students, teachers, and researchers.

Marked by careful scholarship yet free of footnotes and academic jargon, the books in this series are well-written narratives meant to be *read* and *enjoyed* as well as studied.

LIBRARY OF RELIGIOUS BIOGRAPHY

Charles G. Finney and the Spirit of American Evangelicalism

Charles E. Hambrick-Stowe

WILLIAM B. EERDMANS PUBLISHING COMPANY
GRAND RAPIDS, MICHIGAN / CAMBRIDGE, U.K.

© 1996 Wm. B. Eerdmans Publishing Co.
255 Jefferson Ave. S.E., Grand Rapids, Michigan 49503 /
P.O. Box 163, Cambridge CB3 9PU U.K.

Printed in the United States of America

01 00 99 98 97 96   7 6 5 4 3 2 1

Library of Congress Cataloging-in-Publication Data

Hambrick-Stowe, Charles E.
    Charles G. Finney and the spirit of American Evangelicalism /
Charles E. Hambrick-Stowe.
        p.   cm. — (Library of religious biography)
    Includes bibliographical references and index.
    ISBN 0-8028-0129-3 (pbk.: alk. paper)
    1. Finney, Charles Grandison, 1792-1875. 2. Congregational
churches — United States — Clergy — Biography. 3. Evangelists — United
States — Biography. 4. Revivals — United States — History — 19th
century. 5. Evangelicalism — United States — History — 19th century.
I. Title. II. Series.
BX7260.F47H35 1996
285.8′092 — dc20
[B]   96-16697
                                                                  CIP

Contents

v

CHARLES G. FINNEY

Foreword

It would be hard to tell the story of the American republic before the Civil War without giving Charles Grandison Finney one of the starring roles. And yet, pinning down what it was in Finney that made him so important has proven highly difficult. Very few biographers have found much of interest in Finney as a theologian, and even those who hang his importance on his fame as a preacher of mass religious revival usually find little that was permanent or even admirable in Finney's revivals. Finney is most often assigned a niche as a cultural symbol, a sort of religious counterpart to his political contemporary Andrew Jackson. Historians from Whitney Cross and Perry Miller to Timothy L. Smith and Paul Johnson have loved to paint Finney as the perfect Jacksonian democrat, the enemy of aristocratic Calvinism, the apostle of do-it-yourself salvation. By these conventional accounts, Andrew Jackson was the spirit of the age and Finney was his prophet.

And yet, for those who have read Finney beyond his well-known and deliberately provocative *Lectures on Revivals of*

Religion (1835) and *Memoirs* (1876), Finney turns out to be quite a different character. A close reading of Finney's papers, as well as his articles in the *Oberlin Evangelist* from 1838 to 1862 and his less-well-known books, shows him to have been persistently hostile to Jacksonian politics. And, in startling contrast to his reputation as an anti-Calvinist, Finney did not hesitate to speak of himself as a disciple and admirer of Edwards and the New England Theology. No wonder that on rare occasions some modern interpreters, caught between the Finney they read and the Finney they have read about, simply confess an element of bewilderment about the man.

Part of the confusion over Finney has surely been generated by Finney himself. His famous *Memoirs* are rich in self-congratulation over his successes as a revivalist in upstate New York, Philadelphia, Boston, and elsewhere, but they are curiously opaque about his intellectual and theological development. Modern historians have also had difficulty sorting out Finney's complex and idiosyncratic theological vocabulary. In the process, they have written off that vocabulary as just another example of Finney's eccentricities or else have taken it as one more example of his rebellion against conventional theology. But many of these supposed eccentricities are actually rhetorical tag lines that link Finney to a very specific theological context, one that has little relationship to the assumptions of Jacksonian democracy but one that owes a very great deal indeed to the very Edwardsean Calvinism Finney is supposed to have repudiated.

It is one of the major achievements of Charles Hambrick-Stowe in this new biography to have penetrated both of these veils of difficulty. Hambrick-Stowe's account of the life and career of Finney benefits from the first access any major Finney biographer has had to the newly restored full text of the *Memoirs,* edited by Garth Rosell and Richard A. G. Dupuis (Zondervan, 1989), and he has made extensive use of the Charles G. Finney Papers in the Oberlin College Archives and the files of Oberlin's volatile and widely circulated publications

The Oberlin Evangelist and *The Oberlin Quarterly Review*. Hambrick-Stowe thereby discovers a Finney who was certainly no democratic loner. This Finney emerges from the context of New England migration to upstate New York at the turn of the eighteenth century, when the intellectual climate was heavy with the thunderous preaching of the Edwardsean "New Divinity." Hambrick-Stowe then positions the young-adult Finney within a lively coterie of Edwards-influenced "New School" revivalists in the rural New York churches formed by the 1801 Plan of Union (which licensed joint Congregationalist-Presbyterian church-planting efforts in upstate New York). He also shifts the conventional story of Finney's stormy relationship with his Presbyterian mentor, George Washington Gale (in which Gale usually poses as the Calvinistic foil to Finney's sui generis Arminianism), to a much more powerful version of the relationship in which their controversy is transformed into an intellectual sparring contest between the rival Calvinisms of Princeton and New England in the early Republic. Even John Williamson Nevin's acidulous and long-lived denunciations of Finney — that Finney had substituted "salvation by feeling for salvation by faith" — are set in a new relationship through Hambrick-Stowe's account of Finney's connections with dissident German Reformed pastors who were already questioning Nevin and the "Mercersburg Theology." Perhaps the most surprising contribution Hambrick-Stowe has to make concerns Finney's family life — his three marriages, his complex and sometimes wayward children, his own private yearnings to flee from the public limelight to a quiet farmer's life in New York — little of which has been integrated into other Finney biographies.

In the largest sense, Hambrick-Stowe presents a Finney-in-context. That signals an important reversal of the tendency of Finney biographers from G. Frederick Wright (1893) to Keith Hardman (1987) to take Finney at his own word and describe him as a solitary individual who read the Bible for himself, received divine illumination for himself, and labored with no accountability to anyone else but God. In Hambrick-Stowe's skillful hands, Finney becomes a man of numerous theological connections, debts, and borrowings. From this we discover not only a new Finney but a far wider and more varied sense of the culture of the early American Republic. Reading Finney as one of the heirs of the New England theology rather than a lone rebel against it lets us see how rich and numerous were the threads of consistency and continuity between Finney and the Great Awakening of the 1740s and, beyond that, to the shape of modern evangelical Protestantism. The Finney whom we meet on these pages becomes simultaneously more clearly rooted in his own history and dramatically closer to the spirit of modern evangelicalism than we have thought.

Allen C. Guelzo

Preface

Charles G. Finney, born in 1792, was the most widely known of the many great revival preachers in the pre–Civil War United States. His campaigns from 1824 to 1834 in the so-called "burned-over district" of upstate New York and in Philadelphia, New York City, and Boston made his name synonymous with the final stage of the Second Great Awakening as it has traditionally been understood. In 1835, at age forty-three, Finney moved to Oberlin, Ohio, where he became professor of theology and later president of Oberlin College. Oberlin was noted for its abolitionist stance, for its acceptance of black students, and as a pioneer in coeducation for women. Finney and the other faculty also put forth the doctrine of entire sanctification and began to use the controversial language of perfection to describe the life of Christian obedience at the same time that the Wesleyan holiness movement came to life. Finney continued his evangelistic preaching, toured England twice, and served as pastor of the church in Oberlin for thirty-five years. He remained an active preacher and teacher until his death in 1875.

In an era when evangelical Protestantism was defined in

terms of revivalism, education, and social reform, Charles Finney was both a representative American evangelical and an evangelical who was truly a representative American. In *A History of Christianity in the United States and Canada*, Mark Noll ranks Finney "with Andrew Jackson, Abraham Lincoln, and Andrew Carnegie . . . as one of the most important public figures in nineteenth-century America." Theodore Dwight Weld offered a similar assessment in 1829 when he compared Finney with the other preachers of the day: "He rises above them to an overshadowing height."

Charles Finney was an evangelical, and this book uses the story of his life and ministry to open a window on American evangelicalism. The "spirit" of evangelical Protestantism has exercised a powerful influence alongside economic, cultural, and political developments in American history, for both weal and woe. Finney's career embodied that spirit to a great degree. But there are some surprises here. Today many think of an evangelical as a Christian who is religiously and socially conservative. Finney was theologically and socially conservative in some ways yet progressive and even radical in others.

The word *evangelical* has carried with it a broad variety of applications in history. *Evangel*, derived from the Greek word *euangelion*, means "good news." The corresponding English word *gospel* comes from the Anglo-Saxon *godspell* (*god*, a form of "good," and *spell*, meaning "story."). An evangelical is one who believes the gospel of what God has done through the life, death, and resurrection of Jesus Christ as revealed in the Bible. In that fundamental sense, all Christians are evangelicals. The word took on specificity in the sixteenth century when it was used to describe Protestants who embraced the revolutionary spiritual insight of Martin Luther and other Reformers that salvation is available to sinful humanity through the grace of God in Jesus Christ and can be received through faith. *Evangelicalism* thus came to refer to a way of being Christian that was distinct from the more priestly, sacramental, and institutional faith of traditional Roman Catholic Christianity. Evangelicalism relies on the preaching of the gospel of salvation more than on religious ritual and on the personal commitment of faith more than on the church's institutional authority. In the 1600s, the English Puritans espoused this form of Christian faith, and it was Puritan Congregationalists, Presbyterians, and Baptists who first imprinted evangelicalism on the eastern seaboard of North America. While evangelical "heart religion" has characterized the experience of many believers in all three major branches of the Christian family — Protestant, Roman Catholic, and Eastern Orthodox — it has most often been associated with the faith of Protestants.

Today's use of the word *evangelical* goes back to the spiritual awakenings in the British Isles and North America during the early and middle 1700s. In the thirteen Anglo-American colonies that became the United States, these revivals were called the Great Awakening. The leading figures in this revival included the New England Congregationalist pastor-theologian Jonathan Edwards and, in the middle colonies, the Presbyterian evangelist Gilbert Tennent. The most influential preacher of all was the itinerant Church of England evangelist George Whitefield. With his extemporaneous preaching and dramatic style, Whitefield addressed huge crowds spanning all social classes. He presented the gospel in such basic terms that people from every Protestant tradition responded to his message: Each person is utterly sinful and must repent, but salvation may be had freely through faith in Jesus Christ. Whitefield created the modern revival tradition and gave voice to the broad evangelicalism that came to characterize much of American religion.

After the Revolution, American society was freer than in colonial days as states ended the practice of favoring an established church with tax support. Churches vied with one another for members as never before. They also made common cause to win over a culture that they believed was in danger of slipping into atheism and barbarism. At the same time politics and commerce became arenas of competitive human endeavor, religion became competitive. Evangelical revivalism, rooted in seventeenth-century Puritanism and flowering in the Great Awakening, bore fruit in the early years of the United

States. It was a form of Christianity particularly well-suited to the robust young society. In a society alive with religious variety, innovation, and competition, evangelicalism became a common language of faith, a fundamental spirituality shared across economic and geographical barriers.

The term "evangelical spirit" used in the title of this book refers to the religious ethos that pervaded much of the early Republic, including what has recently been called the "evangelical mind." Finney's generation worked hard in the classroom and in print to modify Calvinist theology in ways that enhanced the human response of faith. Evangelicalism was more than an intellectual movement; it was a popular movement, a mass movement. We can thus speak of an American evangelical "mentality" or an American evangelical "culture." Despite its European origins and continued trans-Atlantic connections, evangelicalism appeared to many to have been born in the United States, baptized in its market economy, and married to its national destiny. The career of Charles G. Finney reveals the strength and the limitations of such faith.

Finney is a significant figure, as well, because he managed to hold together a number of elements of evangelical religion that flew apart after his death, by the end of the nineteenth century: urban revivalism, conversion preaching, racial justice, women's rights, education reform, abstinence from alcohol and stimulants, the holiness movement, the second blessing and higher Christian life, baptism of the Holy Ghost, ecclesiastical independence, impatience with doctrinal conservatism, progressive theology, the life of prayer, criticism of government policies, advocacy of civil disobedience, and aloofness from politics. Many of these elements seemed mutually contradictory to Finney's critics during his lifetime, and yet collectively they have shaped American evangelicalism. Charles Finney certainly did not embrace every element of typical evangelical religion (e.g., he was not a premillennialist), but in many ways he was a mediating figure. He held conflicting tendencies together by his zeal for souls, his passion for justice, and his prayerful love of God.

Charles Finney also participated fully in the characteristic divisiveness of the American church. He always had plenty of theological enemies. He was involved in the Presbyterian New School–Old School schism, and he often battled in the no-man's-land between Calvinist and Wesleyan versions of the Protestant gospel. He would not have been surprised that American Protestantism splintered not long after his death with the rise of a number of opposing movements. Fundamentalism stands against liberalism, the Social Gospel and Pentecostalism reflect radically different spiritualities, rival understandings of the authority of Scripture and of the millennium have taken shape, and Christians have taken to the streets and gone to the polls as both liberal and conservative political activists. Finney would have understood all of this and recognized the roots of it in his own era. But he never abandoned his prayer and work for essential, practical Christian unity. To use the language of our own time, Finney was both ecumenical and evangelical.

This book is a biographical study of an influential nineteenth-century Christian. It is also an effort to discern ways in which Charles G. Finney's experience as a typical American on the one hand and as a biblical believer on the other interacted, reacted, and blended together. Although the pre–Civil War United States is scarcely identical to the complex nation of the 1990s, the evangelical faith embodied in Finney's life continues to resonate in many ways with the faith of a vast proportion of the population — across the spectrum from religious right to left.

* * * * *

My interest in Charles G. Finney grew out of a desire to explore the religious experiences of Americans who thought of themselves as heirs of the seventeenth-century Puritans. I appreciated Mark Noll's confidence and encouragement when we discussed my plan to turn my attention to the nineteenth century during breaks at a conference. I am grateful to Roland M. Baumann, College Archivist at Oberlin, for his assistance whenever I came to the institution; I am grateful as well to the

Oberlin College Library for loaning me the Finney Papers on microfilm. The 1992 conference and exhibition at Oberlin College honoring the bicentennial of Finney's birth stimulated my early thinking. Harold F. Worthley and his staff at the Congregational Library in Boston generously made their Finney materials available to me during several visits and by loan. It was a great pleasure to research Charles G. Finney at two sites of his own labors, at the modern library behind Professor Street in Oberlin and in the reading room overlooking Boston's Park Street Church. I also wish to thank the Philip Schaff Library of Lancaster Theological Seminary, the United Church of Christ Archives, and the Shadek-Fackenthal Library of Franklin and Marshall College for providing background materials and facilities in which to review them.

Four scholars participated with me in a lively session on Charles G. Finney at a meeting of the American Society of Church History held at Oberlin College and First Church in the spring of 1994. Our session was conducted in Finney's 1842 meetinghouse, where we spoke from his pulpit. Papers and comments by Allen C. Guelzo, Marianne Perciaccante, Garth M. Rosell, and Barbara Brown Zikmund helped me to build upon my own paper from that conference. Garth Rosell, Allen Guelzo, and Mark Noll read the manuscript of this book with a critical eye and offered many helpful suggestions.

Like Charles G. Finney, I have endeavored to follow a dual calling in life as a pastor and an academic. My understanding of nineteenth-century evangelicalism has evolved through my years of teaching American religious history at Lancaster Theological Seminary. I accomplished my Finney research on mornings taken off from duties at my church over a four-year period, and I wrote the book during a three-month sabbatical that the congregation graciously provided. To the members of Church of the Apostles, United Church of Christ, Lancaster, Pennsylvania, and to my excellent colleague Pastor Glenn J. Rader, I express my deep appreciation. Elizabeth A. Hambrick-Stowe enabled this project to reach fruition by her constant support and, in the writing stage, scrupulous editorial advice.

Religion is the work of man. It is something for man to do. It consists in obeying God. It is man's duty. It is true, God induces him to do it. He influences him by his Spirit, because of his great wickedness and reluctance to obey. . . .

A revival of religion is not a miracle . . . or dependent on a miracle, in any sense. It is a purely philosophical result of the right use of the constituted means — as much so as any other effect produced by the application of means. . . . But means will not produce a revival, we all know, without the blessing of God. No more will grain, when it is sowed, produce a crop without the blessing of God. It is impossible for us to say that there is not as direct an influence or agency from God, to produce a crop of grain, as there is to produce a revival. . . .

A revival breaks the power of the world and of sin over Christians. It brings them to such a vantage ground that they get a fresh impulse towards heaven. They have a new foretaste of heaven, and new desires after union to God; and the charm of the world is broken, and the power of sin is overcome. . . . The worst parts of human society are softened, and reclaimed, and made to appear as lovely specimens of the beauty of holiness. . . .

If there is a sinner in this house, let me say to him, Abandon all your excuses. You have been told to-night that they are all in vain. To-night it will be told in hell, and told in heaven, and echoed from the ends of the universe, what you decide to do. This very hour may seal your eternal destiny. Will you submit to God to-night — NOW?

> Charles G. Finney,
> *Lectures on Revivals of Religion*
> (1835)

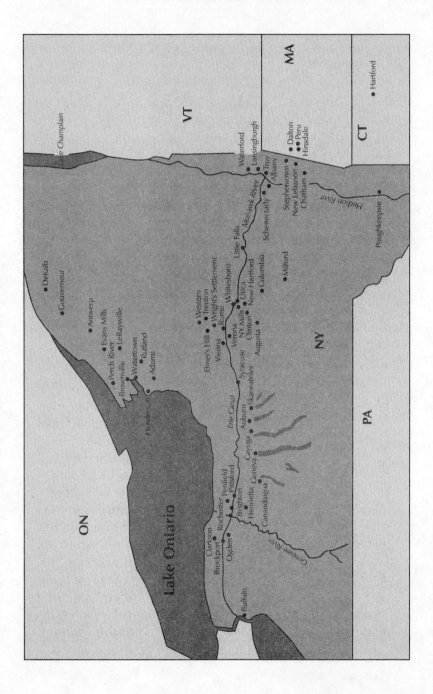

1 This Contest with God

Charles Grandison Finney was born again on the tenth of October, 1821.

In a wooded grove just over a hill outside the northern New York State village of Adams, he resolved, "I will give my heart to God before I ever come down again." Agitated and, as he recalled, "verging fast to despair," Finney sank to his knees convicted that "my *heart* is dead to God, and *will not* pray." Perhaps it was too late. Was he past hope? He looked up with every sound, jittery that someone might be watching. What pride, he thought, that he should be ashamed to be seen in prayer. "The sin appeared awful, infinite. It broke me down before the Lord." As if atoning for his secrecy, he cried aloud, "What! Such a degraded sinner!" A verse of Scripture (Jer. 29:12-13) came to him: "Then shall ye go and pray unto me, and I will answer you. Then shall ye seek me and shall find me, when you search for me with all your heart." Embracing what he later would call faith as "voluntary trust," Finney at last mustererd the courage to pray. He said to God, "*If I am ever converted, I will preach the gospel.*"

He was twenty-nine years old. Finney was still single, although his relationship with Lydia Root Andrews had developed beyond simply being old family friends. He would see her whenever she came north to visit her sister, and Lydia had perhaps let him know she was praying for the salvation of his soul. Having spent his young adulthood completing the equivalent of a high school education, working on the farms of family members, teaching school, and for the last three years apprenticing as a lawyer, Finney knew that this spiritual crisis was also a vocational turning point. Looking back, he attributed his avoidance of religious commitment to fear that God was calling him not to be a schoolmaster or a lawyer but a preacher. The problem was that he had never met a minister he thought he could emulate. He had assumed a posture of intellectual superiority over both the "ignorant" ranting of Baptist zealots and the theological sophistry of seminary-educated Calvinists, with their "humdrum way of reading" sermons. But for "a long time I had a secret conviction that I should be a minister, though my heart repelled it. In fact, my conversion turned very much upon my giving up this contest with God, and subduing this repellency of feeling against God's call."

Charles had grown up with a confident sense of upward mobility about himself. He was an athletic, handsome youth with high cheekbones and a strong nose and chin, sandy hair, and light complexion. His sharp blue eyes always commanded attention. He was endowed with a pleasing voice which he cultivated through musical training, and from an early age he was admired for his powerful, direct speech. At six feet two inches tall, on the ball field or in the classroom he was the natural leader. The engraved portraits and photographs of Finney as a middle-aged and older adult all reveal the prominent forehead and penetrating eyes but suggest a forbidding sternness that fails to account for his early popularity. In two separate oil portraits of the evangelist, both painted in 1834 at the height of his career in New York City, something of young Finney shines through. One can imagine laughter and words of friendship from the pleasantly smiling man in these likenesses.

Young Finney did not despise farming and always did his share of the work, but he had other career plans. The Finneys were a solid Yankee family with roots in the earliest settlements of Plymouth Colony and western Connecticut. Charles's parents, Sylvester Finney and Rebecca Rice (herself from an established Connecticut family), like his grandparents before them, were modest landowners who made their living from farming. They shared something of the cultural aspirations of their generation, however, as they decided to call their seventh son Charles Grandison. They were following a trend here. Ironically, many parents after the Revolution opted for aristocratic-sounding names from English literature or European society instead of ones from religious or family tradition. Among the most popular sources were the novels of Samuel Richardson — *Pamela, Clarissa,* and *Sir Charles Grandison* — all of them published in American editions in the 1780s. *Charles Grandison Finney* in that culture was the equivalent of something like *Bruce Springsteen Finney* or *Michael Jordan Finney* in our own. Richardson's *Sir Charles Grandison* was in essence a handbook on genteel living in an otherwise rude and vulgar world; the name sparkled with virtue and success.

From birth, therefore, Charles Grandison Finney carried with him that expressed desire for an upscale shift in manners and culture in the young Republic that has been termed "the refinement of America." Charles, with his natural gifts and personal ambition, never doubted that he was destined for one of the professions. Among medicine, ministry, teaching, and law, it was the last two that seemed both to afford abundant opportunities and suit him best. At least until October 10, 1821.

In addition to the prospect of turning thirty, at least two other forces were at work in Finney's conversion. One was his study of the Bible. The other was the upsurge of evangelical revivalism in and around Adams.

Several times in his life Finney wrote that "I bought my first Bible as a law-book, and laid it by the side of my Blackstone." He conveyed the impression that he could not trace his knowledge of Scripture back any farther than this. But this surely was not completely so. His recollection of home life as a child does not include much religious instruction ("My parents were neither of them professors of religion"), but the family did attend church with some regularity. Sylvester and Rebecca Finney had migrated with their seven children from Warren, Connecticut, to Oneida County, New York, in 1794, when Charles was two. Itinerant preachers often held evangelistic services in the vicinity. Moreover, in 1805 a meetinghouse was constructed near the Finney farm in Hanover, in the town of Kirkland. Charles heard weekly preaching there from a Presbyterian settled minister during his early teenage years until 1808, when the family moved to the North Country. Garth M. Rosell and Richard A. G. Dupuis show in their recent critical edition of Finney's *Memoirs* how the widely read original published edition established a very wrong impression: it has Finney asserting that in his early years, "I seldom heard a sermon." What Finney actually wrote was, "I seldom heard a *Gospel* sermon from any person, unless it was an occasional one from some travelling minister." He heard plenty of sermons but considered most of them dry, intellectual, and doctrinal — spiritually and emotionally unsatisfying. After his conversion and after his own theological perspective had taken shape, Finney put a label on this (to his mind) unevangelical preaching: Old Schoolism. Even when a pastor identified himself with revival- and reform-oriented New School Presbyterianism, if he did not preach a straightforward evangelistic message with fiery zeal, Finney lumped him with the Old School which rigidly adhered to the Westminster Confession.

Settling on a farm outside the village of Henderson near Lake Ontario, the Finneys attended the First Baptist Church, where Elder Emory Osgood had begun a long-term ministry. Finney listened to Osgood's brash, revivalistic sermons from

4

age sixteen until he was twenty. Although the cynical youth used to chuckle at Osgood's rustic language, it is certain that there was a lot of Bible in his preaching.

Finney next returned to his birthplace in Connecticut and enrolled at Warren Academy. During two years of formal schooling there, Finney sat weekly under the preaching of the venerable and well-loved Congregationalist pastor the Rev. Peter Starr. More precisely, he sat *over* Starr's ministry — in the balcony, where he could watch the old minister's tedious progress through sermon notes stuck in the pages of his Bible. Finney also may have felt more anonymous, or psychologically aloof, in the gallery.

Between 1814 and 1818, while he was teaching school in New Jersey, Finney claimed, "I do not think I heard half a dozen sermons in English," as "the preaching in the neighborhood was at that time almost altogether in German." Presumably he still attended worship and followed as best he could the Bible reading and the sermons preached in German.

At age twenty-six, Finney returned home to Jefferson County, in part because his mother had taken ill, but also to make a fresh start as a clerk for attorney Benjamin Wright in Adams. In his *Memoirs* Finney claims that, having "paid very little regard to the Sabbath," he was at this point "almost as ignorant of religion as a heathen" and had "no definite knowledge of religious truth whatever." Apparently no pastor had given him a Bible, and he had not purchased one on his own. But it cannot be said that he was unfamiliar with the Scriptures and Christian beliefs. He had heard a great deal of biblical preaching as a teenager and young adult. His ignorance was not intellectual but spiritual; the knowledge he lacked was *saving* knowledge. When he attached himself to the ministry of Presbyterian pastor George Washington Gale in Adams, he listened to his sermons with a religiously astute, critical mind, demanding proof for the Calvinist doctrines Gale held forth as gospel.

Charles Finney may not have owned a personal copy of the Bible as a young man but he had certainly read it in school and probably even taught from it. The Bible was the single most widely used textbook in the common schools and academies of the early Republic, used for reading and oral recitation as well as for devotional exercises. Education, both public and private, was an overwhelmingly evangelical enterprise, and Finney was not unschooled. His childhood was not spent on some desolate frontier but in and around rural villages. "The new settlers being mostly from New England," Finney wrote, they "almost immediately established common schools." As a youth Finney was eager for an education, and classmates remembered him as being tops in his class. In addition to his academic ability, young Charles's skill at sports and enthusiasm for rough-and-tumble playground activities stood him in good stead when he himself began keeping school. "I enjoyed the privileges of a common school summer and winter, until I was fifteen or sixteen years old; and advanced so far as to be supposed capable of teaching a common school myself, as common schools were then conducted."

There is some evidence to suggest that Finney may have spent the last two years of his early schooling, prior to the family move north, at Hamilton-Oneida Academy in nearby Clinton, before it was rechartered in 1812 as Hamilton College. His daughter and grandson believed this to have been the case. Although he fails to mention it in his writings, this would partly explain Finney's proficiency in music — especially voice, violin, and cello. The cello or bass viol was customarily used in the early nineteenth century to accompany religious singing — this before the introduction of church organs. Seth Norton, who was both a linguist and a musician, headed the Academy during Finney's student years. Such training and personal references from the Presbyterian-sponsored Academy faculty, together with his experience teaching singing a few years later in Connecticut, would have opened the door for Finney to become George Gale's music director at the church in Adams, a part-time job Finney undertook while clerking for Wright. And enrollment at Hamilton-Oneida Academy would be con-

sistent with the warm friendship apparent in Finney's correspondence with college trustees, students, and faculty in the
mid-1820s. Charles Cushman Sears (who had taught school in
Adams and was a special friend of Finney's) wrote from the
College that "the name Finney possesses some peculiar influence, which whenever it falls on my ear produces within me a
strange sensation." Orrin Gridley, a local trustee, wrote in 1826
that "the Lord appears to be searching the Church at College
in a most wonderful manner" and asked Charles to "please
remember me to Mrs. Finney, your Father and Mother, and all
old friends." On the other hand, scores of people wrote Finney
with similar affection from many places around central and
northern New York State, and no record of his enrollment exists
at Hamilton. If Finney did attend the Academy, he would have
encountered instruction and worship from the Bible, the singing of music based on Scripture, and courses in moral philosophy, along with reading and writing, composition, rhetoric,
mathematics, natural philosophy, introductory Latin, and so
on.

He certainly took courses involving the Bible and Christian thought at Warren Academy in Connecticut. Finney at that
time "meditated going to Yale College," a plan that would have
been far-fetched without his already having completed such
training. Not because Finney was ill-prepared but probably
because of his age, his preceptor, himself a Yale graduate, advised against it. "He said it would be a loss of time, as I could
easily accomplish, at the rate I was then progressing, the whole
curriculum of study pursued at that institution in two years,
whereas it would cost me four years to graduate." After he
became a professor at Oberlin Collegiate Institute, Finney came
to regret that he was "never a classical scholar," but for a
twenty-two-year-old teaching school, or even a twenty-six-
year-old training to practice law, he was well enough educated.
One only has to think of Abraham Lincoln, born sixteen years
after Charles Finney and with less formal education, who became the most successful lawyer in Illinois in the 1840s and '50s.

Finney's schooling, along with his exposure to more than fifteen years of biblical and doctrinal sermons, had prepared him remarkably well for the religious crisis of his twenty-ninth year. He recorded in the *Memoirs* that in the study of "elementary law I found the old authors frequently quoting Scripture," citing Mosaic law as foundational for "the great principles of common law." This is not strictly true if he was referring to William Blackstone's fundamental work on the common law, *Commentaries on the Laws of England.* These four volumes dominated legal training in the days of Charles Finney and Abe Lincoln. Blackstone seldom cites the Bible even when treating such crimes as heresy and blasphemy.

Finney did not need a Bible for his legal education: lawyers typically used the book only as a talisman for oath-taking. Rather, Finney the student felt his mind, and perhaps his heart, stimulated by the *idea* of the law. If Blackstone did not often invoke the authority of Moses, Finney could not help but trace the connections between civil law and God's Law. "This excited my curiosity so much that I went and purchased a Bible, the first one I had ever owned." As Finney eagerly looked up Scripture passages that corresponded with legal topics, "this soon led to my taking a new interest in the Bible." He had read the Bible as a textbook in school, and as a young teacher he had surely used it with his students. But now, hunched over a desk in Benjamin Wright's law office, "I read and meditated on it much more than I had ever done before in my life."

Charles Finney's search for direction in his life involved not only personal study of Scripture but active involvement in the style of corporate religious life that had come to dominate early American society — evangelical revivalism. Finney left generations of readers of his *Memoirs* with the impression that revivalism began with his ministry. His purpose in writing was to tell the story of "the revivals that occurred in central New York and elsewhere, from 1821, and onward for several years." Finney downplayed the effectiveness of the itinerant preachers who worked the villages of Oneida County and the North

Country during his youth. And the revivals associated with the onset of the Second Great Awakening — camp meetings like the powerful one in 1801 at Cane Ridge, Kentucky, and New England revivals about the same time growing out of the efforts of Jonathan Edwards's New Divinity heirs and sparked by the preaching of Timothy Dwight at Yale — may have seemed distant both spiritually and geographically. Finney was about to do a new thing, using new methods, in a new phase of the Second Great Awakening.

We now know that Finney was not in fact the author of revival as many readers of his *Memoirs* were led to believe. He was more a product of American evangelicalism than its creator. Oneida County in the final decade of the eighteenth century and the early years of the nineteenth was no stranger either to Connecticut Congregationalist New Divinity evangelicalism and its New School Presbyterian counterpart or to the more radical, emotional preaching of Baptists and Methodists. Revivalism was even more prevalent in the North Country, where the Finneys moved in 1808 and where Charles as an older teen both worked on the farm and taught school. Early Jefferson County settlers were mostly from western Vermont and carried with them a penchant for emotional extremism in their religion first acquired in the revivals of four and five decades before. In the later stages of the first Great Awakening, northern New England was aflame with Baptist and Methodist enthusiasm, a spirited style of religious life contemptuous of the stuffy formality of the Congregational "standing order." Finney described a Baptist-Congregational union prayer meeting in Henderson, reported to him by his brother George, where this type of fervor was in evidence. The prayer leader, characterized by Finney as "a good specimen of a New England deacon," started in a low tone "but soon began to wax warm and to raise his voice, which became tremulous with emotion." He rocked on his toes and heels with increasing force and then raised and banged his chair in rhythm with his prayer. "The brethren and sisters," kneeling on the floor, "began to groan, and sigh, and

9

weep, and agonize in prayer" until finally they could not rise but "only weep and confess, and all melt down before the Lord."

Over the years, Finney had sampled the wares of every type of preacher, including the Universalists. As varied as their theologies may have been, North Country preachers all employed a popular, evangelistic pulpit style. Except in more urbane Watertown, the people had no interest in studied highbrow sermons read from a manuscript. They liked their preaching extemporaneous, straight from the heart. No preacher who wanted an audience could ignore this reality. The Rev. George Gale, educated at Princeton Seminary, thus felt compelled to modify his homiletics to meet local expectations when he arrived at Adams. He memorized his sermons so he could look the people in the eye while speaking.

About the time Finney was becoming more interested in his Bible, he also began attending a weekly "stated prayer meeting" at the Presbyterian church. By encouraging these meetings and making frequent pastoral calls on Finney at the law office, George Gale adopted methods that would later be associated with the "Finneyite" revivals. In Adams they went so far as to pray boldly for individuals by name, and once, Finney wrote, "I was asked if I did not desire that they should pray for me." He refused, cynically pointing out that he failed to see that it would do much good, since they had been praying for a revival for months and nothing had happened. Poring over his Bible, Finney discovered what he believed was the reason: "They did not comply with the revealed conditions upon which God had promised to answer prayer, that they did not pray in faith in the sense of *expecting* God to give them the things they asked for."

Charles Finney's assessment of spiritual affairs in and around Adams, written down many decades later, was more judgmental than accurate. In fact, periods of revival had sparked the growth of North Country churches throughout the 1810s, and the flame ignited in Adams during the summer of

1821, several months before Finney went into the woods to make his peace with God. That Finney was converted during a community-wide revival is consistent with the prime importance he placed on them for others throughout his career as an evangelist; it would have been odd if his experience had been that of a solitary pilgrim. George Gale wrote in his *Autobiography* that he had been promoting a revival during this period and engaged an aspiring unlicensed young evangelist, Jedediah Burchard, to lead services in June while Gale was absent on a family matter. Burchard succeeded in fanning the fire. After Gale returned, Burchard continued to work with him for a few weeks and then moved on to assist the revival effort in the Baptist church and among nearby towns. Soon after the events of the summer and fall, reports of how "God is pouring out his Spirit" in Jefferson County appeared in the religious press in Boston and Philadelphia. One of these reports was made by the Baptist preacher Emory Osgood (in a far more articulate style of writing than one would expect from Finney's Dogpatch caricature of him), who supplied glowing conversion statistics and called it "the most astonishing spirit of prayer that I ever witnessed." In this northern region long accustomed to evangelistic preaching and fervent religious emotion, Charles G. Finney ended his critical-minded young adulthood and was saved.

During the prayer meeting, Finney became fully convinced that Jesus really meant it when he said "Ask and ye shall receive" and that the Bible is "the true Word of God." The decision was now his to make: Would he "accept Christ as presented in the Gospel, or pursue a worldly course of life?" On Sunday evening Finney resolved to make this decision and "settle the question of my soul's salvation at once." He went to work Monday and Tuesday but spent much of his time praying and reading his Bible — although whenever someone came in, he hastily covered it with law books. Monday evening he went to an inquiry meeting conducted by George Gale. At such meetings, embraced by pastors as a means of extending revivals, sinners hopeful of conversion could receive counsel and prayer. Gale remembered "looking him in the eye" and hearing Finney blurt out, "I am willing now to be a Christian." During the prayers, Finney later wrote, "I trembled so that my very seat shook under me." Gale's *Autobiography* reported almost identical language from Finney in relation to this inquiry meeting. Tuesday night anxiety overwhelmed Finney. If he should suddenly die, he was now convinced, he would wake up in hell. He did not sleep much that night.

Wednesday morning the struggle came to an end. There was nothing more for Finney to do about getting right with God. "I think I then saw, as clearly as I ever have in my life, the reality and fulness of the atonement of Christ. I saw that his work was a *finished* work; and that instead of having, or needing, any righteousness of my own to recommend me to God, I had to *submit myself* to the *righteousness of God through Christ.*" Salvation was not an achievement or a goal but a gift — "an offer of *something to be accepted.*" It was a crucial spiritual moment for Finney, one that suddenly makes his story harmonize with those of countless others throughout the previous two centuries of early American evangelical awakenings. This gospel of salvation by God's free grace has throughout American history been the basic message of evangelists, pastors, missionaries, teachers, and preachers of virtually every denominational description, with only slight variations to reflect theological posture — such as Finney's own emphasis on the consent of the will. Charles Finney walked out of the office door convinced that the Bible made him this promise: "All that was necessary on my part, was to get my own consent to give up my sins, and give myself to Christ." It was a promise, and an exhortation, that he would deliver from hundreds of pulpits before his life was done.

He stopped suddenly in the street when an "inward voice" spoke to him. "Will you accept it *now, today?*" And he answered: "Yes; I will accept it to-day, or I will die in the attempt." Finney's Calvinist opponents always accused him of keeping too much of the self in the work of redemption. One of his most famous sermons was entitled "Sinners Bound to Change Their Own Hearts," after all. And the confessionally and catechetically oriented, most especially Presbyterian doctrinal conservatives, criticized his urgent demand that the present moment was the time for decision. To Princeton minds, Puritanism's fine balance of divine initiative and human responsibility had been completely lost in liberal Boston, was shaky at best in Congregational New Haven, and was in danger everywhere with the rising popularity of Methodism's Arminian belief that Christ died for the whole world and that all people are free and able to accept God's offer of salvation. Finney, they said, was far off in this direction of Arminianism. He tipped the scales too much on the side of the person's choice of God rather than God's choice of the person.

When Charles Finney walked into the woods north of the village and looked for a secluded spot among some fallen trees where he could pray, he did all he could to fulfill his half of the divine equation. Now it was time to pray. "But lo! when I came to try, I was dumb: that is, I had nothing to say to God." It was when he was sunk down in utter shame that the promise that God would come to those who search for him suddenly rang true. "Lord, I take thee at thy Word," he cried out. He "seized hold of" God's promises "and fastened upon them with the grasp of a drowning man." He promised that if God soundly converted him, he would leave his law practice and become a preacher of the gospel. But his conversion was still not finished. Out of the woods on the way back to town, as Finney's agitation completely disappeared, he interpreted his peace of mind as evidence that "the Spirit has left me." He feared he had committed the unpardonable sin; "for such a sinner as I was to take hold of God's Word in that way, was presumption if not blasphemy." Hours later he realized that this feeling of freedom from guilt and lack of "concern about my ultimate salvation" was God's blessing.

Finney found it was noon when he returned to the law

office, but he had no appetite. "I took down my bass viol, and as I was accustomed to do, began to play and sing some pieces of sacred music. But as soon as I began to play and sing those sacred words, I began to weep. It seemed as if my heart was all liquid." Fortunately for Finney, no legal work was required that afternoon — the firm was just then moving to new offices. When the books were reshelved and the furniture was in place and Benjamin Wright had gone home, it all started again. Now, in the darkness of the conference room, "it seemed as if I met the Lord Jesus Christ *face to face.*" Only later did he realize "it was wholly a *mental* state." Finney wept uncontrollably, pouring out his confessions, and then "received *a mighty baptism of the Holy Ghost.*" The experience took him wholly by surprise; its intensity was overwhelming. It "seemed *to go through me,* body and soul . . . *like a wave of electricity,* going through and through me . . . in *waves,* and *waves of liquid love,*" not like water "but rather as *the breath of God* . . . it seemed to *fan* me, like immense wings." This was God in his power, and it was the power of his love: "It seemed to me that I should burst. I wept aloud with joy and love."

Finney's spiritual transformation was evident in the fact that he was no longer shy about his religious behavior as he had been in the woods. One of the members of his church's choir came into the office. Seeing him weeping, he asked if Finney was sick. When Finney replied, "No; but I am *so happy that I cannot live,*" he ran to fetch one of the elders of the church. The elder, an extremely serious man, saw Finney in the throes of conversion and was himself then overcome by the Spirit. "He fell into a most spasmodic laugh . . . *from the bottom of his heart.* It seemed to be a spasm that was irresistible." Then Finney's friend Charles Cushman Sears came in just as Finney was giving an account of his experience, and Sears fell to his knees begging for prayer on his behalf. Finney, for the first time in his life, prayed for the salvation of another soul.

The next morning, after a fitful night during which Finney sensed renewed waves of God's Spirit, "the baptism that I had received the night before returned upon me in the same manner." In his *Memoirs,* Finney recalls having received doctrinal insight to match his spiritual regeneration. He now knew the meaning of *"justification by faith* as a *present experience."* Further, although he stated that he kept this part of it to himself and editor James Fairchild actually crossed out the key phrase on the manuscript and omitted it from the original edition, Finney later asserted that he felt something of "present sanctification." Whether Finney read too much of his later doctrinal development into this spiritual turning point, the fact remains that he was a new person in Christ. "My sense of guilt was gone, my sins were gone. . . . My cup ran over with blessing and with love."

Not every Christian in American history has experienced so dramatic an experience of conversion. Churches that have emphasized catechism and "Christian nurture" have often embraced the vision expressed by Horace Bushnell in 1847, "that the child is to grow up a Christian, and never know himself as being otherwise." But the necessary conversion of one's heart from sinfulness to godliness has been a common and defining element in the broad evangelical stream of religious life in this country from colonial days to the present, even among many believers who also might be described in catechetical or theologically liberal terms. Certainly Finney shared the experience with many Methodists in the new United States. The Methodist evangelist Peter Cartwright described his conversion as a youth in Kentucky in his *Autobiography* (1856) in an account very similar to that of Charles Finney. After feeling convicted of sin, Cartwright "retired to the horse-lot . . . wringing my hands in great anguish, trying to pray, on the borders of utter despair." Grace flashed over him "quick as an electric shock," but a few days later, when he "retired to a cave" on his father's farm, he was still seeking salvation. Finally, three months later he attended a camp meeting, where he "went, with weeping multitudes, and bowed before the stand, and earnestly prayed for mercy." Cartwright heard God's voice offering forgiveness.

When Finney spoke about his own conversion, which he often did in sermons, and when he wrote his *Memoirs* late in life, he was undoubtedly conscious of the way his experience fit a long-established pattern. During the Great Awakening of the 1730s and '40s, ordinary people like Sarah Osborn and Nathan Cole wrote spiritual autobiographies with conversion narratives very similar to Finney's. Finney may not have read many of these, but he had probably heard the stories told again and again in religious gatherings. Almost everyone was familiar with Jonathan Edwards's edition of *The Life of David Brainerd*, first published in 1749 and still in print and enormously popular during Finney's lifetime.

Brainerd's account of his conversion and subsequent spiritual journey became archetypal for many Congregationalists and Presbyterians as they moved west in the 1800s. Brainerd was the model young Christian, the ideal missionary. His conversion narrative was remarkably parallel to Finney's. Brainerd was just turning twenty when "it pleased God, on one Sabbath day morning, as I was walking out for some secret duties (as I remember) to give me on a sudden such a sense of my danger and the wrath of God, that I stood amazed and my former good frames, that I had pleased myself with, all presently vanished; and from the view that I had of my sin and vileness, I was much distressed all that day, fearing the vengeance of God would soon overtake me." For months Brainerd reeled between hope and despair, but finally, "while I was walking in a solitary place as usual, I at once saw that all my contrivances and projections to effect or procure deliverance and salvation for myself were utterly in vain." The following Sabbath evening, "walking again in the same solitary place," Brainerd "was attempting to pray; but found no heart to engage in that, or any other duty." Afraid "the Spirit of God had quite left me," in utter humility he experienced a sudden breakthrough. "As I was walking in a dark thick grove, 'unspeakable glory' seemed to open to the view and apprehension of my soul. . . . I stood still and wondered and admired!" Brainerd's language foreshadows Finney in amazing detail: "My soul was so captivated and delighted with the excellency, loveliness, greatness, and other perfections of God, that I was even swallowed up in him," to the extent "that I had no thought (as I remember) at first about my own salvation." The "sweet relish" of God's love "continued with me for several days" and made everything new. "I felt myself in a new world, and everything about me appeared with a different aspect from what it was wont to do." David Brainerd entered Yale the same year as his conversion to study for the gospel ministry.

Finney's reading of Brainerd's *Life* and Edwards's *Some Thoughts concerning the Present Revival of Religion* (1742) and *Treatise concerning Religious Affections* (1746), in which the great theologian of revivalism describes the evangelical model of God's way of salvation, may have colored the way he told his own story. It is also likely that long before he read any of this material, Finney was conditioned by his youth in upper New York State to anticipate, experience, and reflect on his religion in terms inherited from the earlier New England Awakenings. In his conversion, Finney, and every American evangelical before and since, was a child of the Puritans. The manner in which he was humbled in his sins and saved by God's grace goes back before the Great Awakening to the seventeenth century. Accounts similar to Finney's can be found in the spiritual writings of the founding pastor of the church at Cambridge, Massachusetts, Thomas Shepard ("Walking in the fields . . . the Lord did help me to loathe myself . . . and I saw the Lord gave me a heart to receive Christ . . . and so the Lord gave me peace"), in the confessions of ordinary men and women as they joined Shepard's congregation ("the Lord broke my heart in the consideration of my own vileness and so I saw a necessity of Christ"), and in the more sophisticated meditative poetry of Edward Taylor ("Oh! . . . my Lifeless Sparke! . . . Lord blow the Coal: Thy Love Enflame in mee."). Such first-generation New England divines as Thomas Hooker and John Cotton preached and published sermons outlining "the application of

17

redemption," mapping out the stages of conversion in a way that became part of the culture.

David Brainerd himself had served as a link to this older evangelical piety. He followed the way to conversion set forth in Puritan devotional manuals and in the spiritual narratives preserved in Cotton Mather's *Magnalia Christi Americana* (1702). During the Great Awakening, market-driven publishers came out with scores of new editions of old Puritan spiritual classics, including devotional manuals and personal testimonies. Toward the end of his short life, Brainerd was especially excited as he "read with care and attention some papers of old Mr. Shepard's, lately come to light and designed for the press." He helped with the editorial work on this exemplary Puritan diary and wrote a preface while staying at Jonathan Edwards's Northampton parsonage. Thomas Prince, pastor of Boston's evangelical Old South Church, edited *The Christian History*, a magazine that reported revival news, at the same time Edwards was editing the just-deceased Brainerd's narrative, in 1747. Methodism provided another link with the old piety, for John Wesley's "heart strangely warmed" was kindled by the fires of both Puritanism (through the devotional teaching of his mother, Susanna) and Pietism (Puritanism's Continental cousin).

The tradition of Puritan conversion preaching and intense personal piety became so ingrained in the common language of the people that it sounded completely natural and unrehearsed coming two centuries later from the mouth of a country Baptist like Elder Osgood or an untutored evangelist like Jedediah Burchard up near the St. Lawrence River. It has been a powerful force of extremely long duration in American history. Charles Finney was heir to this well-established way of experiencing salvation in the first decades of the 1800s, and he, perhaps unconsciously at first, devoted his life to its perpetuation and development. By referring to his spiritual struggle as "this contest with God," he may have been thinking by analogy of how he had vigorously argued cases in local courts of law, or he may have had in mind the heated games of "base" or "townball" played on the village square. Either way, Charles Finney's conversion exemplified both early nineteenth-century American vitality and the culture's rootedness in the piety of an earlier day.

Finney knew instinctively from the start that his conversion experience was typical, in the strongest theological sense of that word. It followed the way he had come to understand the Bible's promise of salvation and the pattern of God's conversion of sinners like Saul of Tarsus. Conforming also to the basic lines of the archetypal Puritan pattern, itself rooted in Scripture, Finney's conversion in essence restated the tradition for his generation. He felt that what God had done in his heart was what God also wanted to do for others. That first morning, while Finney was still in the glow of his Spirit baptism, he greeted Benjamin Wright and right off the bat spoke "a few words to him on the subject of his salvation." He told a client on whose behalf he was scheduled to appear in court, "Deacon Barney, I have a retainer from the Lord Jesus Christ to plead his cause, and I cannot plead yours." A famously witty utterance, it is also the kind of line that may have gotten better with each telling until it finally saw print. In any case, Finney's vocational and spiritual direction was now settled.

Charles Finney the new believer "spoke with many persons that day, and I believe the Spirit of God made lasting impressions upon every one of them." He argued with the son of an elder of the church who was toying with Universalism; after Finney "was enabled to blow his argument to the wind," the young man "went into the woods, and . . . gave his heart to God." In the village there were those who had said that if the rakish skeptic Finney were ever converted, they too would believe. When they heard Finney tell what God had done for him and then pray for sinners, "the work spread on every side." Because he had been an acknowledged and admired "leader among the young people," Finney immediately planned meetings and "gave up [his] time to labor for their conversion."

People started going to pray for salvation in the same area of the woods where he had found the Lord, including (after much prideful resistance) the lawyer Benjamin Wright. Together with his brother George, already a believer, Finney converted his own parents back in Henderson. Charles Finney, in short, discovered that there was tremendous force in his story.

Finney's conversion occurred during a general upsurge in the North Country revival, and in turn contributed to its power and extent. One contemporary estimate put the number of converts "over a large part of Jefferson County" at between eight hundred and a thousand. Among the many new members of the Presbyterian Church in Adams were Charles Finney and Benjamin Wright, and they were not the only professionals to come forward. When enthusiasm eventually waned, Finney took the initiative. He had gathered a group of men, including the pastor George Gale, for a daily predawn prayer meeting at the church. When attendance slacked off, Finney began to "go around to their houses and wake them up." In his zeal for souls, he learned to battle with prayer against frustration and disappointment. These early months of Christian life also brought to Finney repeated experiences of what he could only call "divine manifestations," often in the form of intense light, at least one of which he compared to the intensity of Paul's theophany on the Damascus road.

In his preaching Finney constantly referred to his own experience of conversion and of God's continued grace, and he used the salvation stories of others to illustrate his sermons, his history of revivals in the *Memoirs,* and his more formal theological writings. For example, in a sermon published in his 1835 volume *Sermons on Various Subjects,* when he declares that it is not true that "sinners are almost Christians," one hears echoes of his life as a young lawyer in Adams. "The truth is, the most moral impenitent sinner in the world, is much nearer a devil, than a Christian." His warning that "sinners manifest the greatest pleasure in sin. . . . They roll it as a sweet morsel under the tongue" has the ring of personal experience. And Finney knew both from his own experience and his observations of thousands of anxious penitents that "sinners are often thrown into great agony in this life, by the internal struggles, and janglings of their consciences and their hearts." In his preaching he aimed to "let the full blaze of eternity's light be poured upon their consciences." He knew for himself what it was "to resolve on immediate submission to Jesus Christ" and experience the joy of salvation. In his 1835 *Lectures on Revivals of Religion* he advises ministers preparing young converts for church membership to "draw out from them, what they have learned by experience, and not what they may have got in theory before or since their conversion."

When Charles G. Finney was professor of theology at Oberlin, he impressed on successive generations of students the importance of experiencing and then preaching such a conversion as he had himself experienced in Adams. "The Holy Spirit is engaged in a great work within the soul," he lectured. "It is nothing less than to renovate the whole character of life." This renovation, he insisted, would manifest itself in personal experience. "There may be those who cannot tell when their Christian experience began. . . . It may have commenced so quietly and with so little excitement that they did not note its beginnings. Nonetheless if there is a spiritual life it had a beginning. If it is progressing in a world of trial, it must often reveal itself distinctly in consciousness." The ideal beginning was not quiet at all but more like the dramatically soul-wrenching conversions of a Thomas Shepard in the early 1600s and of a David Brainerd in the early 1700s, and like the one in 1821 that launched Charles G. Finney on his great evangelistic career.

2 Pleading the Lord's Cause

In Spirit-filled American religion, charismatic figures can sometimes go from the ecstasy of new birth or new revelation to the pulpit in a matter of days. More often, new leaders begin their work with some practical balance between the immediacy of God's call and the need for theological preparation and institutional endorsement. Even in the case of Joseph Smith, the Vermont-born founder of Mormonism, seven years elapsed between his first visions in 1820 as a teenager in western New York State and the time he reported receiving possession of the golden plates, and it was not until 1829 that Smith formed his new church. Charles Finney started telling sinners about the way to salvation the very day of his conversion, but he did not begin his formal ministry until fully two years later. In spite of the independent streak in his character that forever put him at odds with denominational structures, Finney never dreamed of commencing his work as a preacher apart from the orderly processes of Presbyterian polity. From the spring of 1822 until December 30, 1823, when the Presbytery of St. Lawrence licensed him to preach, Finney devoted himself to theological study under the tutelage of his pastor the Rev. George W. Gale. The last six months, from June 25, 1823, on, Finney was officially "under the care of the Presbytery" as a student for the ministry.

Finney's transition from the practice of law to preparation for ministry took place gradually during the winter months. For one thing, he lost interest in his work as an apprentice lawyer and "had no disposition to make money." But since he had no immediate prospect of income as a pastor or evangelist, he continued going to the office and spent as much time as possible in Bible study, prayer, and religious meetings. His pastor advised him to take it slowly, to test his call to the ministry by undertaking the study of languages and moral philosophy and with prayer.

The greatest lessons for Finney these first months after his conversion were "in regard to *the spirit of prayer.*" In his *Memoirs,* he recounts being "loaded down with great agony" in prayer for a woman lying near death, for another woman who sang in the church choir who "remained unconverted . . . in her sins," and for the magistrate at whose house Finney boarded, who seemed "deeply convicted of sin" and yet resisted conversion. Each case taught Finney something significant for his budding career. The first woman was physically healed and soon embraced salvation in Christ. In the second case, although Finney prayed for the woman's soul and heard "God sa[y] to me, 'Yes! Yes!',", it was some months before she accepted God's grace. Finney had to face disappointment and learn patience in prayer. The magistrate gave up his spiritual quest when he was elected to the state legislature, espoused a vague sense of universal salvation, and, according to Finney, "remained in his sins, finally fell into decay, and died at last a dilapidated man." Meanwhile, Finney and the other "young converts" worried that as spring approached the spiritual revival of the previous year was dying out. They agreed to "observe a closit concert of prayer for the revival of God's work," and, as they prayed in private three times a day, some of them began to fall and "lie prostrate on the floor, and pray with unutterable groanings for the outpouring of the Spirit of God." Attendance at religious meetings again soared, but Finney was astonished that "the older members of the church resisted this new movement" with its more radical enthusiasm. Revivalism could bring dissension as well as unity. Finney knew that his fast-developing prayer life, connected as it was with people and the concerns of the community, was beginning to fit him for his ministry. Throughout Finney's career it would be prayer — especially what he called the "prayer of faith" and "prevailing prayer" — that fueled his life and work.

Theological study was more of a struggle for Finney, in part because of his age and lack of income once he quit the law. It was hard for him to imagine going back to school. Theological seminaries were a brand new way of training clergy, with Andover founded in 1808, Princeton in 1812, Auburn in 1819, and Yale Divinity School, where Finney would have found much in common with professor Nathaniel William Taylor, only in 1822. As with training for the other professions — the first law and medical schools were being established at about this same time — the old apprenticeship method was fast going out of favor with accreditation committees. But the traditional method was still possible during this early period, and it proved to be a far easier, cheaper, and quicker option for Finney.

Charles Finney and George Gale, both writing as old men, published completely different explanations of why Finney opted to study with his pastor. According to Finney, the presbytery committee wanted him to go to Princeton, but he refused, even when they offered to pay his way, because (he told them!) in his view they all "had been wrongly educated" and turned out so badly that they were "not ministers that met my ideal at all of what a minister of Christ should be." As Gale told it, he was helping Finney apply to Andover, Princeton, and Auburn but found that not one of these schools was eager to admit him, at least as a scholarship student. In any case, the presbytery agreed to take Finney under care, assigned him as a student to Gale and Watertown pastor George S. Boardman, and set out an "order of studies." The more staid Boardman lived more than ten miles away and did little or nothing for Finney, but Gale became his preceptor as well as his pastor and friend. Gale had no trouble raising funds to underwrite the cost for Finney to board with his family. The presbytery was apparently not so shackled with Old School formalism and doctrinal rigidity as Finney thought when he looked back years later.

Finney read books from his pastor's library, wrote essays on biblical and theological topics, and engaged with Gale in probing discussions based on his work. Finney's disputatious nature, which legal training had done nothing to soften, made him an aggressive learner. These tutorials involved such lively give-and-take with Gale that the the whole process was finally reduced "as far as he was concerned as my teacher" to "little else than controversy." Finney was convinced that in certain key areas of doctrine, specifically on original sin and the atonement, the traditional Calvinist position officially held by Presbyterians was unreasonable, unbiblical, and, from the viewpoint of evangelical preaching, impractical. The notion that individuals physically inherited their sinfulness from Adam seemed to negate personal responsibility for sin, and Calvinism's doctrine of limited atonement (the assertion that Christ died only for the elect) blunted the imperative to preach the hope of salvation to everyone. According to Finney's account, his theological education consisted primarily of his development of a full-scale assault on Gale's rigid Princeton orthodoxy. But can this exchange between Gale and Finney not also be interpreted as good pedagogy on Gale's part, his effective preparation of a promising candidate for ministry in the conflict-ridden Presbyterian Church and in the super-competitive religious environment of upstate New York? Why else would Gale have promoted Charles Finney as quickly as possible through the ordination process and done the same thing for the controversial Jedediah Burchard, a fiery young revival preacher easily as radical as Finney?

When George Gale fell ill and concluded that he needed a leave of absence from the ministry, he guided events so that Finney could serve as his successor in the Adams church. Even though Finney had been under care for only six months, Gale considered him ready to preach. He suggested to the presbytery "the propriety of licensing Mr. Finney, that he might, for a time or until they could obtain a pastor, supply the pulpit, and this was done." On December 30, 1823, Charles Finney was examined for licensure. He expressed surprise that among its questions the committee asked "if I received the Confession of faith of the Presbyterian church." Although this would surely have been a standard question, it could have spelled trouble for the more practical-minded, rough-at-the-edges former country lawyer. It turned out to be nothing but a formality, however, that was easily satisfied with vague lip-service on the part of the candidate.

It is not that Finney was completely unfamiliar with the Westminster Confession of Faith and Shorter Catechism, which since 1648 had been the theological plumb line of both the Presbyterian and Congregational branches of the Reformed faith. But neither he nor Gale had thought to focus much attention on it. Finney wrote, "I had not examined it; — that is, the large work, containing the Catechisms and Presbyterian Confession. This had made no part of my study." By "the large work" he meant *The Constitution of the Presbyterian Church, in the United States of America* (1788), which included the Westminster standards along with other founding documents. Elsewhere he added, "I had never examined it with any attention, and I think I had never read it through." In response to the presbytery's question, Finney came up with something like "I receive it for substance of doctrine, so far as I understand it" and hoped that that would be good enough to get him by. Later, after he had read the Westminster Confession more carefully and was familiar with denominational politics, he discovered that "I could receive it, as I now know multitudes of presbyterians do, as containing the substance of Christian doctrine as

26

taught in the Bible," although he disagreed with conservatives on "several points." Finney had nothing to fear in the St. Lawrence Presbytery. Most of the elders present — including the Rev. Daniel ("Father") Nash, who would soon become his partner in revival work — were as loose with their Calvinism as Finney was. Many of them would have given an answer very similar to his, expressing no more than "substantial" agreement with the Westminster Confession. Finney even admitted that "I do not recollect that Mr. Gale ever insisted that the Confession of faith taught these principles right out and out." After listening to his trial sermons (perhaps the only two he ever wrote out beforehand), the presbytery voted unanimously to license Charles Finney as a preacher of the gospel.

The terms *Old School* and *New School* were actually not yet in use among Presbyterians in 1822 and 1823, being coined the next year to describe the two emerging parties that would eventually split in 1837 to form two separate Presbyterian denominations. When George Gale had attended Princeton Theological Seminary in the mid-1810s, that institution was not yet the bastion of uncompromising adherence to the Westminster Confession it would later become under the leadership of Samuel Miller and Charles Hodge. Although Finney used "Princeton" as an epithet connoting rigid doctrinal confessionalism, Princeton College had symbolized quite different characteristics just a few decades earlier when it was at the center of the New Side/Old Side controversy. In the 1740s, New Side Presbyterians led by Yale-educated Gilbert Tennent embraced the revivalism of the Great Awakening and promoted a latitudinarian approach to subscription to the Westminster Confession. The early leaders of Princeton College were all products of Yale, and in 1758 the college called as its president New Englander Jonathan Edwards, who exemplified both revivalism and the attempt to reformulate Calvinist theology. In the Revolutionary era, Princeton College's Scottish-born president John Witherspoon successfully suppressed the old rift, although the tensions remained just below the surface.

Now the lines were again being drawn between those who insisted on strict adherence to the tenets of Westminster and those who favored broader interpretations, between those critical of the emotionalism of revivals and those who promoted the new Awakening, between those who distrusted New England's theological experimentation and those who cooperated fully with Congregationalists under the 1801 Plan of Union. In its first years of existence, Princeton Seminary occupied the middle ground, attempting to accommodate both the strict confessionalists centered in Philadelphia and the New England–influenced evangelicals who were so strong in New York. According to the school's original professor Archibald Alexander, the "old moderate plan" of the Seminary was that of "teaching the doctrines of Calvinism" without being "disposed to consider every man a heretic who differs in some few points with us." As a Princeton graduate, George Gale was a moderate Calvinist, trained in the theology of the Westminster Confession but oriented toward the evangelical revivalism of New England theology. Like most of his colleagues in upstate New York, he was a New School Presbyterian, and Finney did not convert him to this position. Finney quickly discovered aspects of Gale's theology with which he disagreed, and he no doubt pushed Gale beyond his previously held theological limits and opened his mind to further revisions of the Calvinist faith, but George Gale, who went on to found Knox College in Illinois as an evangelical, social reform–minded New School Presbyterian institution, was Finney's best theological instructor.

Charles Finney had imbibed a considerable amount of New England theology by the time he moved into Gale's parsonage. He had not yet read Jonathan Edwards or Nathanael Emmons or Samuel Hopkins, but he had heard their views declaimed from a number of pulpits and expressed in countless religious discussions. Most centrally, these New Englanders — and Charles Finney after them — aimed at developing an evangelical theology that would produce conversions in a revival. But even Finney's elevation of post-conversion holiness, for which he owed an obvious debt to Wesleyanism, can be traced in some measure to Jonathan Edwards. Edwards's reflections on the revivals of the Great Awakening led him to place the highest theological emphasis not on conversion itself as an emotional experience but on the effect of salvation in the human heart and in human behavior. "Those affections that are truly holy, are primarily founded on the loveliness of the moral excellency of divine things," Edwards wrote. Virtue or right behavior, while impossible for the unregenerate sinner, shines forth in the life of the redeemed as love for God and for God's creation. Salvation, in a phrase of Edwards's that Finney would echo in his own preaching on spiritual and moral rebirth, consists of conversion from self-love to "benevolence to Being in general." And Edwards identified the locus of human behavior not in the mind or the emotions but in the will. "The moral excellency of an intelligent voluntary being, is more immediately seated in the heart or will of moral agents. That intelligent being whose will is truly right and lovely, he is morally good or excellent." While Finney modified some aspects of Edwards's Calvinism, such as the doctrine of limited atonement, his theological language from the start was thoroughly Edwardsian.

Edwards did not teach that sinners were free to choose righteousness. He maintained that the sin of Adam and Eve rendered the entire human race fallen and placed it in bondage to sin, defined as self-love. Edwards taught that while we are "naturally free" and "naturally able" not to sin, we are "morally unable" to live in righteousness. Every generation and every individual inevitably sins as did our first parents, whose sinfulness continues to be acted out in us. Edwards held that there is no freedom of the will to do good or to love God. Salvation is possible only because God intervenes through the death of Jesus Christ, atoning for human sin, and through the work of the Holy Spirit in changing the hearts of sinners. Finney would follow Edwards in much of this Calvinistic theology, except concerning the ability of the sinner to turn to God. At that point he began to sound more like the "Arminians" or semi-Pelagians Edwards constantly attacked — and like the Methodist preachers who were attracting huge numbers everywhere in the young United States.

Between Edwards and Finney lay more than a half-century of New England theological development often summarized under the terms *New Divinity, Edwardsianism,* or *Hopkinsianism.* Samuel Hopkins, Joseph Bellamy, Jonathan Edwards Jr., and Nathanael Emmons were among the authors of this evangelistic and social reform–oriented reconstruction of Reformed orthodoxy. In addition to their theological writing and pastoral duties, these New England clergy were noted for their support of the patriot cause during the Revolution and for organizing a myriad of missionary and reform societies in the early Republic. These evangelical societies — established to promote Bible distribution, Sunday school attendance, temperance, evangelism and church development, and many other causes — exercised a major influence on New School Presbyterian and Congregational church life in upstate New York under the Plan of Union during Finney's youth. It was one such voluntary society, the Female Missionary Society of the Western District of the State of New York, headquartered in Utica, that commissioned Finney as a missionary to Jefferson County in March 1824 and provided his first financial support as an evangelist.

Finney not only emerged from institutions that had been built by Hopkinsians but was influenced by the New Divinity itself. Moving beyond Edwards, Hopkins emphasized that sin is not mechanically imputed from Adam but is manifested in each human being in his or her own self-centeredness. Salvation frees us for a life of "disinterested benevolence," seeking good for others just because it is good. Like classical Calvinists, Hopkins held that redemption "does not extend to all sinful, fallen creatures," but only to God's elect. But proponents of the New Divinity painted all their doctrines in colors suggesting the "benevolence of the Deity." For example, they held that it is good that sin is in the world and even that some are lost in it, for without sin there would be no salvation from sin. Christ's death on the cross came to be seen not as a payment that satisfied the penalty due God for Adam's sin but as a display of the justice or "moral government" of God.

Hopkins made one theological shift that clearly influenced Finney's thought when he defined "disinterested benevolence" less as a free response and more as obedience to divine law. Further, by thinking of human beings as "moral agents," Hopkins loosened the tie between a fallen Adam and people who sin today. He wrote that "the children of Adam are not answerable for his sin." Though they will necessarily sin, they are responsible only for their own sin: Adam's sin "is not their sin any further than they approve of it, by sinning as he did." Finney would take issue with Hopkins — as he did with his teacher George Gale — on the traditional Calvinist belief that the sinner remained passive in conversion. Still, Hopkinsian preaching allowed much room for "voluntary action" from the very moment the Holy Spirit begins to work, as the believer engages in works of benevolence.

At the same time that Finney was preparing for the ministry, doctrinal developments at Yale pushed New England theology even further in the direction that became Charles Finney's hallmark — human involvement in the work of salvation. Timothy Dwight, president of Yale College from 1795 to 1817, reinterpreted sin and grace by emphasizing human responsibility to seek salvation, live the Christian life, and work for social reform. Dwight's renewed commitment to evangelism at Yale helped spark the New England phase of the Second Great Awakening. Nathaniel William Taylor, who had been the pastor of New Haven's Center Church, began his work as the Dwight Professor of Theology at the new Yale Divinity School in 1822. His so-called New Haven theology was attacked almost immediately for its overly optimistic view of human nature. Critics charged him, as they would Finney, with slipping over into Arminianism.

Taylor took pains to couch his reappraisal of Calvinism

31

in the language of the Westminster Confession. Upholding the doctrine of "entire moral depravity," he nevertheless denied that original sin meant that "God create[s] in men a sinful nature, and damn[s] them for the very nature he creates." Neither did original sin mean our being "corrupted by being *one* with Adam, and by *acting in his act.*" We are all sinners, and each person has a "sinful disposition," but this common disposition is not itself "original sin." The mainspring of New Haven theology was the notion that sin "is man's own act, consisting in a free choice of some object other than God, as his chief good." Finney echoed this interpretation word for word almost from the very start of his ministry. Both Finney and Taylor leaned in the direction of the Methodists who were becoming so powerfully present in both New England and northern New York. Both of them attempted in their theologies to carve out a position that was simultaneously within the Calvinist tradition and progressively and evangelically American.

Taylor made his views fully public in 1828 with the publication of his Yale address to the clergy, *Concio ad Clerum.* It is impossible to say whether, or to what extent, or just how Finney had access to Taylor's ideas earlier than this date. It is barely conceivable that, as he himself would have us believe, Finney owed an intellectual debt to no one and got his ideas straight from the Bible, and hence that the similarity of his theology to that of Nathaniel William Taylor is simply a coincidence. It is more likely that Taylor's ideas were circulating among Congregational and New School Presbyterian pastors in the early 1820s and that Finney drank them in as he did every other piece of information that made its way to the North Country. Old School Presbyterian critics of evangelical revivalism certainly noticed the connection between Finney and Taylor, and they blamed the New School pastors' theological laxness on the infiltration of New England ideas into the Presbyterian household. According to the hostile analysis of Samuel J. Baird in *A History of the New School* (1868), for example, Taylor and Finney represented the worst of both movements — New England theology and New School Presbyterianism — and demonstrated their kinship.

Charles Finney undertook his study of theology with George Gale within this tempestuous religious environment. More sure of what he was against than what he might be for, Finney admitted that his "views took on a *positive* type but slowly." Building on the basic evangelical theology that Finney took to be "unequivocally taught in the Bible," he "gradually formed views of [his] own in opposition to" the Calvinism of conservative Presbyterians. According to the *Memoirs*, Finney locked horns with Gale at precisely those points where Taylor's New Haven theology pushed past Hopkinsianism and where Old School Presbyterian adherents of the Westminster Confession spotted Arminianism. Finney refused to believe that "the human *constitution* was morally depraved"; that Scripture taught the "theological *fiction* of *imputation*" of Adam's sin into every human being; that people were "utterly unable to comply with the terms of the Gospel, to repent, to believe, or to do anything that God required them to do"; or that "God had condemned men for their sinful *nature*." How could the God revealed in Scripture require obedience while knowing that we could not obey and that he was going to punish us for not doing what we were unable to do in the first place? This would make God a monster. Finney felt that if the Presbyterians could not formulate a better answer, they would have to give in to the Universalists.

It was in a debate with a Universalist, when the scheduled speaker George Gale was too ill to mount the platform, that Finney first stated publicly his understanding of the atonement. He presented Gale as holding to Westminster's substitutionary theory whereby Christ's death "was the literal payment of the debt of the elect." If this were true, all the Universalist had to show from Scripture was "that the atonement was made for all men" and it would follow "that all men would be saved, because the debt of all mankind had been literally paid by the

Lord Jesus Christ." It was perhaps testimony to the popularity of both Universalism and Methodism that Finney could state, "The people can easily see that the Bible proves that Christ died for all men, for the whole world of sinners." Finney remembered Gale capitulating to his view of the work of Christ and begging the preacher-in-training to do whatever it would take to refute the Universalist. Finney argued that Christ's death "rendered the salvation of all men *possible*" but "did not of itself lay God under any obligation to save *anybody*." Finney in essence put forth a version of the moral-government theory of the atonement. "Christ died simply to remove an insurmountable obstacle out of the way of God's forgiving sinners," thereby "inviting all men to repent, to believe in Christ, and to accept salvation." Finney argued that "instead of Christ's having satisfied *retributive* justice, and borne just what sinners deserve, he had only satisfied *public* justice, by honoring the law both in his obedience and death; and therefore rendering it safe for God to pardon sin, and to pardon the sins of any man, and of all men, who would repent and believe in Christ." Better than any "Consistent Calvinism" with its own peculiar inner logic, this was a gospel Finney was sure would make sense to ordinary people. He could take it on the road and preach it in any town in America. He would be an evangelist from the Calvinist tradition striving to win souls in a Methodist-saturated and democracy-driven society.

Finney was licensed by the presbytery in order to serve the Adams church, but according to Gale, "some were not pleased" with his preaching. A settled pastorate was not for Finney, at least for the first decade of his ministry. Gale continued to do what he could for his protégé and arranged for the Female Missionary Society, with which he had connections, to support him as a missionary evangelist. The Oneida County group commissioned Finney for two successive three-month periods from March 17 through September 1824, "to labor in the Northern part of the County of Jefferson and such other destitute places in that County as his discretion shall dictate."

In a rare note of humility, perhaps reflecting his inauspicious start at Adams, Finney acknowledged that "having had no regular training for the ministry I did not expect or desire to labor in large towns or cities, or in cultivated congregations. I intended to go into new settlements and preach in school houses, and barns and groves, as best I could."

What struck many people about Finney's preaching was that he sounded like a lawyer arguing his case in court. There is more to the observation than the fact that the new preacher carried over useful skills from his former occupation. Finney was instinctively able in the pulpit to combine hot passion and cold logic. He would present the problem of human sinfulness and the only possible solution as salvation in Jesus Christ, then argue that a decision had to be made immediately or that it could be too late. He addressed the congregation in personal language, using the pronoun *you,* and his tone communicated the dire urgency of the situation. Above all, Finney understood preaching as persuasion. A few years later in a published sermon, he argued against preaching that aimed merely to instruct or comfort without effecting a spiritual and moral change in listeners. "Suppose a lawyer, in addressing a jury, should not expect to change their minds by any thing he could say, but should wait for an invisible and physical agency, to be exerted by the Holy Ghost upon them." At the same time, jury members in a court case bear personal responsibility within themselves to make a decision. In Finney's evangelical preaching, each "sinner, under the influence of the Spirit of God, is just as free as a jury under the arguments of an advocate." Without this active, dynamically reciprocal relationship between them, "in vain might the lawyer plead, and in vain might the jury hear" — and in vain would the preacher exhort. Finney used no notes when he preached (not even the bare outline or "skeleton" he would adopt a few years later). Following the manner of the Baptists, he relied on the Holy Spirit to provide his text and sermon — to the extent that he sometimes did not know what he would say until he stood before the people. Just like a lawyer in front of the jury, Finney felt tremendous power in preaching to people eye to eye, extemporaneously. Finney was, after all, pleading the Lord's cause now.

His evangelistic work began in the villages of Evans Mills and Antwerp. At Evans Mills, the Baptist congregation had a minister, but the Congregational church was without one and welcomed Finney as their preacher on the alternating Sabbaths when they held worship in the "large stone school house" where both churches met. Finney also had access to the school for meetings all other nights of the week, a privilege he was eager to take advantage of. "The people were very much interested, and thronged en masse to hear me preach," Finney recalled. Distressed that they were merely "pleased" with his sermons, after several weeks he began to press them hard with the need for conversion. At the conclusion of an evening service he preached, "You admit that what I preach is the Gospel. You profess to believe it. Now will you *receive* it? Do you *mean* to receive it? Or do you intend to reject it? You must have some mind about it."

For the first time in his career as an evangelist, Finney demanded an immediate response. In a bold attempt to manipulate the course of a revival, he gave the invitation: "You who have made up your minds to become Christians, and will give your pledge to make your peace with God immediately, should rise up." He then told those had no interest in Christ to "sit still." When no one moved, Finney brought down judgment on them: "You have taken your stand. You have rejected Christ and his Gospel." Promising to preach "once more" the next night, Finney then dismissed the people. The villagers were, in Finney's telling of it, "confounded" and "full of wrath," but after spending the next day in fasting and prayer with the Baptist deacon, the evangelist was confident "that that night the power of God would be revealed among the people." In the evening, seeing Finney and the deacon walk through town, people "turned out of their stores and places of business, threw down their ball clubs where they were playing ball upon the green, and packed the house to its utmost capacity." Finney "opened upon them" with a text from Isaiah: "Say to the righteous that it shall be well with him; for they shall eat the fruit of their doings. Wo to the wicked! it shall be ill with him; for the reward of his hands shall be given him." This was a moment of tremendous influence in Finney's life, as his preaching style took shape. "The Spirit of God came upon me with such power, that it was like opening a battery upon them. For more than an hour, and perhaps for an hour and a half, the Word of God came through me to them in a manner that I could see was carrying all before it." The Word of God — and, many would have said, Finney's voice — was like "a fire . . . a hammer . . . a sword."

Finney made them wait until the next night for the resolution of the crisis. Deists, nominal believers, infidels, Universalists, tavern keepers, respectable citizens, and a husband so angry with the evangelist for upsetting his wife that he came to the meeting with a gun swearing he would "kill Finney" packed the schoolhouse "almost to suffocation." As Finney rose to the occasion and "went on to preach with all my might," the conversions began to occur, some accompanied with falling, groaning, and bellowing. Many inhabitants made "heartbroken confessions" and "professed a hope" of salvation over the next days as Finney visited them in their homes and spoke with them in the street.

The missionary preacher "rode on horseback from town to town" and soon achieved similar results among a German Reformed congregation (to whom he taught the difference, as he saw it, between dead catechetical religion and vital holiness) and at Antwerp. He characterized the feeble Presbyterian church at Antwerp as being hampered by Universalist opposition and the general ungodliness of the population. Finney was appalled that "in playing ball upon the green, and in every business place" men were constantly "cursing and swearing." When a large, curious crowd gathered at the schoolhouse to hear him preach, Finney recognized some of the men and took a bold step. "I pointed them out in the meeting, and told what they said. . . . I let loose my whole heart upon them, and my tears flowed most copiously." Feeling *as if I could rain hail and love upon them at the same time,*" he blasted them for being "on *the very verge of hell.*" Despite anger against Finney, which in some people again bordered on violence, he called on the entire population to attend further meetings.

The Antwerp meetings were rowdy even by North Country standards, with "bawling" that passed for singing. At one point "something flashed over the congregation, — a kind of shimmering, as if there was some agitation in the atmosphere itself." A phenomenon associated with the Methodist revivals manifested itself as "the congregation began to fall from their seats; and they fell in every direction, and cried for mercy." Finney presented the hope of the gospel — "You are not in hell yet; and now let me direct you to Christ" — but he could scarcely make himself heard above the din. The preacher himself was caught up in the Spirit, "laughing in a most spasmodic manner" with "a holy joy." Finney now instinctively tried yet another method that was unusual in a public prayer meeting: "I turned to a young man who was close to me, and was engaged in praying for himself, laid my hand on his shoulder, thus getting his attention, and preached in his ear Jesus." The man was suddenly quiet for a moment "and then broke out in praying for the others." Finney moved among the worshipers individually and discovered the same response. As the revival spread, it "penetrated to every part of the town, and some of the neighboring towns shared in the blessing."

The Charles G. Finney evangelistic style and method were born. As he remembered, "the means used were simply preaching, prayer and conference meetings, and much private prayer, much personal conversation, and meetings for the instruction of earnest inquirers." He served as his own song leader, lining out hymns, though singing was never as important in a Finney prayer meeting as it would become for the generation of evangelists that emerged after the Civil War. In

Finney's ministry, other "new measures," including the mourner's or anxious bench, would develop a few years later in Oneida County and in Rochester, although he did remember one occasion in Evans Mills on which, "at the close of the sermon," he "called upon any who would give their hearts to God to come forward and take the front seats." The spirit of Finney's great revivals in the boomtowns along the Erie Canal was present early on in the North Country. There Finney embraced the religious enthusiasm of the common people, although his greatest appeal tended to be with the community leaders who became his friends. He complained that "fanaticism" had made Jefferson County "a burnt district." What he meant by this was that the prospect of spiritual renewal had been seriously damaged, if not entirely burned up, by the ranting of irresponsible preachers. Recent historians, beginning with Whitney R. Cross in his classic study *The Burned-Over District*, have used the term in a positive fashion and in reference to the Mohawk Valley and Finger Lakes area. Finney was referring to Jefferson County and meant it negatively, indicating that the North Country was what modern slang might call a "bummed-out district." It was Finney's calling to rekindle the fire.

Charles Finney never cared for denominational politics, and his revivals involved any church that would participate. Still, there was never a question about his denominational identity. Although he eagerly adopted the enthusiasm of the backcountry Baptists and Methodists — including the Spirit manifestations of falling and "holy laughter" — he also made it clear in the *Memoirs* that he clung to his identity as an evangelical New School Presbyterian in union with Yorker Congregationalists. But he pushed this identity to its limits. He was willing to experiment with baptism by immersion in a stream, for instance, even though he found his administration of the ordinance in the meetinghouse by sprinkling to be more "intensely solemn," "blessed by God," and "acceptable to Him." When Methodists scoffed that "Mr. Finney is a Presbyterian" who dared not preach election and predestination, he did precisely that, arguing that the doctrine of election, properly understood, "was the only hope that *anybody* would be saved." The Methodists and Baptists among whom he labored helped shape Finney, but they did not make him who he was.

Finney proved himself before his own presbytery. That he was a hard worker could not be denied. His report to the Female Missionary Society at the end of his first twelve weeks indicated that he had preached 77 sermons, attended 36 prayer and 13 conference meetings, and made 469 home visits. This pace wore him out at first — he fell ill and even coughed up blood — but he eventually gained strength and developed tremendous endurance. Based on what they knew of his labors, friends among the Presbyterian clergy such as Adams W. Platt, who had served the same missionary society, put forth Charles Finney for full ordination to the Christian ministry. Finney appears to have been nervous about his prospects, but the idea met with universal support. Platt wrote Finney in late June that those he had polled "seemed pleased with the idea." Even George Boardman at Watertown, known for his more formal views, "will make no opposition, but fell in with the idea cheerfully." So at the outset of his second three-month appointment, the Presbytery of St. Lawrence ordained Finney to the ministry as an evangelist on July 1, 1824. He continued to preach and visit at the same breakneck pace into the fall.

Finney's "plain and pointed" manner of preaching was being talked about among the clergy. He aimed, as he said in his report to the Society, to show people that "the religion of such of them as had not been born again, was insufficient, and altogether an abomination to God." He studded his sermons not with literary allusions but with illustrations from "the common affairs of men" in language that could be "understood by the common people." What most intrigued the clergy was the idea that he could "get up and preach on the spur of the moment." Although they had ordained him, some ministers were beginning to feel that, with his brash use of such words as *you* and *hell*, he "let down the dignity of the pulpit." Others wanted to invite him to come and work in their town. At the next meeting of the Presbytery of St. Lawrence, one elder stated, "The people have come together manifestly to hear preaching; and I move that Mr. Finney preach a sermon." Finney did not shy away from the chance; indeed, he admitted, "I *wanted* to preach." He did not let them down. Instead of mounting the pulpit "up against the wall," he stood among the people and announced his text from Hebrews 12: "Without holiness no man shall see the Lord." He explained that "the Lord helped me to preach as I walked up and down the broad aisle; and the people were evidently interested and much moved." At this point he had not yet received any opposition from his predominantly New School colleagues.

Finney generally attended presbytery and synod meetings only when he had some special business in connection with them, and this was the case when the Synod of Albany met in Utica the first week of October. He appeared at the meeting long enough to have his name registered and then left for nearby Whitestown to marry Lydia Root Andrews, to whom he had been engaged for some time. Their friend Adams W. Platt married the couple in Lydia's home church on October 5, 1824. Finney appeared ready to settle down, having given the Evans Mills church "encouragement that I would abide with them at least one year." Lydia completed her "preparations for housekeeping" and was ready for the move north. Shortly after the wedding, Finney went to Jefferson County with the intention of returning with a wagon the next week.

In one of the oddest twists in Finney's life, the evangelist got caught up in a revival at the tiny village of Perch River and forgot about his promise to Lydia. When the revival spread to Brownville, described by Finney perhaps tongue-in-cheek as "a village of considerable size," he wrote to his bride explaining "that such were the circumstances that I must defer coming for her until God seemed to open the way." Through the winter, he admitted, the mail being what it was, "we had seldom been able to exchange letters." Six months later, when spring arrived, he finally set out with his "horse and cutter" for Oneida County, but he did not get far. He had to stop just a few miles down the road in LeRaysville to get the horse shod, and while he was waiting the people prevailed on him to hold a preaching service. One meeting led to another and suddenly, Finney recalled, "we had a powerful revival." He sent someone else to get Lydia.

It is tempting to analyze the behavior of the thirty-two-year-old former bachelor and surmise, at the very least, that he was suffering from a severe case of cold feet. Once they were united, however, the love that Charles Finney shared with Lydia and with the six children they eventually bore and reared (one of whom died in infancy and one in childhood) was obvious to everyone. Lydia became accustomed to the fact that her husband's first and greatest love was for God and for his calling as a preacher of the gospel. In addition to the evangelist's tendency to be preoccupied, the transient nature of his work meant that the couple was essentially homeless. When Lydia joined her husband in LeRaysville, they took up temporary lodging in the home of a prestigious recent convert, Judge Samuel C. Kanady. It was the first of many such homes in which the Finneys lived as guests for weeks or months at a time.

During Finney's time in Jefferson County, he acquired a special friend in the Rev. Daniel Nash. Father Nash, a veteran pastor who had recently experienced a spiritual renewal of his own and was now "full of the power of prayer," became a partner in many subsequent revival campaigns and a mentor to whom Finney looked for spiritual wisdom and support. By what he called "a direct revelation from God to me" that the Lord "was going to pour out His Spirit at Gouverneur," Finney knew that the location of his work was to shift to the northeast in St. Lawrence County. There, too, his partnership with Father Nash became important as they labored together from late April through the summer months of 1825.

The Finney-Nash team entered Gouverneur as if it were a war zone. They battled a cadre of Universalists under the leadership of the local doctor, who was also a trustee in the Presbyterian church, turf-conscious Baptists who forbade their children to attend the prayer meetings, a Deist who believed "the Bible was a fable," and a band of young "roughs" who held religion in contempt. Finney and Nash prayed together in a grove outside town until they "prevailed" with God and "felt confident that no power which earth or hell could interpose, would be allowed to permanently stop the revival." Within the first few weeks "the revival made a clean sweep of them" all. One by one, they "broke down," humbled themselves before God, and were soon "hoping in Christ." Finney exaggerated his success in winning over Baptist converts — this was pointed out when he began publishing some of these revival memories in the New York *Independent* in 1873 — but the Presbyterian church in Gouverneur did experience a tremendous spurt in growth that summer.

Late that summer Finney moved his ministry another sixteen miles north to the village of De Kalb, where Methodist revivals in the late 1810s had firmly established a church and popular support for emotional religion. In De Kalb they knew about the experience of *"falling* under the power of God." Working with the Presbyterians and their sincere but prim pastor, Finney was not impressed with their negative attitude toward Methodist enthusiasm. As usual, Finney organized the revival by neighborhood, "visiting from house to house," holding "meetings . . . in different parts of the town," and encouraging people to pray for their neighbors' salvation. The revival advanced "with a good deal of power." Finney rejoiced when at the end of his sermons people began to fall from their seats — and was even more delighted to learn that they were all Presbyterians.

People came down from Ogdensburg to witness, as one put it in a letter, Finney's "religious performances." These included attorney John Fine, who wanted to employ him "as his

missionary to work in the towns throughout that country."
Finney declined the offer, but the De Kalb revival grew so
powerful that when the Ogdensburg visitors returned north,
they took its spirit with them. At De Kalb the evangelist encouraged individuals to stand and witness to "what the Lord
had done, and was doing, for their souls." It was a practice that
he normally limited to a few well-chosen, articulate believers.
A church leader who had previously been lukewarm in his
piety told how "the Holy Ghost fell upon him, and filled him
as full as he could hold." Others rose to speak, "one after
another," and "the people melted down on every side." Believing the Lord was guiding these events, Finney "sat still and
saw the salvation of God" as "conversions were multiplied in
every part of the congregation."

News of the extravagance of the Gouverneur and De Kalb
revivals reached Oneida County to the south. Charles Cushman
Sears, Finney's friend from Adams who was now studying for
the ministry, wrote from Hamilton College, where a revival
was also in progress. On the one hand, Sears reported having
followed Finney's progress with "the most exquisite satisfaction." Employing language ambitious enough to match the
name "Charles Grandison," he compared Finney to "a Washington, a Bollivar, or Wellington." These heroes may have
saved "a few small colonies from temporary servitude" or "a
few kingdoms from a few days of domineering oppression,"
but Finney's work was even greater: "Saving a soul! immortal!
destined to endure when kingdoms and states, and even
worlds shall have slumbered in their original chaos for myriads
of ages! a soul!"

On the other hand, writing "as a friend to a friend," Sears
also warned Finney against going too far in his zeal. He rebuked him for the judgmentalism he detected in a recent letter
in which Finney wrongly condemned a certain individual for
his "cold heart" and "endless theories." More broadly, he
hoped Finney did not mean to imply "that everything in a
revival was right, and that no degree of rant and passion could

be wrong." Arguing that "the great instrument" in a revival should be prayer and "appropriate appeals . . . to the understanding and conscience," Sears confessed "the unhappiness of differing from" his friend. Let it not be, he pleaded, that "no degree of animal feeling is too great, and that excitement however raised, is to be cultivated and cherished." Charles Finney did not invent the radical form of revivalism that characterized his work in the North Country. He adopted elements of the style of evangelistic preachers who had been in the area for decades. He was the product of the evangelical culture from which he emerged, shaped not only by the revival-oriented theology of New England but also by the spirit of the exuberant Methodist and Baptist popular religion he encountered during his ministry in northern Jefferson County.

Whether Charles Finney's rough way of inciting conversions and his fondness for such expressions of enthusiasm as "falling" in the Spirit, "holy laughter," and reliance on the Holy Spirit to provide a text and sermon at the very moment of preaching would wash in more cultured locations such as Oneida County — or whether the evangelist would adopt smoother methods — remained to be seen. In the fall of 1825 the Finneys traveled to Whitesboro to combine attendance at a church meeting with a visit with Lydia's parents. By chance on the road they met Finney's old pastor and teacher George W. Gale, who was temporarily farming in Western, about nine miles northeast of Rome. Gale enthusiastically invited Finney to stay for a few days and help to lead some prayer meetings. An entirely new phase of his ministry was about to commence. He was prepared in at least two practical ways: the philanthropic lawyer John Fine had sent a tailor to outfit the evangelist with a new suit of clothes and had given him sixty dollars in cash, enough to buy the carriage in which Charles and Lydia Finney were now traveling.

3 Can Two Walk Together?

In late October 1825, Governor De Witt Clinton passed through Oneida County on the festooned canal boat *Seneca Chief*, carrying two kegs of the "pure water of Lake Erie" that he planned to pour ceremonially into the Atlantic Ocean at New York City. Charles G. Finney, who had been in Whitesboro right on the Erie Canal earlier that same month, was now preaching regularly at Western, just to the north. He would soon take his evangelical ministry to the cities of Rome and Utica, then west to Auburn and east to Troy. As a friend wrote in the summer of 1826, "Troy, I think, would open your way to Schenectady, Albany, and New York." Indeed, New School Presbyterian philanthropists in New York City and Congregational clergy in Boston began to take note of his work. The free, highly competitive religious market that flourished in and around the urban centers along the canal embroiled Finney in conflicts and opened to him opportunities that had been impossible to imagine up north in Jefferson and St. Lawrence Counties.

The Erie Canal was complete from Lake Ontario at Buffalo, across the state through Rochester and Syracuse, to the deep waters of the Hudson River near Albany. Clinton's "big ditch" — 363 miles dug by hand though swamp and solid rock and requiring 83 locks — was exceedingly hard and costly to build. But it became land- and commerce-hungry America's first cheap and easy way west past the Appalachian Mountain barrier, and it helped New York City soar beyond its rivals Boston and Philadelphia as the business capital of the nation. Begun in 1817, when the governor persuaded the state legislature to finance the unprecedented seven million dollar project, the canal began paying for itself immediately as sections of it were put into use as soon as they were finished. With shipping costs sliced to a small fraction of what they had been by wagon, farming and manufacturing boomed in the Mohawk River Valley during the early 1820s. By the time its entire length was finished, the cities along the canal had already achieved much economic stability and began to enjoy the luxury of erecting impressive churches and public buildings. The *Seneca Chief*, mounted with a grand portrait of Clinton dressed in a toga as if this were Imperial Rome rather than the Empire State, stopped on Sunday at Utica, where the dignitaries attended church. It was an auspicious month for Charles Finney to begin his work in Oneida County.

Charles and Lydia moved in with George Gale and his wife on their farm in Western, and Finney's transition to urban evangelism took place gradually. If Gale had earlier harbored any misgivings about Finney's theology or style — which in their respective autobiographical writings Gale denied but Finney insisted had been the case — he was now an enthusiastic promoter of the evangelist. Gale, who had retired temporarily from preaching in order to recover his health, invited Finney to go with him to a prayer meeting, hoping this would, as he wrote in a report the next year, "induce him" to "tarry here for a season." Finney had noted that "religion was at low water mark" in the local Presbyterian church and resolved simply to observe the meeting. After enduring a torrent of ineffectual prayers and dismal testimony, however, he could not restrain himself and blasted them for their "mock prayer meeting." The cycle of anger followed by abject repentance that Finney had already experienced countless times repeated itself, and soon "every man and woman present went down upon their knees." For an hour "they all wept, and confessed, and broke their hearts before God." Charles Finney was in his element.

The following Sunday the church was packed and alive with anticipation. "I preached all day," Finney later remembered, "and God came down with great power upon the people." Through the coming week Finney preached "in different parts of the town in school houses, and at the center," following his old North Country pattern. Gale reported that in Finney's sermons "sinners were pressed with the duty of immediate repentance . . . in language plain and pointed." Finney urged people to "pray without ceasing; believing the words of our Lord, that he is more ready to give the Holy Spirit to them that ask him, than earthly parents to give good gifts to their children." In their home visits, Finney and Gale sparked conversions among scores of penitents and found "the spirit of prayer was prevailing, especially among the female members of the church." The wives of two of the church elders were among the awakened, including Sarah Brayton, whose husband was a wealthy businessman and former state senator. Finney's close pastoral work with the Brayton family culminated in the conversion of their children and the cementing of long-term friendships, attested by many letters over the years.

Finney wrote that at Western "it was manifest to everybody that the work of grace had begun." As the word spread, people came out from Rome to hear Finney when he preached at the midway village of Elmer's Hill. Among the visitors who came more than once were the Rev. Moses Gillet, veteran pastor of Rome's Congregational church, and Miss Catherine Huntington, the Sunday school superintendent and stalwart of benevolent causes. Gillet, so taken by Finney's preaching that he said he felt as if he had "got a new Bible," lured the evangelist to Rome by proposing a pulpit exchange. Although "the revival was at its full strength at Western," Finney consented to the plan and immediately discovered that the city was as eager for his message as the villages in the countryside had been. It was December 25, but the people's excitement had nothing to do with Christmas, which at that time was not celebrated in any special way by American Protestants. Preaching that "the carnal mind is enmity against God" (Rom. 8:7), Finney said that he "could see . . . that a great number of them were bowed down with deep conviction for sin." The next step was to appoint an "inquirers' meeting" for penitents. When this was held, Gillet was stunned to see in attendance not notorious sinners but the leaders of his church, the "most intelligent and influential" members, and "the first class of young men in the town." Finney may also have been surprised — with the intensity of the reaction to his prayers and exhortations. In spite of his efforts to limit "any boisterous manifestation of feeling" and to hush "loud shrieking," some penitents "fainted" to the floor, others "partially swooned away, and fell together," and many were reduced to "sobbing and sighing." Moses Gillet, writing soon after the event, described it in identical language: "They partly fell upon each other, and gave vent to their feelings in sobs and groans." Finney and Gillet encountered the same phenomena when they visited families in their homes the next day. Finney insisted, however, that as the revival continued for the next three weeks, it involved no "disorder, or tumult, or fanaticism, or anything that was objectionable."

Meetings were held in Rome almost every day during the first three weeks of January 1826 — prayer meetings in the morning, meetings for inquiry in the afternoon, and preaching services in the evening — in such locations as the large dining room of the hotel, the courthouse, schoolhouses, and the Congregational church. "Worldly business was to a great extent suspended," Gillet reported. Some women who had loved finery, including the beautiful wife of Moses Gillet himself, accepted the Savior and gave up their "trifling ornaments." Believers, and especially groups of women, banded together to make certain individuals "a particular subject of prayer." In a significant move, to follow up on the work of the Spirit more effectively, Finney began asking new converts to "come forward and report themselves" at the end of the evening service. Among the four to five hundred who professed faith in Christ during the revival were numerous civic leaders: merchants, physicians, the bank president (a well-known skeptic), the county sheriff, and every lawyer in town. The reputation of Charles Finney spread abroad as ministers and church leaders arrived, some from places as distant as other states, to witness the excitement in Rome. At least as significant as the number of conversions was the affection the people of Rome developed for Finney. One woman wrote Lydia the next summer, after the scene of his ministry had shifted to Utica and Auburn, to say "How it would gladden our hearts to once more hear Mr. Finney . . . from that sacred desk, in that sanctuary, where . . . God was present by the convicting and converting influences of his Holy Spirit."

Charles Finney worked in Oneida County from late 1825 through the summer of 1826 essentially as a member of an evangelistic team of preachers, most of them settled pastors of congregations. He was also still working in many of these meetings in partnership with Daniel Nash, although he strangely failed to mention this in his *Memoirs*. Besides George Gale at Western and Moses Gillet in Rome, the group included Noah Coe at New Hartford, Samuel Aikin at Utica, Oliver Wetmore at Trenton, and John Frost at Whitesboro. These men wielded great power in the presbytery. Finney formally joined them by transferring his membership from St. Lawrence to the Oneida Presbytery, and the presbytery — with a few dissenting clerical voices — gave him its full support. These New School pastors in turn were allied with other revival-minded Presbyterian and Congregational clergy both to the west and the east along the Canal. They began a pro-revival periodical, *The West-*

ern Recorder, edited by Thomas Hastings and published in Utica. Moreover, they promoted revivals in their communities before Finney arrived and continued them after he moved on. They viewed him, in Gillet's nice phrase, as "a distinguished instrument in promoting the revival" but never identified the effort solely with his ministry. To encourage the revival, these pastors wrote and gathered firsthand reports, publishing the collection as *A Narrative of the Revival of Religion, in the County of Oneida, Particularly in the Bounds of the Presbytery of Oneida, in the Year 1826* (Utica, 1826).

The *Narrative* overwhelmingly demonstrated the extent to which Finney's theology and methods were broadly shared among New School pastors. Oliver Wetmore, who served in a village Finney visited only once, stated in language strikingly similar to that employed by Finney himself that the "means" used in the revivals were "prayer and the preaching of the gospel," with "meetings of inquiry" and "prayer meetings" in which "Christians . . . have prayed for particular individuals." They offered "the prayer of faith" as the means of receiving salvation. The distinguishing doctrines were identified as "the holy sovereignty of God . . . the divine law, with its penalty . . . the atonement, total depravity of the heart, and the duty of immediate repentance and reconciliation to God." All the New School pastors had by now renounced the Old School emphasis on the divine initiative in salvation, which seemed to them to wipe out any chance for human response. They wrote that in the revivals "no excuse, on account of human depravity, or human dependence and divine agency, has been allowed." Wetmore pointed to "the great guilt of sinners in making excuses, that they *cannot* repent, and *cannot* love God, and *would* if they *could.*" Every one of these pastors joined Charles Finney in rejecting the traditional Calvinistic disparagement of human ability and utter reliance on God's sovereign initiative in the experience of salvation. They preached, "You *can!* You *must! Now!*"

Charles Finney began his ministry in Utica at the end of

January 1826 with this spirit of cooperation among the New School pastors. At the same time, he became increasingly aware of rising conflict with both theological and methodological conservatives. Opposition to the Oneida revivals from Old School Presbyterians, most of them outside the county and even the state, involved revulsion at both theology and method. Meanwhile, some New School Presbyterians in central New York and a few prominent New England clergy were beginning to write against what they saw as the crude barbarism of Finney and his colleagues. Finney appears not to have relished the conflict, but neither did he shy from it. He simply advanced with his mission as he understood it. Samuel Aikin reported that before January "there was but little of the spirit of prayer" in Utica, but that began to change when "daily reports of what was doing in Rome" stirred some to go hear Finney there. Aikin and his elders visited in homes and engaged in "pointed" conversation and prayer, and "one of his principal ladies" devoted herself entirely to prayer for revival. As Finney saw it, "the work had already begun in her heart," and he committed himself to the booming canal city of about five thousand inhabitants. The revival exploded in Utica with the arrival of the evangelist.

"When the Rev. Mr. Finney came to Utica," Samuel Aikin wrote, "as in other places, his plain and pungent and faithful preaching was attended with evident and wonderful success." Finney pressed the people with their sinfulness and "the necessity of a broken spirit" and followed with the promise of the gospel. "They were urged to seek [the Holy Spirit] as a blessing which God has promised, and will certainly give to those who seek it with faith." Among the scores of conversions were several, noted by Finney in his *Memoirs*, who became significant figures in their own right: Dr. Garret Judd, who sailed a year later as a missionary to the Sandwich Islands and subsequently turned his energy to Hawaiian political leadership; a skeptical school teacher visiting from Newburgh, Miss Fanny Thomas, who then married the missionary Peter Gulick and sailed on the same ship with the Judds; and an outspoken Hamilton College student named Theodore Dwight Weld. Weld had made no secret of his contempt for revival preaching and for Finney in particular, and the evangelist spared nothing in his frontal assault on Weld's unrepentant sinfulness, reportedly telling him, "Puke it up, Mr. W——, puke it up!" Weld soon "made public confession before the whole congregation" and became an ardent coworker with Finney through the summer months. Weld's presence at Utica serves as a reminder of the connection between the New School revivals and the social reform side of evangelical benevolence that Weld would later come to embody. While his devotion to the abolition movement was at this point perhaps latent, Weld even then was a supporter of women's rights. He immediately promoted female testimony in mixed prayer meetings, a practice that was common among Methodists and had been going on to a lesser degree at the Presbyterian-led revivals. Finney did not disapprove of this liberty but had frankly not given it much thought. Along with most other evangelicals, Weld was also a vigorous advocate of temperance. A note at the end of *A Narrative of the Revival* states that profits from sales of the volume would go to fund an annual prize at Hamilton College for "the best essay on the subject of *intemperance*."

Finney preached during the spring at all the churches served by his New School friends in the villages surrounding Utica and in such public places as a textile factory on Oriskany Creek at New York Mills where Lydia's brother was superintendent. In the mill, Finney used his imposing height and piercing eyes to humble the girls and young women, often reducing them to tears. The factory owner stopped production and called for a series of prayer meetings. Finney wrote in the *Memoirs* that "in the course of a few days nearly all in the mill were hopefully converted." He omitted any mention of the local Methodist minister's activity in this revival, although it was his church that benefited most from new members. The Methodist, in turn, left Finney out of his autobiographical account of the event as if the evangelist's presence were incidental. The authors of *A Narrative of the Revival* were perhaps more honest when they estimated that during 1826 *"more than three thousand"* were "indulging hope" of salvation, with "about half this number" having joined Presbyterian, Congregational, Baptist, and Methodist churches. Charles Finney did not single-handedly create the revival mentality in Oneida County; rather, a broad-based revivalist environment welcomed the ministry of Charles Finney.

Finney experienced some opposition to the revivals within Oneida County, and this proved to be an omen of future conflict. He simply ignored the outlandish rumors that he was a bigamist and the father of illegitimate children. Some said he beat children to drive them to repentance. Crude jokes about the evangelist circulated. More seriously, Finney consistently encountered opposition from Universalists and deists. He had relished the intellectual thrill of exposing their theological inconsistencies since the first days of his Christian life. Unitarianism was largely restricted to the financial and intellectual elite of urban New England, but Universalism was a popular and often evangelistic movement with great appeal among common folk, and so he focused more of his attention on that error. Dismissing both the Universalist assertion that all would be saved and Calvinist restrictions on the human capacity to seek salvation, Finney trumpeted his own version of the gospel. Christ died for all, but each sinner had better come to the point of repentance and belief or face a fiery hell. Finney routinely disregarded criticism from those who felt he tarnished the dignity of the pulpit, though in sermons he often lashed out at these enemies of revivals.

A published assault entitled *A "Bunker Hill" Contest, A.D. 1826,* though, was particularly vicious and could not be ignored. Written by a Unitarian lay leader in Trenton, in eastern Oneida County, the tract depicted Finney as "High Priest" of a " 'Holy Alliance' for the Establishment of Hierarchy and Ecclesiastical Domination over the Human Mind" and a wild-eyed fanatic with frightening powers bordering on the occult. It charged that the evangelical revivals amounted to a conspiracy against "Free Inquiry, Bible Religion, Christian Freedom, and Civil Liberty." It was partly in response to these outrageous charges that the New School pastors published *A Narrative of the Revival of Religion*. The *"Bunker Hill"* description of Finney's preaching is beautifully vivid, if laced with sarcasm: "You breast yourself to the work like a giant. You open the attack with Jupiter's thunderbolt. You take the doctrine for a damning fact — declare you know it — raise your voice — lift high your hand — bend forward your trunk — fasten your staring eyes upon the auditors — declare that they know it to be God's truth; that they stand upon the brink of hell's gaping pit of fire and brimstone . . . unless they repent forthwith." This part of the barrage was in fact so true to life that the published defense could only say it was "a little caricatured," that it was not, as claimed, mere theatrical gimmickry.

Criticism from closer to home came from three Congregational ministers, led by William R. Weeks of the Paris Hill church. Their *Pastoral Letter of the Ministers of the Oneida Association . . . on the Subject of Revivals of Religion* (Utica, 1827) condemned a long list of "evils" in the way the revivals were being carried out. Old School Presbyterians objected, of course, to Finney's un-Calvinist rejection of the imputation of Adam's sin and his emphasis on human ability to choose Jesus as Savior, and the *Pastoral Letter* was read with approval and republished in Philadelphia. But Weeks and his colleagues were not Old School Presbyterians. They were evangelical Congregationalists adhering to the New England theology of Hopkins and Emmons, whose language of disinterested benevolence and governmental theory of atonement Finney shared even as he modified their view of human ability. This attack on the Oneida revivals had to do with the perceived glorification of "mere animal passions," lack of decorum, and judgmentalism in "calling men hard names." They rejected the practice of "female prayer and exhortation in promiscuous meetings," urging women rather to "be active and diligent in their own sphere" (i.e., in women's meetings). These were methodological rather than theological objections, representing a critique of the manner and tone of the revivals and not an Old School condemnation of revivalism itself.

Similarly, opposition by Hamilton College president Henry Davis was hardly on Old School Presbyterian theological grounds, as Davis was a New England divine who graduated from and taught theology at Yale College before assuming the presidency of Middlebury and then Hamilton. Finney's lack of unambiguous support from the Congregational pastor in Clinton, Asahel S. Norton, was likewise methodological and not theological. Insisting to friends that he did "fully approve" of Finney's preaching, Norton hosted the evangelist at his church and promoted the revival at the college. He drew back, however, from full personal participation in the work. H. H. Kellogg, who had actually invited Finney to Clinton, complained that Norton "appears desirous of doing his duty, but he is not plain, telling sinners to repent, and *that immediately.*" After Norton was exposed to three weeks of Finney's preaching in June, Kellogg reported some improvement, noting that he was preaching "rather more pointedly" since Finney left, although he could not bring himself to call for immediate repentance and commitment — "still he does not do *the thing.*"

When Finney moved the site of his work out of Oneida County to Auburn, west of Syracuse at the head of Owasco Lake, he again found tension between support for the revival and antipathy toward the methods his name was coming to symbolize. Dr. Dirck C. Lansing, the distinguished pastor of the Auburn church and a trustee and teacher at the New School Presbyterian seminary there, invited Finney west after he had gone to hear him in Utica. Charles and Lydia lived as guests in Lansing's manse in July and August while the evangelist preached in Auburn and villages along the Finger Lakes. It was not an unpleasant spot for the Finneys to spend the summer.

However, Charles was by now aware of a hostile network of correspondence established by "ministers east of Utica" and stretching west at least as far as the lake district. Their goal, he was confident, was to prejudice church leaders against him and "to hedge me in, and prevent the spread of the revivals in connection with my labors." At Auburn friends revealed that "a system of espionage was being carried on," involving at least one student at Auburn Theological Seminary, to supply opponents with potentially damaging information such as cases of emotional excess and female exhorting during prayer meetings.

Finney gave the spies plenty to report back east. The evangelist gave himself anew to "closet prayer" and was rewarded with such a sense of God's presence that he felt as if he were Moses on Mount Sinai. "The Lord showed me as in a vision what I had to pass through. He drew so near to me . . . that *my flesh literally trembled on my bones.* I shook from head to foot, like a man in an ague fit." Never had Finney been elevated with such confidence as he went to the pulpit. He likened himself to the prophet Jeremiah, who preached, "The Lord is with me as a mighty terrible one; therefore my persecutors shall stumble, and they shall not prevail." The revival spirit filled Auburn just as it had the cities and villages of Oneida County, and Jefferson County before that. Lansing's was a wealthy church, "a large congregation, and a very intelligent one," but the more rough-and-tumble popular style of religious experience lay just beneath the cultured veneer. When Finney preached one Sunday morning against men who prevented their wives and children from attending prayer meetings, he proclaimed, "Probably if I were acquainted with you, I could call some of you by name who treat your families in this manner." Suddenly, "a gentleman cried out in the congregation, 'Name me!'" He "threw his head forward on the seat before him" and "trembled with great emotion."

Spontaneous and passionate emotional responses bubbled up from within the previously reserved Auburn worshipers. During an evening service a man, suddenly convicted of sin as Finney spoke, fell to the floor "from his seat near the broad aisle" and "cried out in a most unearthly and terrific manner." The congregation was "very much shocked." Finney spoke quietly to him as he stayed "on his knees with his head on his wife's lap . . . weeping aloud like a child, confessing his sins." When Finney announced to the congregation the identity of the penitent, "it produced tears and sobs in every part of the house." Dirck Lansing, who worked as hard as Finney to promote the revival, was himself not immune from the popular upsurge. After Finney preached that people must give up their worldliness and turn to God, he called upon the pastor to pray. When Lansing reiterated the point of the sermon "a man arose in the gallery and said in a very deliberate and distinct manner, 'Mr. Lansing I do not believe that such remarks from you can do any good whilst you wear a ruffled shirt and a gold ring on your finger, and whilst your wife and the ladies of your family sit as they do before the congregation dressed as leaders in the fashions of the day.'" The charge struck the pastor down, and he "cast himself across the side of the pulpit and wept like a child." People dropped their heads and wept quietly as the sanctuary became "profoundly silent." Lansing remained motionless. Finney at last prayed briefly and dismissed the people. In an effort to resolve the spiritual crisis in an orderly fashion, Lansing drew up a general confession for the whole church that was officially adopted and presented in worship. The people "stood, many of them weeping, while the confession was read." Not everyone approved of all this. Some members called for Lansing's dismissal and, failing at that, withdrew to form another church.

Auburn Seminary had been established seven years before as an evangelical Presbyterian institution, and it came to symbolize, in contrast to Princeton, the theological stance and benevolent activism of the New School movement. Dirck Lansing, Auburn's leading light, was in full fellowship with Charles Finney's Oneida County revival colleagues. Finney notes in his *Memoirs,* however, that "some of the professors . . . were taking an attitude hostile to the revival." President James Richards, a product of Connecticut Congregationalism and Yale College who also had earned a master of arts degree from Princeton College, was among those who regarded the revivals as "to a great extent, spurious excitement," according to a biographer. Richards, like others in the anti-Finney network of correspondence, did not differ from him so much on theological grounds. It was the style and tone — the bad manners — of the revivals to which they objected. "Doing *the thing,*" as H. H. Kellogg in Clinton called it, seemed to them religious vulgarity. The confrontational methodology and extreme urgency, Finney's way of calling for immediate repentance and immediate commitment, represented for them a change from the older Edwardsian and Hopkinsian New England awakenings and the old Puritan "means of grace." Opposers began to use the term "New Measures" to denounce what they did not like about the methods employed by Finney and his colleagues.

Charles Finney knew the names of those "ministers east of Utica" who were writing letters against him: Asahel Nettleton and Lyman Beecher. Nettleton, ten years older than Finney, had spent his career as an itinerant evangelist in the northeastern United States, with most of his work in Connecticut. He was a soberly conservative revivalist whose theology was solidly in the Edwardsian-Hopkinsian tradition. In 1833 he joined with other Hopkinsians to found Hartford Seminary as a bulwark against Nathaniel William Taylor's more progressive or diluted Calvinism at Yale. Before being stricken with typhoid fever in 1822, Nettleton was the most powerful promoter of revival the New Divinity had produced. He was still a force to be reckoned with in 1826 and 1827, as is evident in Lyman Beecher's deference to him in the face of the upstart rival Charles G. Finney. But Nettleton's health was poor, and it is not hard to detect in his approach to Finney the defensiveness of one whose star was falling.

Lyman Beecher, on the other hand, was already a national

figure whose career would take him in ever wider circles in the coming years, culminating in the presidency of Lane Seminary in Cincinnati. In 1826 he made a dramatic move from an influential pastorate at Litchfield, Connecticut, to Hanover Street Church in Boston, one of the few orthodox Congregational churches left in that predominantly Unitarian city. Serving on the boards of countless mission and reform societies, Beecher was a major leader in evangelical Protestantism's benevolent empire. Theologically, Beecher emerged from the Edwardsian tradition shared by most Yale graduates and many upstate New York Presbyterians, but he was already drifting toward "Taylorism" — which was practically indistinguishable from what at least a few church leaders were beginning to call "Finneyism." Still, Beecher was outraged by the wild reports of fanatical behavior associated with the Oneida County revivals and vowed that their influence must not advance any further east or west.

Finney first heard that he had attracted the attention of the New England clergy when he was at Utica in the spring of 1826. Nettleton wrote several times to the Utica pastor Samuel Aikin outlining "what he regarded as objectionable in the conduct of those revivals." The Oneida County pastors replied that "no such things were done," but they were fudging. Finney conceded in his *Memoirs* that it was true "that occasionally females would pray in the social meetings," but he maintained that no one had complained and that "I had no agency in introducing that among their people." Dirck Lansing's wife informed Lydia Finney in a letter in November 1826 that there arose "more of a spirit of prayer among the females since you left and we have had some meetings at the Session house where male and female voices have both been heard successively and the spirit of the Lord was indeed among them." Word of this no doubt also found its way to Beecher and Nettleton. Several letters from both Nettleton and Beecher to a number of Finney's upstate New York colleagues dated early in 1827 were published later that year in evangelical newspapers. Finney suggests that there were many more letters in the summer and fall of 1826 passing on the stagecoaches serving Boston, Albany, and the western cities.

As though drawn to a magnet, Charles Finney completed his work in Auburn and, after some stops back in Oneida County, responded to persistent invitations to move his ministry to Troy. Troy is located at the point where the Mohawk River flows into the Hudson, not far from the Massachusetts border. In reaction to the presence of "the madman of Oneida" at the gateway to New England, Nettleton hurriedly left a revival on Long Island and began a campaign in Albany, little more than five miles south on the opposite bank of the Hudson River. The meeting of New York and New England did not occur instantly, however. Finney took a considerable amount of time coming to grips with his destiny.

Invitations for Finney to move east began to arrive in the spring and summer of 1826. The Young Men's Missionary Society of Albany wanted him "to labor as a missionary in this city." Nathan S. S. Beman, pastor of Troy's 1,200-member First Presbyterian Church and a leader of the New School wing of the denomination, wrote, "Many in this city would be glad to see you here; the church is cold." State Supreme Court Judge Jonas Platt and his son Zephaniah, both awakened during the revival in Utica, urged Finney to consider an even larger field: "Some of our New York [City] churches are in readiness for *your preaching.*" Other correspondence from old friends in such places as Ogdensburg, Adams, Rome, and Clinton begged, "Can you not come? Does not duty call this way?" Plainly, the evangelist stood at a major fork in the road. Just as formerly remote villages like Utica were being introduced to the national market by the Erie Canal, Charles G. Finney was now emerging as a participant in the national religious marketplace. Many letters of invitation echoed Acts 16:9 in their request that Finney "come over and help us." And like Paul, who increasingly received calls from the more prominent commercial centers of the Roman

61

Empire as his ministry expanded, Finney increasingly received calls from the larger towns and cities in the state.

Beman and his supporters had to work hard to persuade Finney to come to Troy. Beman's invitation, dated June 9, was followed a week later by one from a lay leader describing the situation into which Finney would step. "A considerable portion" of Beman's congregation had "begun to complain of his preaching 'hard things,' and are disposed to quarrel against the *manner*." Others, however, were "beginning to *pray* — and it is believed that a crisis of some kind is at hand." Beman wrote the evangelist again on August 3, pleading for a response, and then again on September 23. "The state of things here is alarming," he wrote. "Our church has never been thoroughly awakened, and I fear this week that those who have felt the most are going back. . . . They need to hear some voice besides mine. . . . If something is not done *immediately*, the revival is over!" Finney's agreement to come to Troy and this letter must have crossed in the mail, because two days later Beman wrote urging his presence at "an anxious meeting appointed for Wednesday evening," appending the blessing "May the Lord prosper your way."

Finney began his ministry in Troy on the first of October 1826. Predictably, some found his style of preaching abrasive and "his gestures too violent," but others fully approved of what they heard. A friend wrote to Lydia, who remained with her parents in Whitesboro, "I never heard Mr. Finney when he was *greater* than he was yesterday." A month later, however, he was back with Lydia and preaching in Utica, leaving Father Nash to work with Beman. Then a significant letter dated November 6 arrived from his attorney friend J. P. Cushman in Troy: "We hear this evening that Mr. Nettleton is in Albany, and preached for Mr. Weed yesterday. . . . He wishes to see *you*." Cushman appears not to have been at all sarcastic when he called this "glad news." Finney was back in Troy by December 5. Before the end of the year, he would meet face-to-face, probably on two occasions, with Asahel Nettleton in Albany.

Finney reported to several friends and later wrote in his *Memoirs* that he entered the conversations with Nettleton with a kind of naive confidence that the two of them could work together in the same way he had worked with so many New School Presbyterian pastors in central New York. Although he had never admitted to seeking the advice of anyone before, he said, "I had the greatest *desire* to see him, so much so that I had frequently dreamed of visiting him and obtaining from him information in regard to the best means [of] promoting a revival." Finney claimed that he now "felt like sitting at his feet, almost as I would at the feet of an apostle." As Finney tells it, the discussion between the two men touched only lightly on the key doctrinal issues that often divided Protestants — including "the voluntariness or involuntariness of moral depravity" — but reported that on these points Nettleton "entirely agreed with me." In fact, "there had been no complaint by Dr. Beecher or Mr. Nettleton of our *teaching*." They objected only to "what they supposed was highly objectionable in the *measures* that we used." But in the end, Finney's optimism about the meeting was not rewarded. He quickly sensed that Nettleton was nervous about being seen with him or even having him attend his evening service. Sitting in the gallery, "I saw enough to satisfy me that I could expect no advice or instruction from him, and that he was there to take a stand against me."

For his part, Nettleton perceived Finney as having approached him with a belligerent attitude. On the second of January he wrote to Beecher imploring his help in organizing opposition to Finney and his abrasive, divisive, irreverent, and judgmental brand of revivalism. He sent a copy of a revised version of this letter to Finney's friend Samuel Aikin in Utica and to twenty other central New York pastors. He charged Finney and Beman with having provoked "a civil war in Zion." Indeed, the Presbyterian community in Troy was spinning in chaos and conflict. Beman brought in Horatio Foote to preach in January, and he offended the disaffected even more than Finney had. Members of the anti-revival faction split from First

Church to form Second Presbyterian Church. But many were not content simply to withdraw. They succeeded in dragging Nathan S. S. Beman before the presbytery in late January and trying him on charges not of heresy but unclerical conduct — unprofessional behavior in the promotion of a revival. Joseph Brockway, who had just moved to Troy from Vermont and whom Finney denounced as "an outside influence" and "a spy," published *A Delineation of the Characteristic Features of a Revival of Religion in Troy* (1827). This was followed quickly by *A Brief Account of the Origin and Progress of the Divisions in the First Presbyterian Church* (1827), in which the pastoral work of Beman, Finney, and Nash was excoriated as verbal abuse, their preaching ridiculed as "theatrical," and their prayers caricatured as mindless repetition. The presbytery acquitted Beman, but the case was pressed at synod and finally at the General Assembly in 1828.

In his *Memoirs*, Finney stated that "in the meantime I went on in my labors in the revival" except for "a week or two" when "my wife was in a state of health" that required attention. This is not strictly true, for shortly after his conversations with Nettleton he retreated once more to Whitesboro for over a month. On January 1, 1827, the Oneida Evangelical Association issued Charles G. Finney a carte blanche commission "to labour in such places as your best judgment shall direct" for the coming year at a salary of $600. The question in the evangelist's mind must have been where his best judgment and his sense of God's call were now directing him.

Nathan S. S. Beman appealed to Finney back in Whitesboro on January 8: "It is strange, say many, that Brother Finney don't write. What are you doing?" After finally receiving a letter from him, Cushman and Beman wrote on January 12, "Brother Finney, when will you be here? You must come soon. . . . *Come!*" Again on the eighteenth: "Why do we not see you? I beg you don't delay. Every hour is important." And on the twenty-third: "Why should you have turned aside so suddenly and preserved so unbroken a silence toward Troy we are altogether ignorant." Cushman importuned, "The place is ripe for your visits from house to house, and were you here to strike I do feel that a great movement would take place." Not until almost February did Charles Finney find it within himself to resume the work in Troy.

Despite the controversy, the revival in Troy produced a multitude of heartfelt conversions, and, as was often the case with Finney's revivals, many community leaders were among the awakened. Finney made side trips to New Lebanon on the post road near the state line, where Daniel Nash was already working with the local pastor, in mid-February and again in mid-March. There, he again noted, "the most cultivated and influential of the inhabitants were converted." The tension with Asahel Nettleton and the opponents of the Beman-Finney revival, however, was never far below the surface. Finney preached two notable sermons in Troy during March that illustrate the situation. "The Blessedness of Benevolence," delivered on March 17, gave expression to the vast amount of common ground shared by Finney, Nettleton, Beecher, and all the New School Presbyterians and Congregationalists who stood in the evangelical Edwardsian tradition. Finney's exposition of Acts 20:35 — "So laboring ye ought to support the weak, and to remember the words of the Lord Jesus, how he said, It is more blessed to give than to receive" — characterized the reformist theme of the Christian life as one of "disinterested benevolence." The other sermon, which Finney had tested in Utica in January and now preached in Troy while the presbytery was in session, drove a wedge between those who promoted the revivals and those who opposed them. *A Sermon Preached in the Presbyterian Church at Troy, March 4, 1827*, published at the request of the presbytery with fifteen sponsors, addressed the question of Amos 3:3: "Can two walk together except they be agreed?" It was Finney's first publication.

Finney asserted that before Christians could walk together, they had to be agreed not just "intellectually" but "in feeling and practice." That largely described the rift between him and his friends on the one side and Nettleton, Beecher, and their allies on the other. He argued that the difference exhibited the quality of the spiritual life of each side. Those who were moved by "the fire of eloquence" in political speechmaking or a "fine piece of harmony" in music, he said, would find that their "feelings" would be "grieved and distressed" by a sudden switch to "drier" discourse or the "din" of martial music. Similarly, if "your heart is glowing with religious feeling" and "you hear a dull man *preach or pray*," you will be "disgusted with his coldness." On the other side, if "you are luke-warm, and carnal" and you hear a "spiritual" preacher, "you are annoyed with the *manner*, and fire, and spirit of the man." Finney went a step further and suggested that this division explained "why luke-warm professors and impenitent sinners have *the same* difficulties with *means*, in revivals of religion. . . . It is the fire, and the spirit, that disturbs their frosty hearts." Finney denied that "animal feeling" was the issue. Admitting that "this kind of feeling is sometimes excited in revivals," he nonetheless argued that it is the "spiritual" that offends. "Let it not be thought," he preached, "that we advocate or recommend preaching, or using other means, with *design to give offense*." But offense will come just as it came to the prophets, and Christ, and the apostles. The question is, which side are you on? Finney's conclusion gave the text a hard twist: "If we walk with the lukewarm and ungodly, or they with *us*, it is because we are agreed. For two cannot walk together except they *be agreed*."

Finney's sermon was heard as a war cry. Nettleton and others took it personally that he thought of them as lukewarm and no better than impenitent sinners. They published rebuttals in the religious press charging Finney with censoriousness and spiritual pride. Lyman Beecher had a better idea. He called for a grand convention at which, he hoped, the two sides could settle their differences, agree to correct abuses in the conduct of revivals, reaffirm the New England–New York evangelical alliance, and return to their common task of winning sinners to Christ. A rehearsal for such a meeting actually took place at the Oneida Presbytery meeting the second week of March. In response to "the letters from the east," revival issues were debated, resolutions passed, and consensus was achieved. On the key issues — "females praying in the presence of men" and "praying for individuals by name except where requested" — the presbytery agreed these practices should "ordinarily be confined to small circles which you know with few exceptions they have been with us." George Gale wrote to Finney, "You will be satisfied no doubt with the result."

Oneida County pastors wanted to find middle ground without losing their zeal for souls. Noah Coe was ready to concede "that a great many things are wrong in these revivals"; Moses Gillett admitted to Finney, "You and I have both been too free in 'denouncing' cold ministers and cold professors of religion"; and George Gale confessed that a few radicals on the fringe had been "a little latitudinarian" on female prayer and prayer for people by name. On the other hand, Harriet Gillet wrote with scorn, "Mr. Nettleton has had some letters from this vicinity that must cut him to the heart, if he has any feeling left, from those that used to be his warm friends." They felt strengthened by the presbytery's achievement of harmony and ready to argue that the revivals continued the best Congregational-Presbyterian tradition. A Utica merchant chided those who worried so "about new things and new measures" for being asleep "like Knickerbocker's dutchman." A pastor advised Finney: "I do not wish you to appear before the public as an advocate for any *new measures.* Say what is true, that you have introduced no new measures but have followed such as you found in the church when you entered it." Another, however, warned him, "You stand as a mark for everyone to shoot at."

Asahel Nettleton and Lyman Beecher continued to shoot. In letters to clergy, Nettleton aimed to kill, while Beecher fired warning shots over Finney's head. In a letter to Beman, Beecher condemned such Cane Ridge–like "extravagances" as "falling, and groaning, and laughing" but affirmed "energy and warmth" in revivals and expressed faith that "if Brother F. will take counsel, he may be an invaluable blessing." In letters both to Oneida County pastors and Nettleton, Beecher presented his goal: to bring Finney "upon common ground on which we can sustain him" and to keep the revivalists "within their orbit." He especially worried that evangelical dissension provided the real enemy — Unitarians and Universalists — with ammunition in the far more important war for America's soul.

A number of Oneida County friends helped interpret events to Finney through the spring. John Frost wrote from Whitesboro that, unlike Nettleton, "Dr. Beecher . . . is lowering his tone." Herman Norton reported on April 30 yet another Nettleton circular letter that "manifests a very bad spirit," and on May 15 one from Beecher "written with a pretty good spirit." According to Norton, "The Dr. acknowledges that he has been mistaken in some things," including his understanding that Finney invaded congregations without the pastors' consent. Two Utica merchants reported positive firsthand impressions of Beecher in Boston — he "preached without notes" in a dramatic style something like Finney's. Nettleton, meanwhile, obdurately resisted all attempts to arrange a meeting between the two sides. Beman expressed the view that "he is getting farther and farther off" and "will not be able to carry all the world with him, nor even all New England. If Dr. Beecher does not ultimately forsake him, I shall be much disappointed."

Nathan Beman went to Boston, where he and Lyman Beecher arranged the New Lebanon Convention. It was not convened as a synod with any ecclesiastical authority, nor was it an "eastern" plot to crush "western" revivalism, and it was certainly not a "trial" of Charles G. Finney. Asahel Nettleton attended only reluctantly, and when he saw that it was none of these things, he slipped out of the meeting. The convention was designed, as stated in its first resolution, to hammer out a New York–New England and Congregational–New School

Presbyterian consensus "in regard to principles and measures in conducting and promoting revivals of religion." Emotions were high. As her pastor Moses Gillet left Rome for the meeting, a friend wrote Lydia Finney, "Our revival ministers should feel a holy anger against opposers." She reported that "next Wednesday [when the convention was set to begin] is to be observed by this church for secret prayer and fasting." Charles Finney, who had no taste for church meetings, could not avoid attending this one.

The New Lebanon Convention, held in a large private home, began the morning of July 18, 1827, and ran for a full week. The nine participants from each side have generally been described, as in Finney's *Memoirs*, as representing the "east" or the "west." Two ministers aligned with Beecher and Nettleton, however, were from Oneida County — Asahel Norton and William Weeks, who had recently published a devastating anti-Finney tract. Albany-area pastors were divided, with Henry Weed on Beecher's side, but Beman and two others with Finney, Gillet, Lansing, Frost, Gale, and Aikin. Leadership seemed stacked in favor of Beecher, as Heman Humphrey, president of Amherst College, moderated the sessions and Weeks acted as secretary. The location, however, was Charles Finney's turf. His revival preaching had completely won over New Lebanon and the neighboring villages of Chatham and Stephentown. Asked "what I find amiss in your preaching here," Chatham pastor Joel Benedict responded, "I cheerfully say *nothing*." Moreover, Finney began receiving supportive letters from pastors across the border in Massachusetts and Connecticut.

The minutes of the convention were published in the evangelical *New York Observer* but also appeared with derisive editorial commentary in a Universalist booklet published in Ithaca and in the Unitarian *Christian Examiner*. What the minutes reveal, as resolutions were proposed and amended and as successive votes were taken, is a body of Christian leaders who shared fundamental beliefs and differed minutely on tone and practice. The initial agenda was well organized, with Justin Edwards of Andover Seminary proposing a set of resolutions that passed unanimously. The first of them stated, "Revivals of true religion are the work of God's spirit, by which, in a comparatively short period of time, many persons are convinced of sin, and brought to the exercise of repentance towards God, and faith in our Lord Jesus Christ." Everyone agreed that revivals combine divine initiative and "human instrumentality," that "variety in the mode of conducting revivals" is no problem, and that "indiscretion and wickedness" can creep into otherwise good revivals. Consensus on other matters, however, was not so easily attained.

The two sides pulled and tugged on the resolution, "In social meetings of men and women, for religious worship, females are not to pray." Heated discussion ensued on what women were actually doing in the western revivals, with the Oneida pastors demanding to know the source of the exaggerated reports that had poisoned "eastern" understanding. They knew full well that the culprit was sitting among them, but Nettleton refused to say, and William Weeks sat in silence. The brethren wisely then "united in a season of prayer." A number of substitute resolutions were attempted — including Lansing's motion, "There may be circumstances in which it may be proper for a female to pray in the presence of men" — but vote after vote split down the middle. According to Finney's account, Nathan Beman delivered a powerful defense from Scripture of female prophesying but at the end of the convention pulled back to try one last compromise: "In public meetings for religious worship, composed of men and women, females are not to pray." Finney and his friends voted yes on this, but Beecher and his friends declined to vote, and no one was happy with the outcome. The convoluted wording of motions and the odd way votes split reveal just how cautiously conservative the revivalists were on the women's issue.

The ministers were more successful with the matter of prayer for individuals by name. Such prayer was to be "carefully avoided" in public meetings but was acceptable "in small social circles" if "practiced with great caution and tenderness." This was essentially the wording arrived at the previous March by the Oneida Presbytery. A motion that "audible groaning" be deemed "improper" in public prayer passed after it was softened to say merely that such groaning should "be discouraged," and that only "in all ordinary circumstances." Finney and Beecher joined the large majority that also characterized "violent gestures and boisterous tones" in public prayer as "improper." When Edwards moved to proscribe the practice of calling ministers "cold, stupid, or dead . . . unconverted, or enemies of revivals," Beman stepped in to add, "heretics, or enthusiasts, or disorganizers . . . deranged, or mad." Approval was almost unanimous. Some final partisan jabs — a resolution that "great caution should be exercised in listening to unfavorable reports" and one that "attempts to remedy evils which exist in revivals . . . may . . . do more injury and ruin to souls, than those evils which such attempts were intended to correct" — failed to land. But the Oneida County pastors were making their point.

Nettleton gave up after the Saturday session and failed to return on Monday morning. His absence not only hurt the "eastern" party's voting power but was taken by everyone as a sign of personal weakness. Beecher persuaded him to return for the final session on Thursday. Finney recalled that he was "manifestly very much agitated" as he entered and took his seat. In one final attempt to make his case, Nettleton read what he called "an historical letter" that laid out "the facts, upon which he had founded his opposition." This turned out to be the letter he had sent to Samuel Aikin in January, and Finney had a copy in his possession at the convention. Finney stood and "affirmed that so far as I was personally concerned, not one of those facts mentioned there and complained of, was true." The others from the west backed him up, and Weeks again remained silent. Finney wrote, "No one there pretended to justify a single sentence in Mr. Nettleton's historical letter." A final attempt by Justin Edwards to coerce Finney and his colleagues into condemning objectionable revival practices was met with a proposal by Finney to condemn "lukewarmness in religion." Neither was enacted. It was a frustrating way to end, but the ministers did then join in a final "season of prayer."

The stalemate actually amounted to a victory for Charles G. Finney. Although subtle differences — and some not so subtle — remained between him and the more formal Congregational and New School Presbyterian clergy, he had held his own at New Lebanon, and revivalism in general had received unanimous endorsement. In his *Autobiography*, Lyman Beecher remembered that he issued a warning at the convention: "Finney, I know your plan, and you know I do; you mean to come into Connecticut and carry a streak of fire to Boston. But if you attempt it, as the Lord liveth, I'll meet you at the State line, and call out all the artillerymen, and fight every inch of the way to Boston, and then I'll fight you there." Finney did not recall him making this famous statement, but he agreed that it summed up Beecher's feelings at the time. As it turned out, though, Beecher soon lost interest in supporting the work of Asahel Nettleton, warmed up to Finney, and actually welcomed Finney to Boston. Beecher's friendship with Nathaniel William Taylor drove him further from Nettleton, who sided with Bennett Tyler in the doctrinal war against Taylor's New Haven Theology — a system of thought remarkably similar to that which was apparent in the preaching of Charles G. Finney. In American evangelicalism, identity is sometimes established by those one is willing to walk with and sometimes by those one walks away from.

Charles Finney gained a significant quality at New Lebanon. He demonstrated that, together with his Oneida County colleagues, he was fully capable of engaging in a week-long conference including civil but sharp-witted debate, savvy compromise, humble prayer, and a measure of consensus. In so doing, he achieved dignity in the eyes of the wider American church. Even his detractors — and there would be more of them — now had to recognize that here was an intellectual and spiritual force to be reckoned with. They had to respect him.

Charles Finney was thirty-five years old. Since his arrival in Utica in October of 1825 only two years before, he had preached hundreds of sermons, visited thousands of homes, prayed with a multitude of seekers and penitents. The cities along the canal were growing more sophisticated as commerce moved east and west; so, too, was Finney. His old teacher and friend George Gale, who knew him well in the North Country and supported him in Oneida County, could see how he had matured. Gale wrote in the aftermath of New Lebanon, urging the evangelist to continue this process of "correcting" any earlier excesses and smoothing the rough edges in his behavior. He also warned him, "Do not abandon any important principle." Knowing that Finney would soon be speaking on grander platforms in larger cities, Gale promised, "Your friends at the west will never abandon you so long as they see you laboring to serve God in the best manner."

4 Make You a New Heart

Charles Finney moved on in December 1827 to Wilmington, Delaware, and then to Philadelphia, having concluded his ministry in New Lebanon and Stephentown in New York State. With over 100,000 inhabitants, Philadelphia was still the largest city in the United States. The evangelist also had powerful friends in New York City with whom he corresponded regularly and whom he consulted in person whenever his travels took him through the city. There was talk of a New England tour, and some began to imagine Finney in Boston. Charles and Lydia returned to the Mohawk Valley on occasion, especially to visit her parents in Whitesboro during the summers, and a major revival was soon to occur in Rochester, but the metropolitan east now commanded Finney's attention.

Charles and Lydia Finney were not alone in their carriage journeys back and forth among the towns and cities of the northeast. Nor were they alone in seeking their fortune in the larger urban centers. Americans in the 1820s and 1830s were an irrepressibly mobile people. Later rootless generations would create the myth of an age in which children grew up in the same neighborhood as their grandparents and played with their cousins, but in the United States that experience was never the norm. For men on the make in business and families striving to improve their lot in life, the burgeoning nation's roads and canals — and soon its railroads — were a more fitting symbol than the village green. The "representative men" of antebellum America, including such figures as Andrew Jackson, Abraham Lincoln, and Charles Grandison Finney, were all engaged in what is today called upward mobility. And upward mobility usually required geographic mobility. For many, opportunity beckoned in the west, and a few members of Lydia's family had already moved to Ohio. For others it meant going east. The lives of many Americans — especially those involved in commerce, law, politics, or the national marketplace of religion and ideas — followed a zigzag path across the country. Finney's first promoters in New York City, for example, were two prominent Oneida County attorneys who moved their practice to Manhattan after the 1826 revivals. Jonas Platt, a former State Supreme Court judge and member of Congress, and his son Zephaniah, whose legal career would later take him to the Midwest and the Reconstruction South, carried on an active correspondence with the evangelist and opened many important doors for him.

Thanks to the New Lebanon Convention, Charles Finney rose in the estimation of many Presbyterians, Congregationalists, and other evangelicals throughout the northeast. It was apparent to them that the evangelist was now a significant religious leader. As a supporter at Andover Theological Seminary said in a letter to Finney, "God has been with you." Invitations multiplied, including one from the church in Plymouth, Massachusetts. George Gale rejoiced at the thought of Finney preaching at "the rock where the good old pilgrims first set their feet" and imagined "the spirits of those pious souls hovering around with immense delight, should the Spirit of God attend as he has sometimes done your labours." But Finney's old mentor advised against New England and pointed him to New York and Philadelphia. "Let Doctor Beecher . . . fight Unitarians," Gale wrote. "The Presbyterian Church furnishes an ample field, which is the field where you have been born and nurtured." Although inquiries had already come from both major cities, Finney made the decision to go first to Wilmington after he and the Rev. Eliphalet Gilbert discovered a kindred spirit in one another when the Delaware pastor was in New Lebanon on family business. Moreover, Asahel Nettleton was in New York after the Convention arranging publication of his anti-Finney letters and was on his way to Philadelphia. Gilbert wrote, "Philadelphia, large as it is, would not be large enough for you and Mr. N. at once."

Eliphalet Gilbert drew Finney to Wilmington with the promise that "the elders of the church and the leading females here are very anxious for your coming." Just to the south, he added, Finney would be welcomed in New Castle by the Rev. Joshua Danforth, who was a New School "revival man, the most of any one in our presbytery." Although he was "a child of Mr. Nettleton," Danforth had just returned from a visit to the Troy area, where "a number of your friends . . . removed nearly all his difficulties." Gilbert reported that some of the ministers who were "Scotchmen, and pretty stiff in the Old School system," were also eager for a revival. "However sticklish for doctrine," they "would be glad to see an awakening in their bounds even by a Hopkinsian!" Indeed, he wrote again later, "even the Quakers are inquiring after you." This may have been so much salesmanship, but it was indicative of the environment into which Finney now advanced. In Delaware and Pennsylvania he would encounter real Old School opponents for the first time in his career. Despite the impression conveyed in his *Memoirs*, however, doctrinal conservatives could not present a united front. Presbyterianism in and around Philadelphia was deeply divided. The welcome accorded Charles Finney in his new field demonstrates just how much influence New School Presbyterians enjoyed in the supposed bastion of traditionalism itself.

Finney was in the habit of describing any Presbyterian who had not abandoned a strict interpretation of the Westminster Confession's doctrine of original sin and human inability as an adherent of the Old School. That Eliphalet Gilbert held New School views before the evangelist arrived in Wilmington is evident from his letters to Finney, in which he refers to other pastors in negative terms as "Old School" and to Hopkinsianism (which he seems to have assumed was Finney's position) with approval. Still, Gilbert had not yet stepped over to the quasi-Arminian Taylorite-Finneyite view of a human ability to respond to God's call. For this reason, Finney disparaged the Wilmington congregation for being paralyzed by "the oldest of the Old School views of doctrine . . . that God would convert sinners in His own time" and insisted that "nothing could be done unless Brother Gilbert's views could be changed on this subject." Finney says he spent several weeks talking theology with Gilbert before his host's eyes were opened and the way was clear for Finney to preach his full gospel. As soon as Finney felt free to issue the call for immediate repentance and salvation, "the work went forward," with Mrs. Lydia Gilbert as first convert and most zealous promoter. Finney noted that "Brother Gilbert's views became greatly changed; and also his style and mode of preaching." Gilbert told Finney in a letter that he wanted more and more of the "Oneida fire." His shift, and that of Joshua Danforth in New Castle, received comment by nearby Old School critics of the revival as well.

James Patterson of Philadelphia, meanwhile, had been seeking for some time to persuade Charles Finney that he would "have an opportunity of doing good on a larger scale here." An evangelical, Patterson was eager to save souls, and he believed that revival preaching was the most effective means to that end. Finney described Patterson as "a tall man, of striking figure and powerful voice" who preached "with the tears rolling down his cheeks." Revivals were nothing new to him; he "used to have a revival of religion every winter up to the time when I labored with him." Patterson also hoped to tip the scales of Presbyterian opinion and power to the side of New School "revival sentiments." In a letter he wrote shortly after Finney had begun in Wilmington, Patterson reminded him that "Philadelphia is the great centre of Presbyterianism in the U.S.A." If he imagined Finney was the least bit interested in denominational politics, he was wrong, but the evangelist was certainly ready for the larger platform Patterson's church would provide. Finney began gradually, taking the steamboat up the Delaware River twice a week for the evening meeting, "thus alternating my evening services between Wilmington and Philadelphia."

Finney naively thought of James Patterson as an Old School Presbyterian, just as he had Eliphalet Gilbert and, years before, George Gale. In his *Memoirs* he complimented Patterson, however, for caring "a great deal more for the salvation of souls than for nice questions about ability and inability," and he was pleased to note how "his wife held the New England views of theology" with "a general as opposed to a restricted atonement." When Finney opened up on the congregation with his version of the gospel, Patterson "expressed no surprize" and "did not at all object to it." Finney remembered that Mrs. Patterson would "smilingly remark" to her husband, "Now you see, Mr. Patterson, that Mr. Finney does not agree with you on those points upon which we have so often conversed." He presents Patterson as tolerating his distinctive spin on the Westminster Confession because it was obvious from the results that "the Lord *blesses* it" but also as worrying that "if the presbyterian ministers in this city find out your views . . . they will hunt you out of the city." This was manifestly an inaccurate picture of Patterson and of his plan for Finney in Philadelphia. Patterson the New School leader wanted Finney at his church precisely because he could use the added firepower against Old School conservatives. Patterson knew full well that many New School and moderate Philadelphia pastors would open their pulpits to Finney and, conversely, that Old School pastors would disapprove of his preaching.

When Finney moved from Wilmington to Philadelphia in mid-January 1828, he placed himself at the geographical center of Presbyterian factional disputes. He did not create the conflict that would split the denomination a decade later; rather, he was brought to Philadelphia because he was undeniably part of it.

Patterson's congregation, First Presbyterian Church of the Northern Liberties, had grown under his evangelical ministry from humble beginnings in the poor outskirts of town into the largest congregation in the city. At the other end of the spectrum was Philadelphia's conservative fortress, Arch Street Church, under the Rev. Jacob Janeway. Ashbel Green, president of Princeton College from 1812 to 1822, had previously served Arch Street and now lived in the city, where he edited and served as primary writer for *The Christian Advocate.* Among his many articles defending the Old School position, Green wrote out his old lectures advancing a strict interpretation of the Westminster Confession and published them in this paper.

Green took unfavorable notice in *The Christian Advocate* of Charles Finney's presence while he was still in Wilmington, characterizing both his theology and his methods as false and dangerous. While Finney was no stranger to hostility against the so-called "new measures" in his revivals, this was the first time he experienced at close range an attack on his theology. He had given the venerable Dr. Green and the Old School an easy target with the most powerful sermon he had delivered in Wilmington. It was a sermon he would deliver again many times over the next few years. Frustrated that "garbled extracts" were appearing in hostile periodicals and pamphlets, he finally wrote it out in 1834 for inclusion in the collection *Sermons on Various Subjects.* It was based on a text from Ezekiel 18:31, "Make you a new heart and a new spirit, for why will ye die?" The published version appeared in two parts, "Sinners Bound to Change Their Own Hearts" and "How to Change Your Heart." It was a signature Finney sermon. The next year, a friend in Philadelphia heard a pastor emulating the Finney style; he must have chuckled as he wrote that the pastor "preached . . . last night a Hopkinsian sermon . . . showing the obligation of sinners to *make themselves new hearts.*"

Finney's sermon amounted to a radical reinterpretation of the Westminster Confession at certain key points. Finney shared the New Divinity of so many ministers with Connecticut roots, which rejected the Confession's notion that because Adam and Eve were "the root of all mankind, the guilt of [their] sin was imputed, and the same death in sin and corrupted nature conveyed to all their posterity." Finney insisted that, while every human is absolutely a sinner, each of us is responsible solely for our own sin. New England theology had also modified the Calvinist doctrine that Christ died only for the elect "for whom Christ hath purchased redemption." He died to make salvation possible for all, said Finney, though only the elect will embrace it. Now Finney (and Nathaniel William Taylor in New Haven) took the next revolutionary step, over-throwing the Confession's pessimistic view of human nature and erecting in its place a republican anthropology of hope. Finney advanced the basic tenet of Whig political ideology — namely, that just rule must be with "the consent of the governed" — into the realm of theology. God, whose rule is perfectly just, will govern only with the full participation of his people. Salvation, said Finney, involves "a change in the choice of a *Supreme Ruler.*" Ashbel Green doggedly argued in the language of the Confession that "man, by his fall into sin, hath wholly lost all ability of will to any spiritual good accompany-ing salvation" and "is not able, by his own strength, to convert himself, or to prepare himself thereunto." To Finney's way of thinking, Old School theology made salvation impossible be-cause it autocratically denied the chance for sinners to respond, and all are sinners.

The evangelism of Charles G. Finney was based on his conviction that every person "has the power and liberty of choice" in the matter of who they will serve and how they will live. In his trademark sermon on making yourself a new heart,

Finney put forth his case that "all holiness, in God, angels, or men, must be *voluntary*, or it is not holiness." God's moral government of the universe requires that human beings as free moral agents render voluntary obedience to divine law. Sounding like a lawyer, Finney argued, "The blame-worthiness of sin consists in its being the violation of an obligation." The contention that "we are under an obligation to do what we have no power to do," therefore, involved phony logic. "Suppose God should command a man to fly; would the command impose upon him any obligation, until he was furnished with wings?" The answer to the problem of sin is not "a constitutional alteration, and the implantation of a new principle, in the substance of [our] soul"; it is, rather, "a change of heart" that "consists in changing the controlling preference of the mind in regard to the *end* of pursuit." Finney preached, "You have all the powers of moral agency; and the thing required is, not to alter these powers, but to employ them in the service of your maker." With sin defined in typically Hopkinsian terms as "preference of self-interest to the glory of God and the interests of the Kingdom," Finney's converts possessed a "new heart" in the sense that they now embraced God and others in selfless benevolence.

Finney resolutely denied the Old School charge that he left God out of the equation. Turning the tables, he argued that the idea of salvation as the implantation of a "new principle" eliminated any need for the ongoing work of the Holy Spirit. "Those who have a new heart, find [the Holy Spirit's] constant agency is as indispensable to their perseverance in holiness, as it was to their conversion." Finney insisted that, far from robbing God of his glory, his was "the only view of the subject that gives glory to God." The sinner "never does, and never will turn, unless God indures him to do it; so that although the act is the sinner's own, yet the glory belongs to God, inasmuch as he caused him to act." Finney employed in this sermon his famous and often-used illustration of the man saved from going over Niagara Falls. Suppose you are standing by the

Falls, he preached, and "you behold a man lost in deep reverie, approaching its verge unconscious of his danger." He is about to "take the final step that shall plunge him in destruction," and you "cry out, *Stop*." Later at the public house he says, pointing to you, "That man saved my life." Later he reflects, "*Stop!* how that word rings in my ears. Oh, that was to me the word of life." So it was "the *word* that aroused him, and caused him to turn." Still later the man expresses the act as his own — "had I not turned at that instant, I should have been a dead man." And finally he sees the hand of God in it, saying, "O the mercy of God; if God had not interposed, I should have been lost."

Finney presented all these philosophical "causes" coming together in the preaching of the evangelist. "Not only does the preacher cry *Stop*, but, through the living voice of the preacher, the Spirit cries *Stop*. . . . The Spirit pours the expostulation home with such power, that the sinner turns." Thus, "the actual turning, or change, is the sinner's own act," but "the agent who induces him, is the Spirit of God" and "a secondary agent, is the preacher," while "the truth is the instrument, or motive, which the Spirit uses to induce the sinner to turn." Old School critics punched holes in Finney's logic and remained unconvinced that he had shown "the sense in which it is the work of God, and also the sense in which it is the sinner's own work." But the masses easily grasped — and were gripped by — Finney's explanation. Tears came to their eyes and they fell to their knees in anguished repentance when he looked them in the eye and said, "The fact is, sinners, that God requires you to turn, and what he requires of you, he cannot do for you. It must be your own voluntary act. . . . Another moment's delay, and it may be too late for ever."

Finney recalled in his *Memoirs* that he and James Patterson were "greatly surprised that I met with no open opposition from the ministers or churches on account of my theological views." He preached a sermon on Jesus Christ as the Mediator who "gave himself a ransom for all" (1 Tim. 2:5), presenting the New School case for universal atonement, in seven churches on seven successive evenings. Dr. Thomas Harvey Skinner, the New School pastor of Fifth Presbyterian Church who would later become a professor at Andover Seminary, eagerly promoted Finney among the churches. Dr. Gilbert Robert Livingstone of the Dutch Reformed Church "sympathized with my views," welcomed Finney to his pulpit, and supported him in the community. Then, from mid-August 1828 until January 1829, Finney entered a formal arrangement with Samuel Helffenstein and the German Reformed Church on Race Street, which had the largest auditorium in the city, to preach every Sunday afternoon and evening and on Thursday evenings. The fact that his "orthodoxy did not prove a stumbling block" in Philadelphia testified in part to Finney's new urbanity and tact. (John Frost advised Finney in the spring of 1828 to "keep humble," on the grounds that "no one is in so great a danger of overstating his talents and graces as a successful evangelist.") It also revealed the power and influence of the city's New School pastors, despite Ashbel Green's published Old School criticisms.

Evangelical women played a key part in the promotion of a revival in Philadelphia, as they had in the revivals associated with Finney's ministry in upstate New York. James Patterson pointed to the support of "leading females" in his invitation to the evangelist. Finney considered especially significant the conversion of women who had initially been opposed to his preaching, and he identified the wives of several pastors as important supporters. In fact, such pastors' wives as Lydia Gilbert and Lydia Finney herself were more than behind-the-scenes supporters of their husbands. The many letters to Lydia Finney from women friends and revival colleagues in New York State reveal her role as organizer. Specifically, she and other leaders organized evangelical women as bands of visitors who worked the neighborhoods more deeply than the evangelists had time to. In homes they counseled families and prayed with women for the conversion of their husbands. They organized women's prayer groups that would continue long after the evangelist had moved to another town and the church had returned to its normal routine. Women continually wrote Lydia asking for advice and, most of all, for her prayers in support of their work. These women (including Lydia Finney) were on the cutting edge of attempts to secure the right of women to speak and pray in "promiscuous" or mixed-gender meetings.

Every conversion story Finney recounted in his *Memoirs* of the work in Philadelphia, except his description of how lumbermen would come down the river and attend meetings in the spring, involved a woman as the prime actor. The wife of a German tobacconist was "thoroughly converted" but then obstructed from attending meetings by her husband, a man "of hasty temper, and . . . athletic frame." Finney advised her that "her first obligation was to God; that she was undoubtedly under obligation to obey His commands, even if they conflicted with the commands of her husband." After she defied her husband, he attacked her with "a dagger" and was at the point of killing her when her prayers prevailed and he was brought to his knees. He "begged God, and begged her, to forgive him" and became "a wonderfully changed man." Finney tells of a young woman with a complicated spiritual condition who finally became a "beautiful convert," and of another whose physical beauty led her easily into vanity until she tossed her "ornaments" into the fire and "gave herself to Christ." The latter became an evangelist in her own right, presenting the gospel to a "richly dressed lady at market" until she confessed her pride. Finney encouraged her to continue "to warn her own sex against that which had so nearly ruined her own soul." Finney's sermons at Race Street Church in the fall of 1828 attracted hundreds of the Sunday school teachers, women from all denominations, who made Philadelphia the vanguard city in the American Sunday School Union. This rising level of participation by women in religious affairs was encouraged, sometimes cautiously and sometimes boldly, by Charles Finney and his Presbyterian and Congregationalist colleagues in concert with Methodists and other evangelicals.

Lydia Finney gave birth to a daughter, Helen Clarissa, in Philadelphia on June 10, 1828. A month later Charles and Lydia took the baby home to Oneida County for a visit with her family on the farm in Whitesboro. Evangelical women had a special word of caution for motherhood as well as for vain finery, as Lydia discovered in a letter from a friend in Troy. Pronouncing the baby "a lovely child," she warned, "No doubt you are in danger of loving the little creature too exclusively, as every mother with one darling or a dozen is in danger of idolatry." The friend advised Lydia to take special care and "connect your watchfulness with prayer."

Finney preached his way north from Philadelphia and back again, speaking in New York City, Rome, and Troy, while Lydia remained with her parents. When she rejoined her husband in Philadelphia in October, Finney was in the middle of his stint at Race Street Church. It was not the evangelist's first experience with a German Reformed congregation, for early on he had preached successfully to such a community in Jefferson County. However, the arrangement with the Race Street consistory was somewhat unusual in that the church essentially was being used by New School Presbyterians as a city-wide nondenominational preaching post for their most powerful evangelist. Pastor Samuel Helffenstein at Race Street was a leader in the German Reformed Church in the training of young men for the ministry and was one of the organizers of that church's new seminary in Chambersburg. The Synod elected him to the position of professor of theology in 1823, but he declined the offer. When John Williamson Nevin and Philip Schaff assumed the professorial chairs in the early 1840s after the seminary moved to Mercersburg, they promoted steady, systematic use of the Heidelberg Catechism and formal liturgy as the basis of sound religion, and they criticized the baleful influence of Charles Finney and quick-conversion "Anxious Bench" revivalism in the strongest terms. Philadelphia pastors led the evangelical, less confessional side of the denomination in that mid-century controversy. In the fall of 1828, however, the lines were not so sharply drawn among the German Reformed, and Helffenstein and his elders had no trouble welcoming Finney's ministry. Despite signs of tension between the evangelist and his less charismatic host that may have hastened his decision to move on, the church leaders on January 5, 1829, wholeheartedly thanked Finney "for the zeal, fidelity, and truth with which he has assisted the Pastor of this Church in his Evangelical labours."

"Go on dear Brother," a supporter wrote. "Go where the Lord directs you, should it be into the center of German Pennsylvania." Finney did just that during the first half of 1829. He was unimpressed with Henry Muhlenberg, the distinguished Lutheran pastor in Reading who, as Finney saw it, reduced religion to a few easy duties — "simply to learn the catechism, and to be baptized and partake of the communion." German pietism and Anglo-American and Scots-Irish evangelicalism had flourished in Pennsylvania during the Great Awakening, but Finney saw little evidence of it during the winter and spring he spent in the area. In southeastern Pennsylvania's inland cities he found "religion in a very low state" and had to battle against the notion that conversion, family prayer, and secret prayer were "only fanaticism."

The city of Reading, he wrote in his *Memoirs*, "had never seen a revival, so far as I could learn." The Presbyterian pastor, the kindly and pious Dr. John Ferguson Grier, had written Finney for months begging him to come. He had also, it turned out, been praying earnestly for a revival for a long time, believing that if the church could be awakened, his lifework could be fulfilled. Finney preached three times on Sunday and four nights a week for about three weeks before calling for an inquiry meeting. When he sensed the time was right, he announced such a meeting, explaining that it was only for those "seriously impressed with the state of their souls" who "had made up their minds to immediately attend to the subject . . .

of what they should do to be saved." Grier, who admitted "know[ing] nothing about such a meeting as this" and let Finney handle the work, was astonished at the size and makeup of the gathering.

The large roomful of people gathered on that Monday evening, January 26, 1829, included men and women from all strata of society. Grier was delighted to see among them "the most respectable and influential portion of his congregation." Finney made an opening statement and then, following his usual practice, moved among the seekers speaking in low tones with each of them about their spiritual "symptoms." Grier "was greatly moved. . . . His excitement was intense." The evangelist then preached for about forty-five minutes on the need for immediate submission and consecration. He called on those who were ready "then and there to pledge themselves to live wholly to God . . . then and there to commit themselves to the sovereign mercy of God in Christ Jesus . . . then and there to give up all sin, to renounce it forever in every form," to kneel down and just do it. Finney himself knelt and prayed, with Grier kneeling by his side. The "awful solemnity" was palpable, with "sobs, and sighs, and weeping" audible throughout the room. When the prayer was complete, Finney dismissed the people. Dr. Grier then went home and died in his sleep! His friends said that his prayer had been answered, that, like Simeon, he had been permitted to "depart in peace."

Finney admired Grier's faith but complained that his death "proved a sad diversion of the public mind." It was more than a week before the revival got back into its "proper channel." Without a pastor now, the full work of the church fell on Finney's shoulders. He visited penitents, including a proud, muscular man known for his courage who was "torn to pieces" by a sermon, "writhing in agony, grinding his teeth, and literally gnawing his tongue" in confession of sin when Finney arrived at his home. Finney himself was shocked and remembered exclaiming, "If this is conviction, what is hell?" But the man was "persuaded to trust the Savior, and he came out free and joyful in hope." Others included a prominent lawyer whose soul, Finney told him, had been shackled by Ashbel Green's Old School spiritual counsel when he was a student at Princeton. A whiskey distiller immediately closed down his business when he, along with many members of his family, embraced Christ. He was a sick man, however, and Finney visited him regularly. Finney's fondness of recalling the man's deathbed scene, and for the people themselves, is evident in the tender language in his *Memoirs*. "Give my love to Brother Greer when you get to heaven," the evangelist-pastor said. The dying man "smiled with holy joy" and asked, "Do you think I shall know him?" Finney replied, "Yes, undoubtedly you will know him. Give him my love, and tell him the work is going on gloriously." The next Sunday the family received the Lord's Supper with a mingling of joy, sorrow, and "holy triumph" as Finney reminded them that their "husband, and father, and brother, and friend, was sitting that day at the table of Jesus on high, while they were gathered around his table on earth." Finney's account was a perfect marriage of the old Puritan ideal of a good death with rich nineteenth-century sentimentality.

In one of his few references to political figures or events in the *Memoirs*, Finney noted that Lancaster was "then and until his death the home of the late president Buchanan." The reader would have no inkling from his narrative that during the year and a half Finney spent in and around Philadelphia, American politics was being remade. Finney arrived in Lancaster in 1829, shortly after Andrew Jackson was inaugurated as president while the jubilant masses partied in the Federal City. Congressman James Buchanan, who occasionally attended and later joined Lancaster's First Presbyterian Church, where Finney preached for a month, had helped put Jackson in the White House. Charles G. Finney and Andrew Jackson shared so much of the boisterous popular spirit of the 1820s and 1830s — the "Age of Jackson" — that the evangelist has often been thought of as a "Jacksonian" and his revivals as accomplishing in religion what Jackson's new Democratic party did at the polls.

Applying any strict definition of terms, this could not be further from the truth.

Voter turnout more than doubled from previous levels in the presidential election of 1828, with almost 55 percent of eligible white men casting ballots, but Charles G. Finney did not vote. As a transient with no permanent address who lived with friends for a month or two at a time, he had no way to register with a local election board in any state. Pennsylvania, still operating under its 1790 Constitution, restricted the franchise to free men who had resided in the state for two years and had paid state or county taxes at least six months before the election. Even if he had somehow been registered at his parents' home in Henderson, New York, or at Lydia's family home in Oneida County, absentee balloting was not yet possible in the era of "Jacksonian democracy." In any event, Finney had little personal interest in politics at this time. While evangelicals have often merged their faith with political causes, and this would increasingly happen north and south in the decades before the Civil War, a countervailing apolitical or even antipolitical mood has sometimes controlled the behavior of American believers. The mudslinging election of 1828 may have galvanized much of society, but Charles Finney considered the spectacle to be a distraction from the real work of saving souls.

Finney actually mentioned the New York State election of the previous year, 1827, in his *Memoirs*. He was in the midst of the revival at Stephentown and "looked forward to the election day with considerable solicitude, fearing that the excitement of that day would greatly retard the work that was going on." The off-year state election had turned into a raucous preliminary version of the presidential campaign. Ever since Andrew Jackson lost the presidency to John Quincy Adams in 1824 when the election was thrown into the House of Representatives, Sen. Martin Van Buren from New York had worked in Washington to build a North-South Jackson coalition that would succeed in 1828. Although many evangelicals were being drawn to anti-Masonry and other reformist political movements, Van Buren was reelected to the Senate in 1827 and engineered the election of other Jackson supporters to state offices as well. Finney exhorted believers not to go out and vote but to "watch and to pray greatly, that the work might not be arrested by any excitement that should be got up on that day." Finney held a prayer meeting after the polls closed on the evening of election day. There he preached with such power, and with such pointed criticism of the animosity unleashed by the campaigns, that two of the "gentlemen who had sat at the table to receive votes during the day" were immobilized by their "conviction of sin." The evangelist counseled with each one individually and prayed with them, and they were "manifestly converted."

Finney's sermon rang with a rhetorical tone similar to that employed by the candidates on the hustings. Scholars have drawn the connection between revival preaching and the rise of popular political oratory in the early Republic, suggesting that candidates learned how to speak from Methodist and Baptist evangelistic preachers. Influence flowed the other way, too, and Charles Finney constantly advised stuffy, seminary-trained clergy to preach more like vote-hungry politicians.

Nor did Finney hesitate to use political activity as a parable for his own entirely spiritual purposes. An example of the kind of illustration he might have used in that election night sermon is found in "Sinners Bound to Change Their Own Hearts," an early version of which he preached just a few weeks later in Wilmington. Finney painted a word-picture of the dealings that had marked American politics since the "corrupt bargain" between John Quincy Adams and Henry Clay in the House of Representatives that secured the presidency for Adams in 1824. "If a man change sides in politics, you will see him meeting with those that entertain the same views and feelings with himself; devising plans and using his influence to elect the candidate he has now chosen." Finney's listeners that night had seen much of this at the local level during the

campaign and had read about more of it in their highly politi-
cized newspapers. Building on the fact that politics had to do
with such alliances, he continued, "He now has new political
friends on the one side, and new political enemies on the
other." The same kind of choice must be made in relation to
sin and salvation. By 1827 and 1828 there had emerged "two
great political parties" — and so it was in the realm of the spirit,
where each person must choose between "Satan's empire" and
Jesus Christ. "So with a sinner; if his heart is changed, you will
see that Christians become his friends — Christ his candidate!"

The politics of such men as Martin Van Buren, James
Buchanan, John C. Calhoun of South Carolina, and all those
who had banded together to support Andrew Jackson for president was abhorrent to Charles Finney. As much as some may
have saluted Jackson as the hero of the common man and hailed
his new Democratic party as the champion of freedom, northern evangelicals like Finney saw it otherwise. They denounced
Jacksonian democracy as little more than freedom to own
slaves and liberty to drive Indians ruthlessly from their rightful
land in Florida. Northern Jacksonians like the doughface poli-
tician James Buchanan were not only willing to compromise
with southern states over slavery but seemed eager to support
its existence.

"Finneyites" were not the "Jacksonians" among northern
Protestants when it came to actual political support. Old School
Presbyterians were the ones who tended to vote for Jackson
and other Democratic candidates, while New School Presbyterians were more likely to vote against Jacksonian candidates.
Evangelicals were among those who in the decades between
1830 and the Civil War organized the new Whig, Anti-Masonic,
Liberty, Free Soil, and Republican parties. The Old School tilt
south could be seen in denominational politics as well. Many
New School ministers were beginning to involve themselves in
the abolition movement and would soon agitate for an official
antislavery position in the Presbyterian Church. The mission
and reform societies supported so generously by evangelicals

adopted an increasingly activist posture against slavery. Old School Presbyterians, with a numerical center of gravity south of the Mason-Dixon line, meanwhile tried to forestall debate on the slavery issue on the grounds that as a secular rather than a spiritual matter it had no business in the church.

Charles Finney's approach to personal salvation — based on an assumption of the ability of each person to renounce sin and choose to follow Christ — has seemed to many to embody the can-do individualism of Jacksonian democracy. There were other similarities between Finney and Jackson as well. Like many of their contemporaries, both were entrepreneurs in their respective fields, and they both promoted the belief that individuals were responsible for their own future. But in every one of his sermons, prayers, and lectures, Charles Finney warned the American people against striving for self-interest and self-gratification. Indeed, in his sermon on the text from Ezekiel, "Make you a new heart," preached while Jackson was on the campaign trail, Finney described sin in terms that sound very much like the "Jacksonian" virtue of pursuing one's own self-interest. "God has established a government . . . yet [the sinner's] wicked heart consists in setting up his own interest in opposition to the interest and government of God."

Jacksonianism was for Finney the apotheosis of sin — each individual "aiming to promote his own private happiness, in a way that is opposed to the general good." Finney defined sin quite simply as selfishness. Still no doubt reflecting on the recent election and the current campaign, he denounced selfishness as "hateful . . . the discord of the soul . . . the jarring, and dissonance, and grating of hell's eternal anguish." Despite the competition of the religious marketplace, in which every evangelist strove to establish his voice, Finney's message was one of cooperation, service, and a "public spirit." He held up the old-fashioned Edwardsian-Hopkinsian, Revolutionary-era Whig, and always countercultural virtue of "disinterested benevolence" as America's evangelical hope and the individual's only hope for salvation. The evangelical-Whig spirit was in process of being reborn in the late 1820s. The political and social reformist implications of "Finneyite" religion would soon become manifest. In 1828 Charles Finney was definitely no Jacksonian.

Finney took part in one important bit of church politics at the May 1828 meeting of the Presbyterian General Assembly while he was in Philadelphia. He never went out of his way to attend such gatherings, and in the *Memoirs* he says he cannot remember adding his name to the paper Lyman Beecher held in front of him — but sign it he did. The document was a cease-fire agreement between Beecher and some of his "eastern" friends on the one side and the leading evangelical pastors from the Mohawk Valley on the other. It acknowledged that bickering had hurt their common cause of revival, that adequate consensus on revival methods had been reached at New Lebanon, and that the signatories would hereafter publish nothing negative about the other side. Beecher's olive branch could only help Charles Finney's ministry as he considered the many invitations that were piling up on his desk from all over the northeast and especially New York City.

Charles and Lydia Finney enjoyed spending as many weeks as possible every summer at the farm in Whitesboro under what the family called "the paternal roof." In late June and July, they made their way slowly north, with Finney preaching for several weeks at Troy and Albany. Summer doldrums seem to have set in, however, and after Finney left for Oneida County, Albany pastor Edward N. Kirk wrote that "some of the people are amusing themselves with the fact that 'Mr. Finney went out of town in the night, mourning that he could get so few to hear him.'" Kirk suggested that Finney come back when the legislature was in session. Finney preached "four day meetings" here and there and may have visited his parents in Jefferson County. In Columbia, Herkimer County, he worked in a German congregation with a recently converted young pastor from Pennsylvania and "found his views evangelical and his heart warm." He was back in Rome and Utica in late September and early October. All of this, however, was simply a comfortable interlude on home territory before the evangelist's first major effort in New York City.

Charles Finney's friends from Utica, Manhattan attorneys Jonas and Zephaniah Platt, had long been trying to arrange for him to preach in New York. In December 1827, when Finney was on his way south to Wilmington, they convened a number of highly influential laymen to meet with him over a period of several days. This group of leading businessmen and philan-thropists included dry-goods merchant David L. Dodge, man-ufacturer Anson Phelps, and William E. Dodge. They were related to one another through membership on the boards of mission and reform agencies, personal friendship, and family ties — the younger Dodge was married to Phelps's daughter. Finney greatly impressed these men, successfully countering the negative campaign waged against his reputation in the city by Asahel Nettleton. In a remarkable stroke, they convinced the dignified Dr. Gardiner Spring to invite Finney to preach at his prestigious Brick Presbyterian Church the following sum-mer (July 1828) when he was on his way to Whitesboro for vacation. Finney preached again in New York on the return trip to Philadelphia in August at the Laight Street Church. The invitation came from the church's governing body via the prominent merchant-philanthropist Arthur Tappan, but unfor-tunately the session acted without the knowledge of the va-cationing pastor Samuel Cox. Apart from the irate Cox, New Yorkers were impressed with Finney and ready for more.

The evangelical "association of gentlemen" in New York took ecclesiastical matters into their own hands. These men were all aggressive businessmen, and most of them were trans-planted Connecticut Congregationalists who knew something about lay authority in the local church. Ignoring Presbyterian protocol, Anson Phelps, Arthur Tappan, and others who had belonged to the Brick Church withdrew and attempted to as-sume leadership of the Bowery Presbyterian Church. When internal tension made that situation untenable, they withdrew again and decided to form a church of their own with pastoral leadership from the Mohawk Valley. Phelps went to Albany, where he met with Nathan S. S. Beman, Samuel Aikin, Edward Kirk, and other pastors. The invitation came in a letter from Aikin dated October 12, 1829, to Finney in Whitesboro. On October 17, Charles, Lydia, and Helen Finney arrived in New York City, and Finney was in the pulpit the next morning.

Aikin explained in his letter how Phelps and his friends had separated from the Bowery Church and were "going to build, but in the meantime shall occupy the Vanderwater Street Church which they [had] hired." The plan was for Beman to become their pastor, but he would not be able to move "for several months." The men were now inviting Finney "to come on without delay and occupy their pulpit which is now wide open for you and will be at your entire disposal." Aikin wrote that his colleagues at the Albany meeting were "very desirous that you should accept" and that he had "this morning seen Brother Lansing and he is of the same opinion." He assured Finney, "We all think that a wide and effectual door is now opened for you in New York City, and that the voice of Providence is, Arise and enter." Beman added a note of urgency from Troy: "The call from New York for revival preaching has become *loud* and commanding. . . . They look to you and to me." He concluded, "You and I must meet and consult on this subject." But Beman's letter did not reach Finney in time and had to be forwarded to New York City.

Finney's congregation organized with thirty-five founding members and named itself the Union Church. They met through the fall in the Vanderwater Street building but relocated in December when Phelps was able to purchase a vacant Universalist meetinghouse at the corner of Prince and Marion streets. The church was the first of several to bill themselves as "Free Presbyterian Churches," which meant that a free seating policy was adopted in place of the traditional method of charging annual pew rents. The intention was charitable, to make poor and transient people feel welcome in worship. The name also connoted something of the spirit of congregationalism and Yankee self-reliance espoused by the businessmen who were at the church's helm. This group of wealthy philanthropists in essence became Finney's collective patron. On previous visits to New York, the Finneys had stayed with the Platt family, but now they lodged for a few months with the Phelpses before moving to the home of the merchant William Rockwell.

Finney received supportive letters from upstate friends, many of them studded with bits of cautionary wisdom. Beman confessed that he "was nearly provoked" with Finney for not stopping in Troy to "talk over New York." He warned him "how important it is for you to have God with you," since now "you have no Lansing, no Aikin, or Frost, or Gillet, or Beman to stand by you, and assist you" — as if Finney had not been on his own and relied on God in Philadelphia. Everyone had helpful advice: Don't make Beecher's mistake in New York and try to use "anything like *wit* in the pulpit." Don't be like Nettleton, who "became proud and lost a spirit of prayer, in consequence of being patronized and flattered by great doters." Don't "preach too much against [other] ministers." Remember "your old friends as well as your new ones." Preach so as to convince them "that you are not a barbarian." Don't be distracted by "the business, the bustle, the dissipation, the etiquette" of the big city. Don't "seek to be a great intellectualist." Don't let "the revival spirit seem to evaporate." And so on.

Relations between the lay leaders and Nathan Beman as their potential permanent minister soured. He wrote on New Year's Day 1830 complaining of his frustration "respecting a call for me" and told Finney to "say to them, no call could be accepted by me now." Beman had been getting more and more touchy with Finney — he once added in a postscript to a letter, "What do you deform the outside of your letters to me for, by sticking on D.D.? Do you do it to insult *me*, or to make the Post Master think you correspond with some *Great Man?*" In his New Year's letter he simply added, "You are doing better without me than with me now." Still, when Charles and Lydia had their second child in New York City on March 28, they named him Charles Beman.

Finney built up the Union Church congregation with his regular pattern of a full preaching schedule, prayer and inquiry meetings, and pastoral visitation. In his *Memoirs* he provided few details and only one unusual conversion story from these nine months in the city. He simply noted, "Many very interesting conversions took place, as persons came from every part of the city and attended our meetings." *The New York Evangelist*, a pro-revival paper founded by the Platt-Dodge-Phelps-Tappan consortium, reported that by the spring of 1830 "more than 200 have been hopefully renewed by the power of the Holy Ghost" through Finney's ministry. When summer arrived and it was time for the annual trip to Whitesboro, Finney was certain he would not return in September. He wrote Beman, who confirmed that he was not a candidate but suggested another central New York friend of Charles and Lydia Finney, Herman Norton. Arrangements were made, and the congregation called Norton to assume pastoral responsibilities in the fall.

What Finney did remember in his *Memoirs* about that first time in New York was the deep impression made upon him by the businessmen who took such an active role in the religious affairs of the city. He was awed by the piety of Anson Phelps, with whom he lived for some months, and especially "his interior life as it was manifested in his outward life." He recalled one time going downstairs after midnight to get something for the baby and finding his host "sitting by his fire in his night gown" engaged in his "secret devotions." Phelps then told him how, with "business pressing me during the day," after a brief nap, the early morning hours became "a season of communion with God." He even kept a journal, in authentic Puritan tradition, recording "the secret workings of his mind, and the real progress of his interior life." Finney also related the conversion story of Lewis Tappan, who came from Massachusetts to join his brother Arthur in the New York business in early 1828. A Unitarian who thoroughly believed the trumped-up stories of Finney as a "half-crazed fanatic" propagated in the anti-revivalist press, Lewis Tappan had berated his brother for his gullible admiration of the evangelist. Arthur promised Lewis the substantial sum of five hundred dollars if he could produce "credible testimony" that would hold up in a court of law on the veracity of any of the tall tales. When a Unitarian investigator hired by Lewis utterly failed, his liberal faith was shaken, and he restudied the entire literature of the Unitarian-Orthodox controversy. Arthur pressed the need for repentance and salvation upon his brother, Lewis was converted, and the two became a powerful team in support of evangelical benevolent causes.

In the Christian businessmen of New York City, Charles Finney discovered his model of the ideal male convert. Exemplary female believers had abounded in his upstate New York ministry. Once they confessed their sinfulness and embraced the Savior, they never hesitated to busy themselves as missionaries in their own churches and neighborhoods. It was the Female Missionary Society in Utica that gave Finney his first financial support in the ministry back in Jefferson County. Letters from women friends to Lydia fairly bristle with news of prayer meetings, recent conversions, and foreign and homeland mission work. One letter that reached the Finneys in Pennsylvania from "Charlotte" in Troy, for example, reported the organization of a new local Temperance Society. When "appeal was made to females to lend their influence," the friend rejoiced to say that "all but one or two" joined. But with few exceptions, as Finney told it in his *Memoirs,* the men who came to Christ went nowhere with their faith beyond the reformation of their character. When he became friends with Anson Phelps, the Dodges, the Tappans, and their colleagues, Finney caught a new vision of what it could mean to be a man and a Christian.

Most impressive to him was the energetic way these evangelical businessmen incorporated the old virtue of "disinterested benevolence" into their commercial, philanthropic, church, and family lives. Although they were wealthy, they expressed genuine concern for the poor and sought ways to improve their lot and bring them faith. They were devoted to the church and supported it with enormous amounts of time and money. They committed themselves to leadership in voluntary organizations for the spread of the gospel, education, and the reform of every social evil they could identify. They did all this not as ordained ministers but as laity. In fact, it often seemed as if the motive behind their drive to succeed in the business world was to produce income for religious and benevolent causes. Finney would take this model of the ideal male convert with him as he planned his next steps as an evangelist.

Finney called men of the world to this kind of Christian accountability in a sermon that appeared later in print (in *Sermons on Important Subjects,* 1836). Preaching from Luke 16:2 — "Give an account of thy stewardship" — he argued that in managing property people are "merely [God's] agents, and not the *owners* of the property." It is nothing but sin and shame if a wealthy man should "use it for his own private interest . . . or the aggrandizement of his family." All people must give God an account "for their *time* . . . of their *talents* . . . for the *influence* [they] exert . . . for the manner in which [they] use *the property in [their] possession.*" Finney went on to say, "You have God's money in your hands. . . . The world is full of poverty, desolation, and death; hundreds of millions are perishing, body and soul; God calls you to exert yourself as his steward, for their salvation, to use all the property in your possession, so as to promote the greatest possible amount of happiness among your fellow-creatures." Men like the Platts, Anson Phelps, and the Tappans had a special responsibility to put universal benevolence into action on the grandest scale possible.

The "association of gentlemen" had already set in motion events that would help determine where the next step would be taken. In their effort to establish churches in poorer sections of New York City, they brought together enough families to form the nucleus of a congregation that would meet in a vacant building on Thames Street near Broadway. They invited a mission-minded revivalist pastor, Joel Parker of the Third Presbyterian Church in Rochester, New York, to serve as minister of this new Free Presbyterian Church. Finney may have participated in the arrangements, for he visited Rochester the first week in February 1830, three months before the laymen sat down with Parker when he was in New York for the annual meeting of the major mission boards. Parker began his work in New York near the end of June, leaving his Rochester pulpit open.

Finney received scores of letters during the first half of 1830 — from New England, Wilmington, Philadelphia, all around New York State, and from Cleveland, Ohio — urging his presence. The idea of moving into the void created in Rochester by Joel Parker's departure seemed far-fetched at first, since it could be construed as a retreat to a smaller, more provincial market. Finney languished for some time during the summer. "I remained at my father-in-law's, and considered the subject until I felt that I must take hold and work somewhere." On faith, Charles and Lydia packed their trunks, went to Utica, and asked a group of trusted friends for advice and prayer on where to go. Finney recalled in his *Memoirs* that everyone agreed that Rochester was too insignificant a city "to be put at all in competition with New York or Philadelphia." Finney "should go east from Utica, and not west." Charles Finney agreed with them; we do not know what Lydia felt. It certainly made sense for the evangelist to continue his work in the largest urban setting possible. After praying with their friends, Charles and Lydia and the children were prepared to "take the canal boat . . . and start for New York."

5 The Anxious Seat

Charles and Lydia Finney surprised their Utica friends early that September morning, the evangelist recalled in his *Memoirs*, by boarding the "packet canal boat" that was heading "westward instead of eastward." They would spend the year, from September 10, 1830, through mid-June 1831 in Rochester and western New York.

In fact, Charles Finney never decided for the west over against the east. They would go east again in August of 1831, first to Providence, Rhode Island, and then to Boston, where he preached from September 1831 until May 1832. In addition to widening his field of evangelism to include the entire northeastern United States during these years, Finney adopted the pattern of conducting a revival campaign from autumn through spring of each year. The rhythm of his work seemed to require a mental and physical break in the summer, with a change of scenery in the fall. (Charles and Lydia's second and third children were both born in March, in 1830 and 1832, respectively, nine months after their vacation at her parents'

Whitesboro farm.) With each annual cycle, Finney continued to develop his style and method as an evangelist. While he did not modify his basic approach or purpose, there is no question that after more than two years in Philadelphia and New York City he had acquired a more polished manner than had characterized his earlier preaching. Penitents still came to Christ through tears and agonizing prayer, but they were not falling to the floor in the Spirit as they had in the early years. In 1830 and 1831, moreover, two "new measures" developed out of his traditional revival method — the anxious seat and the protracted meeting.

"Something seemed to question me," Charles Finney wrote in his *Memoirs,* concerning the decision to turn away from Rochester in the fall of 1830. Before retiring for the night, still uneasy, he spent more time in prayer. That "something" compelled him to list again the arguments against going to the flourishing mill town on the Genesee River near its mouth on Lake Ontario. His opportunities in a small city could not compare with those in New York or Philadelphia. He could "readily enumerate" the problems that he had heard plagued Rochester. "Religion was in a low state" at Third Church, the congregation that was calling him. An elder of Third Church, a wealthy businessman, had busied himself in the affairs of both First Presbyterian Church and Second Church, stirring up discontent against the pastors and plotting their dismissal. The city may also have seemed "too uninviting a field of labor" because of the boomtown vices — greed, sex, and "ardent spirits" — associated with commerce on the Erie Canal, which crossed the Genesee at Rochester. The inner voice demanded, "Are these *good reasons?* Certainly you are *needed* at Rochester *all the more* because of these difficulties." It crystallized in Finney's mind that the reasons not to go there were really "the most cogent reasons *for* my going." Finney demonstrated remarkable restraint in identifying the "something" that turned his attention to the west. At several times in his life he testified to immediate revelations of God's will by the Holy Spirit. Here, however, his will appears to have been turned to what he believed was God's will by the operation of his own subconscious good sense followed by the application of faith-guided reason. The decision was as much a mental as a spiritual process, and when he resolved to go to Rochester, he wrote, "it was strongly impressed on my mind that the Lord would be with me, and that that was my field."

Rochester turned out to be the ideal site for Charles Finney's revival preaching. The city contained more than enough New England–rooted Yorker men and women of the sort that typically responded to his evangelism so readily, and there was enough social stress to ignite an explosive revival. Rochester was the fastest growing city in the United States during the 1820s, a regional entrepôt that had been transformed by the commercial revolution connected with the completion of the Erie Canal. The city was a manufacturing center, with workshops and small factories producing necessities and a few luxuries for the surrounding countryside, but its economy was based on agriculture: it was inseparable from the surrounding villages and farms. Wheat was the commodity responsible for Rochester's wealth, and the city's mills increased their annual production of flour at a meteoric rate. Before the Canal, Rochester was a village with fewer than one thousand residents and carted out twenty-six thousand barrels of flour a year; by the time Finney arrived in the fall of 1830, it had attained a population of more than ten thousand and was shipping about a quarter of a million barrels of flour annually. At the lower end of society, young laborers arrived and left the city with some regularity, but the enterprising merchants, millers, and master craftsmen were remarkably stable and worked as hard at building the city's churches and social institutions as they did at their own businesses. Society was becoming more stratified as the working classes no longer lived in the same households and neighborhoods as their employers, and the commercial middle class worried about loss of social control. But Rochester was still a small town where face-to-face contact among the populace was the daily norm. Rochester gave Charles Finney yet another chance to achieve a community-wide impact.

In Philadelphia and New York, after four years in villages and small cities where his preaching often enjoyed the full spotlight, Finney for the first time had experienced only relative success. He drew crowds of hundreds or even thousands, occupying as he did Philadelphia's largest church building, but many other pastors with no connection to Finney also boasted large followings — some larger. Rochester appeared ready to give Finney its undivided attention. Indeed, the spiritual awakening had already begun during the summer of 1830, with church attendance rising in many congregations and a powerful Methodist camp meeting ablaze nearby. Finney succeeded quickly in becoming the focal point of a broadly cooperative evangelistic effort that involved all the churches and reformed the city's social fabric.

Charles Finney stepped into the tension-filled center of Rochester's church and business life on his first day in town. Entrance into the city by canal boat was itself a dramatic experience, as passengers crossed the Genesee River and millraces on the stone aqueduct with its view of the falls and an impressive skyline of mills, bridges, and church steeples. It was early in the morning when their boat moored at the landing and the Finneys disembarked. The family made its way toward fashionable Fitzhugh Street, where they were to stay with Josiah Bissell, the evangelical businessman who had issued Finney the invitation from Third Presbyterian Church. Finney suddenly recognized his cousin Frederick Starr on the street. Word had gotten on ahead of the canal boat by stagecoach that the evangelist was on his way to Rochester, and Starr had plans for ensuring that the revival would not be limited to Third Church. Starr, himself a manufacturer and an elder in First Church, invited the Finneys on the spot to stay with him. Finney wrote that his cousin was "anxious to have his Pastor Dr. Penny meet and converse with me and be prepared to cooperate with me in my labors." After Finney explained that they were to stay with Bissell, they continued to his large home, settled in, and were served breakfast. It was their host Josiah Bissell, an elder at Third Church, who had engineered the ouster of Second Church's pastor and was now politicking within First Church and with presbytery leaders to remove Penney. No sooner had the family finished eating than Starr arrived and informed Finney "that he had arranged an interview between myself and Dr. Penny, at his house at that hour."

Finney credited his cousin with the behind-the-scenes work necessary to establish the cooperation of the churches in Rochester. "Mr. Starr exerted himself to bring about a good understanding between the Pastors and Churches and a great change soon manifested itself in the attitude and spiritual state of the Churches." Finney played an important role in the reconciliation as well. He "hastened to meet the Dr." that first morning and "had a cheering Christian interview." By maintaining a working relationship with Bissell, whom he viewed as the local counterpart of Anson Phelps and the Tappan brothers, and with all the pastors as well, Finney brought harmony where there had previously been division. Bissell was a tough case, because his devotion to evangelical social reform had crossed the line from zeal to offensiveness. He was particularly committed to sabbatarianism, the strict observance of Sunday as the sabbath in business and every area of public life including mail transport. He had founded the Pioneer Packet and Stage Companies as a sabbath-keeping line and condemned as un-Christian any individuals who dealt with the competition. His intrigue against First Church pastor William James stemmed from the fact that Bissell had spotted him riding on a rival stage coach. Bissell's Pioneer Line was a financial disaster and went out of business in a year, but he continued his arrogant meddling in church affairs. It took Finney's revival to bring peace. As they united in a common effort, Finney wrote, "the difficulties between Brother Bissel and Dr. Penny were healed; and all the distractions and collisions that had existed there were adjusted, so that a spirit of universal kindness and fellowship pervaded all the churches."

Finney mounted the pulpit at Rochester's Third Presbyterian Church and received an invitation to preach at First Church as well, and the conversions began immediately. An astonishing event interrupted the revival less than three weeks later, however, just as he was to preach at First Church. Finney was kneeling at the sofa behind the pulpit as Penney offered the opening prayer, when suddenly a sound like the crack of gunfire and "the jingling of glass" commanded attention. At first Finney thought it was from a militia training event that was going on in the city, but it turned out to have been the collapse of a roof timber. As plaster dust filled the sanctuary, panicked worshipers scrambled out of the building any way they could. Finney described how Penney "leaped from the pulpit over me." An elderly lady held a window open while some "leapt out into the canal" on the banks of which the church was built. Some men jumped from the gallery; others ran along the tops of the pews. The evangelist cried out for order, not realizing the seriousness of the situation, but soon everyone evacuated the building. Some injuries were reported, but no one was seriously hurt or killed. Unknown to Finney, citizens had worried for some time about the safety of the structure, which had been undermined by dampness from the canal. Other churches threw their buildings open to Finney, including the Episcopal. Meetings soon began alternating between Second and Third churches. Finney expressed fear that the excitement would distract people from the work of the revival, but he need not have worried. If anything, the catastrophe united the three Presbyterian congregations as never before. "Christians of every denomination generally seemed to make common cause, and entirely united in their efforts . . . to pull sinners out of the fire."

Among the early converts in Rochester was Mary P. Matthews, whom Finney described as "the wife of a prominent lawyer" and "a lady of culture and extensive influence." A godly female friend brought her to the evangelist for counsel when she appeared humbled for her vanity by his preaching. Seeing that she was indeed "bowed down with great conviction of sin," Finney "pressed her hard then and there to give herself to Christ." They knelt in prayer, in which Finney invoked Jesus' call to "be converted and become as little children." She fixed on the phrase "as little children," repeating it like a mantra as Finney "besought the Lord to convert her, to make her as a little child, to put away her pride and her loftiness of spirit." Finney prayed with confidence. This was what Father Nash had called "agonizing prayer" and the "prayer of faith" — believing with certainty "that the Lord was doing the very work that I asked him to do." When he finished his prayer, Mary Matthews's face was "turned up toward heaven, and the tears streaming over her face." She arose a new woman and immediately became "zealous for the conversion of her friends." She also threw herself into temperance, Sunday School and abolition work, and Bible and tract distribution. Charles Finney was at the top of his form.

Mary and Selah Matthews were Charles G. Finney's kind of people. After the first few weeks with Bissell, the Finneys lodged with a lawyer named Elisha Beach, whose house was "in a more central position" in the city. The first order of business was to convert Beach's sister, "an impenitent girl . . . of fine appearance, an exquisite singer." Finney was most at home not with the rough and dirty working class but with young and middle-aged business and professional people, upwardly mobile master craftsmen, and women from the better families. Finney boasted that at Rochester "it was soon seen that the Lord was aiming at the conversion of the highest classes of society." It would be wrong to describe evangelicalism, or the 1830-1831 revival in particular, in reductionist fashion as the product of tensions among social classes. Nevertheless, an analysis of the Rochester revival by social historian Paul E. Johnson, aptly titled *A Shopkeeper's Millennium*, confirms this connection between evangelical religion and business and professional families with commercial ties to the surrounding countryside. Finney believed that when the city's leaders were won to Christ, reform would pervade every neighborhood, and the lower classes could then be brought in as well. Mary P. Matthews later wrote Charles and Lydia that she and her husband were considered Rochester's "greatest *Finneyites.*"

Strange as it may seem, Charles Finney introduced the anxious seat during the Rochester revival as a "new measure" particularly suited to the best educated and most sophisticated of the population. From the start of his ministry, he had offered special inquiry meetings to encourage penitents to give themselves to Christ. At these gatherings he typically moved among those kneeling to counsel and pray with them personally. In every place he worked, he visited penitents in their homes and welcomed them at his lodgings for individual prayer. On occasion, perhaps inspired by the Methodist practice of an altar call, he had invited those "anxious for their souls" to stand or to come forward for special prayer. Business and professional people, who tended to be "too proud" to make their spiritual anxiety known, were naturally shy about all this. But Finney did not believe that this tendency should be accommodated by a retreat into more private counseling. These were public people, he reasoned, and they needed to be pushed into "some public manifestation or demonstration that would declare to all around them that they abandoned a sinful life then and there, and committed themselves to Jesus Christ." In Rochester, Finney called those ready to renounce sin and embrace Christ "then and there" to occupy some reserved seats at the front of the church "while we made them subjects of prayer." He was pleased that a large number came forward, and especially the "prominent lad[ies] . . . lawyers, physicians, merchants, and indeed all the most intelligent class of society."

The anxious seat became a standard feature of Finney's religious meetings and, with its cousin the camp meeting altar call, of American evangelical revivalism in general. Finney explained the rationale behind this call for an immediate response in *Lectures on Revivals of Religion,* a published version of a series of lectures he delivered in New York City in 1834 based on his experience at Rochester and elsewhere. First of all, he insisted, preaching must be targeted at the individual. "You must make a man feel that you mean *him,*" that God is provoked at "the individual's *particular sins."* In counseling, the pastor should "find the *point where the Spirit of God is pressing* a sinner." Finally, when individuals could be termed "anxious sinners" who were ready to come forward, they should be "regarded as being in a very *solemn and critical state."* Finney saw them as having "come to a turning point" at which "their destiny is likely to be settled forever." Every sermon was to include this note of urgency: "Will you submit to God tonight — NOW?" It was critically important that this submission be made in public, overcoming the "powerful tendency to try to keep [religious feelings] private." Finney knew that "if you can get him willing to make known his feelings, you have accomplished a great deal. . . . When a person is borne down with a sense of his condition, if you can get him willing to have it known, if you can get him to break away from the chains of pride, you have gained an important point toward his conversion." Moreover, the commitment has to be made in public because conversion brings with it social responsibility, commitment to a life of public benevolence. In anti-ritualistic evangelical Protestantism, the anxious seat may be said to have provided a public liturgy of repentance and rebirth that involved individuals together in community.

Charles Finney's gospel preaching engaged the market-oriented ethos of Rochester on its own terms. A high school student who heard nearly every one of Finney's Rochester sermons recalled more than four decades later, in 1876, at a memorial service after Finney's death that the evangelist had possessed "the dignity and majesty of one of the old prophets." The message delivered by "that clarion voice" was "fearful . . . searching, scorching, withering." One sermon in particular, on Romans 6:23 ("The wages of sin is death"), etched itself in the youth's mind. "You will get your *wages*," Finney assured his congregation; "just what you have earned, your due; nothing more, nothing less; and as the smoke of your torment, like a thick cloud, ascends forever and ever, you will see written upon its curling folds, in great staring letters of light, this awful word, wages, *wages*, WAGES." Whether or not many common laborers who worked for daily wages got the message, the young convert, who subsequently joined Third Church and went into the ministry, felt his heart stand still.

Nor was this pious teen the only one, for high school classes were suspended as enthusiastic students gave their full attention to the revival. The notoriously skeptical head principal was converted, and the female principal years later counted forty graduates who went on to become ministers and missionaries. Businesses closed early so employees and customers could attend prayer meetings. In his *Lectures on Revivals* a few years later, Finney reflected on how, "if we do our business for God," Christian businessmen would willingly close their doors for a few hours or even days and "consider it in the light of a holiday." The newspapers, especially the *Rochester Observer*, were enthusiastically supportive of the revival and of evangelical social reform generally. Men were converted in larger numbers than ever before in Rochester and joined their wives, who had been prodding and praying for them, in church membership. The theater and the circus were purchased by wealthy believers and closed down on the grounds that they encouraged dissolute, self-indulgent behavior. In his *Memoirs*, Finney wrote that a lawyer converted in the 1830-1831 revival, a future district attorney, connected "the wonderful influence that that revival had had upon the community" with a dramatic drop in the level of crime in the city. To a greater extent in his ministry than anywhere else, as Finney put it, in Rochester "public sentiment has been molded." Many were to say that it was the greatest local revival in American history.

Reading Finney's *Memoirs*, one would never know that the primary means by which individual salvation led to social reform in Rochester was the wedding of the revival with the temperance movement. Lyman Beecher established the American Society for the Promotion of Temperance in 1826 in the conviction that alcohol consumption was behind such problems as violent crime, poverty, domestic strife, and individual failure. As divisions between the managerial and working classes grew deeper in communities such as Rochester, temperance societies were founded by leading men and women at least partly in an effort to secure greater social control. Temperance was the child of evangelical Protestantism, and in Rochester it was linked explicitly with revivalism. Charles Finney was forever chary of any diversion, no matter how worthy in itself, from the work of saving souls. Nevertheless, he himself consecrated the marriage by inviting one of his prize Utica converts to Rochester. Theodore Dwight Weld, now in his mid-twenties and studying for the ministry, had achieved a reputation as a powerful Temperance Society speaker.

Finney introduced Weld to the neighborhood prayer meetings and at Third Church had him deliver his message that alcohol was at the root of America's social ills. Weld's crusade reached its apex at First Presbyterian Church on New Year's Eve in a four-hour lecture, backed on the platform by Methodist and Baptist clergy alongside the Presbyterians. He demonstrated how drink led inevitably to ruin not only for those who were already lost in wretchedness but for well-to-do still-respectable moderate tipplers. Weld then issued a thundering call to abandon and boycott all business activity related even remotely to the liquor trade. Dr. Penney followed up with a specific demand that local merchants, many of whom were present, immediately halt liquor sales. The next day shopkeepers smashed barrels in the streets or dumped their contents into the canal. Economic pressure from evangelical politicians and business leaders, newspaper editors, and ordinary believers forced even the most reluctant vendors to discontinue sales or face bankruptcy. The effectiveness of Finney's revival in Rochester can be measured both in church membership statistics and in the soaring power of the temperance movement.

Finney did not bring temperance to Rochester; he promoted it and built upon it to advance his own primary work of evangelism. The city was already well known as a center of evangelical reforms — especially sabbatarianism and opposition to Masonry — before Finney arrived, and he endorsed them all. But as the collapse of Bissell's Pioneer stage line showed, sabbatarianism was a complex issue that fostered conflict rather than united commitment among the churches. And opposition to Masonry was too political for Finney's purposes just now. It was born as an organized movement in 1826, when William Morgan, a former Mason, mysteriously disappeared after publishing an exposé of Masonic secrets. Evangelicals and others who saw the lodge as a cabalistic attempt by a wealthy elite to grab control of the American economy and government accused the Order of murder. Francis H. Cuming, a local Episcopal rector and Masonic Grand Master, was implicated in the kidnaping. He was also related by marriage to the family of Nathaniel Rochester, who, along with many other Episcopalians and Masons, was a political leader in Martin Van Buren's Bucktail Republican party. This political faction in the city was decidedly pro-Jackson in 1828. All of this exploded in Cuming's face when controversy rocked St. Luke's Church — some members were anti-Jacksonian evangelicals with good friends across courthouse square at First Presbyterian Church — and Cuming was forced to resign. Finney himself was strongly anti-Masonic in temperament. He had joined the Masonic Order as a young man but quit shortly after his conversion and thereafter considered it antithetical to Christianity. Still, the anti-Masonic movement, which had spawned a major political party in 1828, was so divisive that Finney seems to have sidestepped it in Rochester. Other issues, such as abolition or women's rights, were similarly problematic; they would have motivated some believers but alienated others. Finney might actually have omitted any mention of Weld's role in the Rochester revival in the *Memoirs* because a few years later Weld became so radically committed to abolition and feminism that he abandoned the church and traditional Christian faith. But the cause of temperance united evangelical Protestants in America like no other social movement had, and it would continue to do so for almost a hundred years.

The Rochester revival "spread like waves in every direction," Finney wrote, as visitors who came from nearby villages and farther-away cities returned home with the spirit. The evangelist himself preached occasionally at villages along the canal and throughout Monroe County, making a regular Wednesday visit to Pittsford, where Asa Mahan was pastor. Finney wrote his colleague Edward N. Kirk in Albany that when he went out to the villages, "in every instance, the Lord has come down and commenced a work upon the spot." Indeed, during 1830 and 1831 a fresh awakening seemed to ripple throughout the northeast, and even at the time observers pointed to Rochester as the epicenter. Of course, revivalism was omnipresent in America quite apart from the contribution of Charles G. Finney in Rochester or anywhere else. Even so, Finney and Rochester acquired symbolic power as news of that city's revival reached far and wide. As Finney observed in his *Memoirs*, "the very *fame* of it was an efficient instrument in the hands of the Spirit of God." He gloried in quoting Lyman Beecher that the nationwide revival sparked by Rochester was "the greatest work of God, and the greatest revival of religion, that the world has ever seen in so short a time." Contemporary estimates, which may have been fairly accurate, put the number of new church members in the northeast at about 100,000; some went as high as 200,000. "The waters of salvation had risen so high," Finney wrote, that opposition was silenced. Widespread acceptance of revivalism was due in part to the political power of evangelicals, and perhaps also to the gentrification of the revivals as they overtook (and were overtaken by) mainstream America. Finney was glad to report that at Rochester "I am not aware that there was ever any complaint of any fanaticism, or anything that was to be deplored in its results."

The protracted meeting was adopted as a means of promoting revivals around the time of the Rochester revival. Finney's correspondence during this period contains reference after reference to a "four day meeting" being held here and a "three day meeting" planned for there. The idea for this "new measure" may have dated from the summer of 1828, when Finney received a letter from New Lebanon proposing a week-long *"great meeting . . . this summer"* with "some half dozen ministers whose hearts the Lord has opened." The schedule would include "three sermons a day and as many prayer meetings . . . in the courthouse if the weather is bad and on the green if it is good." Planners insisted, "You cannot call it a *Camp Meeting*," because "it varies in the principal features." They may have meant that congregants would not be sleeping in tents and that there would be less singing and no altar call. By the 1820s the camp meeting had been so thoroughly taken over by the Methodists that these Presbyterians had forgotten that the practice was brought to America from Scotland a hundred years before. The protracted meeting as Finney's associates developed it in the early 1830s was an urban and village evangelistic program. Several ministers would join forces for an intensive campaign with meetings in the morning, afternoon, and evening. In his *Lectures on Revivals,* Finney listed protracted meetings along with inquiry meetings and the anxious seat as an essential revival "measure." He insisted, however, that they were really "not new," having developed naturally out of the evangelical tradition. "New measure" or not, Finney endorsed the practice. During the last week of February 1831, for example, William Wisner of Ithaca was in Rochester to work with Finney in a "four days meeting."

Wisner found Charles Finney physically worn out. For six months, his daily round of visitation, counseling and prayer, preaching, and travel had continued unabated. His friends were concerned for his health; physicians thought he would soon die of consumption. When the evangelist decided to accept an invitation from President Eliphalet Nott to preach at

Union College, Wisner and Josiah Bissell traveled with him on the stage as far as Geneva, where Wisner begged him to come home with him and rest. Disregarding Wisner's advice, and with Lydia remaining in Rochester, Finney pressed on as far as Auburn. The atrocious springtime condition of the road tired Finney even more, however, and he finally succumbed to his fatigue. He stopped to rest overnight at the home of the Auburn district attorney Theodore Spencer, a "very dear friend" who had been converted during Finney's 1826 revival. Finney never made it to Schenectady. When he awoke, he was presented with a petition to stay "signed by a long list of unconverted men, most of them among the most prominent citizens in the city." He noted that these men had vigorously opposed his work five years before. The church added its voice to the invitation, and Finney agreed to stay, but only under conditions that would enable him to recuperate. He would preach "twice upon the Sabbath and two evenings during the week" and spend the remainder of the time resting. Others would do the counseling, visiting, praying with penitent sinners, and leading of other meetings. The revival ignited again in Auburn, this time with no opposition. The "unconverted men" were the first to come forward to the anxious seat.

Finney himself was revived by spending March and April in Auburn. His physical strength was restored. Attending a synod meeting in Rome, he met with many old friends and colleagues. Catherine Huntington wrote Lydia on April 4, "The Romans had a strong satisfaction of seeing your husband here last week." Invitations poured in daily, from Lewis Tappan, Joel Parker, and others in New York City; from Albany and Syracuse; from Timothy Dwight Jr. in New Haven, Connecticut; and from the North Country — "O Brother Finney, cast your eye to the Land of your Spiritual Birth!" Finney had apparently made some promises to the Presbyterian church in Buffalo, for the Rev. Sylvester Eaton wrote impatiently, "Your leaving Rochester and going to Auburn instead of coming here, after having excited our expectation, is an event which I have been utterly unable to comprehend." Theodore Weld argued for Buffalo against New York City: "Go to Buffalo and the intermediate towns between there and Rochester. Once get that region thoroughly soaked and all hell can't wring it dry." With Lydia and the children, Finney stayed in Buffalo for a month from early May to early June. In what was by now the familiar pattern, the revival took hold first and most firmly among the lawyers, judges, merchants, and commercial leaders, including a pioneer of the hydraulic power industry, Reuben Heacock.

In the spring of 1831, Finney's friends in New York urged him to return to the city. Herman Norton, who took his place at Union Church, conceded that the clergy were less than enthusiastic — "the great majority of the ministers say that it is inexpedient for you to come" — and that "Parker's pulpit and mine are *the only ones that are absolutely open.*" Nevertheless, he wrote, "the city is ripe." Because men were always in New York on business, "one sermon affects perhaps a hundred congregations in different parts of the U.S." He predicted large crowds: "1000 would now hear you." Meanwhile, plans for a New England tour were taking shape. On April 2 Finney wrote to New Haven indicating his willingness to come. Return mail assured him, "You will be received cordially. . . . Our revival is in progress." Dirck Lansing of Utica wrote in May, "You are called to Hartford. The door seems to me to be open for all New England. You can play with perfect ease between Hartford and New Haven. . . . Dear Brother Finney, it does appear to me time for you to go East, and may God go with you." Then a specific invitation came from Boston's Union Orthodox Church. The writer savored the delicious anomaly of the occasion. Casting aside Boston's icy anti-Finney bias, he exclaimed, "What hath God wrought!"

Congregationalist leaders like Leonard Bacon of New Haven's prestigious First Church were full of friendly advice on how Finney should prepare himself for New England. Bacon explained that his colleagues had been slow with an invitation "not because we have wanted confidence in you as a preacher of the gospel, or as holding the same view of the gospel with ourselves," but because of the "prejudice which you know has existed in many places." Finney would be well advised to take a slightly different tack in approaching this new field. New Englanders, influenced strongly by Unitarian rationalism and characterized by their literary sophistication and reserved temperament, would not react kindly to being insulted or embarrassed. "Your views of doctrine and of measures . . . are our views with one exception," wrote Bacon. "We are decidedly of the opinion that *here* it is not advisable to try any such thing as calling on impenitent sinners to pledge themselves by standing up before the congregation." Call for immediate repentance, yes. Inquiry meetings, yes. Anxious seat? Bad idea. Oh, and in New England it is better to stress "the *goodness* of God in Christ," which is "the great motive which leads to repentance." Bacon was certain that reports of Finney's "severe and threatening style" were grossly exaggerated. Bacon rejoiced that "these blessed revivals are fast putting to silence the miserable outcry against *Taylorism* in one quarter, and *Finneyism* in another." Such advice must have given Finney pause, but he remained determined to head east.

Charles Finney left Buffalo for the east in early June 1831. He first joined Lydia and the children, who had departed earlier, in Whitesboro for their annual vacation on the farm. He preached in and around Utica (Daniel Nash wrote that in the village of Western "folks think you are under at least half a promise to return there") and then in the Albany-Troy area in July. It appears that Lydia remained with her parents through the summer. An August 17 letter to her there expressed concern for "the protracted illness of dear Helen." Finney seemed ready for New England, and his friends believed he would go there directly. Instead, he went to New York City for three weeks. Edward Kirk wrote on August 9, "How strange it is, after all that occurred in Mr. Willard's parlor on the day on which you went to Troy, that I should now be addressing you in New York instead of Boston or New Haven." New England was on

117

everyone's mind, for the conversation in Albany had included Catherine Beecher's "theory of virtue," and Kirk now wondered if Finney had "anything more to say" on the topic. At the same time, Finney laid the groundwork for an extended ministry in New York City after the New England tour. He preached to his old congregation at Union Church. But his main item of business was to explore with the Tappan brothers their idea of renting a major hall or even erecting an impressive new church building in which to showcase Charles Grandison Finney.

Finney began his work in New England on August 10 at a protracted meeting in Providence, Rhode Island. Staying for about three weeks with the wealthy textile merchant Josiah Chapin, Finney preached three times on Sunday and led meetings every evening of the week with the Rev. James Wilson at Beneficent Congregational Church. In the characteristic style of the *Memoirs,* Finney selected one remarkable conversion in a leading family to highlight the effectiveness of his work in Providence. In some ways Mary Ainsworth topped them all, for she was indisputably "the most beautiful girl in Providence" and was blessed with "a fervent nature, a strong will, and an uncommonly well-balanced and cultivated intellect." After a series of counseling sessions in which the evangelist sought "to show her the depravity of her heart," she confessed her sinful pride and "selfish motives." She finally "gave herself unreservedly to Christ," married a wealthy businessman, and was ever after "a very interesting Christian," by which Finney meant she showed a sincere interest in piety and church work. Finney rarely wavered from his belief that successful evangelism should aim high in society and benefit the poorer classes primarily through the benevolent work of able converts. He practiced, as it were, trickle-down evangelism.

The most significant turn of events in Providence was the espionage of Benjamin Wisner, pastor of Boston's Third Church (Old South). The leadership of Boston's trinitarian Congregational clergy included Lyman Beecher of Bowdoin Street

Church and his son Edward Beecher of Park Street Church. Wisner went as their agent to bring back a firsthand assessment of whether Finney's preaching would be acceptable in Boston. He arrived during the second week of August, in time to observe a four-day protracted meeting. He kept his presence in the congregation secret, listening through three sermons before revealing himself to the evangelist. His report would be crucial, because events in Boston had put Finney's trip there on hold.

After the lay leaders of Boston's Union Church had issued their invitation to Finney during the summer, the clergy association at their August 1 meeting attempted to block it. They declared the planned visit "inexpedient" and Finney's "manner of presenting truth" potentially embarrassing. Lyman Beecher, Finney's old adversary, followed up on August 2 with a fawning letter in which he praised Finney's "power of intellect" and stated, "You possess our confidence and affection." Putting aside "past differences of opinions about measures," Beecher wrote, "you and I are as much, perhaps even more, *one*, than almost any two men whom God has been pleased to render conspicuous in his church." It was just that "Boston was not the *best* point of entrance for you into New England, nor the *present* the best time for you to visit Boston." Beecher then had his daughter Catherine add a page explaining that, as eager as she was that "you and father should be brought together," it was better not to outrage the Unitarians, who were "on the look out for every indiscreet expression, or impolitic movement that may be trumpeted in their newspaper." She explained that "for *your comfort*, as well as your usefulness . . . Hartford or New Haven would be a better location for you than Boston." Finney wrote Union Church that he would not come without the "hearty concurrence" of Boston's orthodox clergy. The church urged him to come anyway, at least for "a few Sabbaths," to demonstrate that he could preach without being "obnoxious to the particular feelings of this community."

Finney wrote an important letter to Union Church on August 8 explaining his refusal to come without full clergy support. "I have been extensively supposed by New England ministers to be a kind of interloper crowding myself in here and there where I was not wanted. Dr. Beecher himself has viewed me in this light and accused me of floating upon the tide of popularity." Finney still chafed from Beecher's vow to keep him out of New England. He was not about to come until Beecher himself agreed. "Having no evidence that Dr. Beecher had changed his purpose I do not see how I could consent to visit Boston." Moreover, after his experience of interchurch cooperation in Rochester, Finney asserted, "I don't think that my coming would be productive of sufficient good to balance the evil that would result from disunion."

Benjamin Wisner's trip to Providence demonstrated the seriousness with which the trinitarian clergy of Boston took Charles Finney. Many of them were feeling pressure from their own members, in addition to pressure from the lay leaders of Union Church, to bring him to Boston. Park Street Church deacons, for example, wanted Finney to preach there while their pastor took time off to move into a new house. Whatever Wisner's expectations may have been, Charles Finney thoroughly won him over. When the clerical spy finally introduced himself to the evangelist, he shook his hand and expressed his complete approval. On August 15 Lyman Beecher, Benjamin Wisner, and the other ministers co-signed a letter with Union Church leaders opening their doors to Charles Finney. The next day the Old South pastor wrote personally, voicing his delight that all the ministers' objections had been "fully removed." He urged Finney to begin his Boston ministry at both Park Street and Union Church, "then decide in which place you will labor, which will no doubt be in Park Street" — the more commodious auditorium. Wisner invited Finney to stay in his home on Milk Street.

Charles Finney arrived in Boston at the end of August 1831. On September 5 the arrangements under which he would labor in the city were made official at "a meeting of all the ministers and ten brethren from the Orthodox Congregational

Churches." The association voted that "Mr. Finney should come, not as the stated supply of any particular congregation but as a general laborer among the evangelical churches in this city" and that his salary be raised "by subscription in the different congregations." Finney returned to Oneida County for his wife and children. A friend wrote Lydia, "I often, *very often*, think of you and your many *trials* and *privileges*." Fresh invitations arrived from Philadelphia almost every week, but Finney committed himself to what Benjamin Wisner in a letter had called "a steady and a good long pull" in Boston. Anson Phelps wrote Finney on behalf of his old Union Church congregation in New York City with the prayer "that the Lord may give you strength in body and mind equal to your day."

Charles G. Finney based his ministry in Boston from September 1831 through April 1832, rotating his Sunday preaching among the orthodox churches and holding forth regularly at Park Street evenings during the week. Numerous requests to attend three- and four-day protracted meetings throughout the area also poured in, though it is unclear how many of these he honored. An invitation from Keene, New Hampshire, for example, stated, "Some of our merchants have heard you in Boston, and they would be much gratified if you could come." When he preached at Andover during the Seminary's fall convocation, his sermons diverted attention so powerfully that the main program had to be adjusted. Finney was not pleased with the progress of the revival in Boston, however. In his *Memoirs* — using the bell curve established in Oneida County, New York City, and Rochester — he gave Boston believers low marks for their "spirit of prayer" and "strength of faith." He confessed disappointment that when he "began to preach some searching sermons" he "found that these sermons were not at all palatable to the Christians of Boston." Instead of increasing in the early weeks, attendance at Park Street Church became "less and less." Finney was shocked. "This was *new to me*." He never imagined that the fault was somehow his, explaining that "it was evident that they somewhat resented my plain deal-

121

ing." The problem obviously centered in Lyman Beecher, who was guilty of "letting down the standard of orthodox piety and preaching" in the interests of "getting the people into the churches."

Finney was especially annoyed when Beecher would attempt to soften the impact of his call to radical submission to Christ. There was at least one incident at an inquiry meeting in the basement of Bowdoin Street Church when Finney called for penitents to renounce their worldly wealth and Beecher quickly assured the people that when they did so God would "give it right back" to them. Still, Finney conceded that Beecher never overtly obstructed or objected to Finney's work. In fact, he gave it his enthusiastic support, making numerous public statements of full agreement with Finney's theology and his evangelical methods. Gradually, the crowds grew larger, and Finney felt that the Bostonians not only became accustomed to his "searching preaching" but "came to highly appreciate it." Finney's ambivalent evaluation of the situation was mirrored in a letter from Benjamin Wisner to a friend in Utica. "Mr. Finney is here, preaching almost every night of the week, to immense congregations and to great acceptance. Great results are not yet seen, but . . . we expect them."

Lyman Beecher convinced himself prior to Finney's arrival that the evangelist had mellowed enough to find acceptance in Boston society. Finney had bristled at the thought, warning Union Church leaders not to "encourage this idea." Finney wrote "that in this he is mistaken, that my views in regard to doctrine and revivals of religion are not that I know of materially changed." Perhaps Finney himself knew better, however, as the word "materially" might suggest. He went on to say, "I hope that like other men I make some advances in knowledge and gain advantage from experience, but to encourage the idea that my views of doctrine or of measures (under similar circumstances) are changed was to do wrong." Circumstances do vary, Finney acknowledged, and he had indeed made some changes in his practice, though whether they were "advances" or not was a matter of opinion. For one thing, the evangelist had begun to preach from notes. It is not clear exactly when he began to do so — perhaps in New York City, perhaps in Rochester. Gone were the days of total reliance on the Holy Spirit, waiting until he stepped into the pulpit even to think of a text. Now he prepared "skeletons," sermon outlines with numbered topical heads and major points written on small cards, usually front and back. Even so, he still considered his preaching "extemporaneous," in that he never preached from a manuscript, and the outline was indeed brief.

The aged and ailing Daniel Nash in Oneida County was worried. Referring to him as "dear Charles," Father Nash reminded Finney of the old revivals when "I wanted to hear you preach, to keep me alive" and how "I [would] pray for you and thus keep you alive." Each was to the other "a friend, to whom we could say everything." Now in November 1831 he wrote, "I should advise you to be careful about using skeletons in preaching. Whatever may be the effect on you, I am persuaded they would injure my spirituality. . . . If you choose to write them, for the sake of digesting a subject, write. If you wish to look at them at home, to refresh your memory, do it. But, when you preach, throw yourself entirely on God." A few weeks later, friends wrote with the news of Nash's death: "Beloved Father Nash prayed himself away to the throne." Finney continued to write out skeletons and used them in the pulpit for the rest of his life. In Albany, Finney's colleague Edward N. Kirk saw the benefit of such outlines. Suffering from revival burnout, he complained that he had no time to read or prepare sermons anymore. "I have pulled on the old chord until I am expecting every day to hear it snap. . . . Send me some skeletons!" Charles Finney may have felt something like Kirk as the Boston work dragged on.

Finney shifted his headquarters to Essex Street Church, the pastor of which, Samuel Green, was in Europe on sick leave during the winter. In the *Memoirs* he praised God for the "blessed work of grace" in that congregation and reported that "the work was more or less extensive" as "a large number of persons were converted in different parts of the city." The accuracy of this assessment was in dispute even at the time. Pro-revival newspapers in New England lauded the effectiveness of Finney's work and listed respectable church membership increases. Asa Rand, a Congregational minister working as editor of the Hopkinsian monthly *The Volunteer* at the time, offered a different account. According to him, Finney wore out his welcome at just about every church in town and in the end was left with only Lyman Beecher as a supporter. The truth may lie somewhere in between. Finney complimented the Boston ministers as "true men" who "had taken hold of the work as well as they knew how." But there is no sparkle in his Boston narrative in the *Memoirs,* except when he mentions the birth of his third child, Frederic Norton. In telling the Boston story, he could not think of a single exemplary conversion with which to illustrate the work. An Oneida County friend wrote Lydia, "We have heard that the churches where Mr. Finney preaches are crowded, but it cannot be said there is a revival." After Rochester, where "the waters of salvation had risen so high," the Boston effort must have been for Finney a tremendous letdown. When it was time to leave, he wrote, "I had become fatigued."

Asa Rand, a moderate supporter of revivals and a conservative Calvinist along the lines of Edwardsian-tradition New England theology, took it upon himself to attack Finney's work in Boston. In the pages of *The Volunteer* he criticized "New Measures" revivalism for its methodology. Finney was quite accustomed to that and had successfully dealt with such opposition at New Lebanon and elsewhere. Rand also systematically ripped into Finney's theology. Throughout his career, Charles Finney had been accepted as a garden variety New School Presbyterian when it came to doctrine. In upstate New York, despite controversy over the propriety of his methods, Finney always worked among friends who more or less shared his slant on the evangelical Protestant version of the gospel:

each individual's utter sinfulness, free moral agency, the urgent need for penitents to embrace Jesus Christ and make God their highest good, and the active life of disinterested benevolence. Even in Philadelphia in 1828, Old School Presbyterians had remained silent and let Finney do his work, tolerating him as yet another New School preacher with a New England Hopkinsian accent. In New York City a second and then a third presbytery had been formed so that New School and then even Free Presbyterian pastors could avoid doctrinal hassles with Old School clergy, affiliating by "elective affinity."

Theological controversy had recently heated up, however, among both Congregationalists and Presbyterians. In Philadelphia, the Rev. Albert Barnes, a pro-revival New School pastor with a view of sin and salvation akin to that of Nathaniel William Taylor at Yale, was called in 1830 to the pulpit of First Presbyterian Church. Having failed to block his call, Ashbel Green and his Old School colleagues charged Barnes with heresy before the presbytery in 1831, and he was found guilty. Barnes successfully appealed to the General Assembly, but, while the national body found him innocent of heresy, they agreed that some of his doctrines were "objectionable." Meanwhile, in New England, conservative Edwardsians attacked Nathaniel William Taylor for abandoning Calvinist orthodoxy after he delivered and published his bombshell *Concio ad Clerum* in 1828. Bennet Tyler, with Asahel Nettleton and Asa Rand as major allies, engaged Taylor in a vitriolic "paper war" and in 1833 founded the Theological Institute of Connecticut to counter Yale's errors. Charles G. Finney provided an important link, like an electrical connection, between the Presbyterian and Congregational conflicts. When Asa Rand published his critique of Finney's shortcomings (revealingly entitled *The New Divinity Tried*) and Finney's friends jumped to his defense, the young and powerful Princeton Seminary professor Charles Hodge published a review of the controversy that pushed Rand's criticism even farther to paint Finney as heterodox.

Asa Rand took notes in Boston when Finney preached his

signature sermon from Ezekiel 18:31, "Make you a new heart." Writing in *The Volunteer*, he prefaced his own "strictures" of the evangelist's theology with an "Abstract of the Sermon" from his own notes. While Rand's summary is remarkably fair, Finney's friends objected that he left out some key points and worded it to put Finney in the worst light with respect to his views on God's initiative in salvation. For example, Rand reported Finney's concluding sentence as flagrantly humanistic: "To change your own hearts will save you; nothing else can; and on that point is suspended your eternal destiny." He thus unfairly implied that in Finney's gospel the death and resurrection of Jesus Christ and the gift of the Holy Spirit were irrelevant to the plan of salvation. As much as Finney demanded the anxious sinner's response to God's offer of grace, he never reduced it all to human effort. Benjamin Wisner borrowed Finney's "skeleton," the brief outline from which he preached, and wrote up a set of corrections which he demanded that Rand publish. Rand appended Wisner's notes to his articles when he published them as a pamphlet, *The New Divinity Tried*, but he conveyed the false impression that Finney now approved Rand's version of the sermon. Charles Finney began to consider preparing his own published edition of this and other sermons, and he finally did so in 1834 with *Sermons on Various Subjects*.

Asa Rand expressed agreement in gentlemanly fashion with many of Finney's beliefs but identified "the grand defect of this sermon" as its "very inadequate notion of the moral depravity of revolted man." He criticized Finney for confusing the "freedom and power of man . . . *as God made him*" with "man in a state of revolt and moral ruin . . . under bondage to sin and satan." Rand was working within the same paradoxical anthropology as Finney, but he balanced the scale in a more traditional Calvinist manner. Rand argued that "the depravity of man reduces him to a bondage or inability exclusively *moral*. He *can* turn to God, but *will* not; and that perverse *will*, controlled by a *wicked heart* or *vile affections*, is so strong, that he is lost forever if the special grace of God do not interpose." Although Finney upheld the doctrine of total depravity in every sermon he ever preached, Rand argued that because he refused to define original sin as "transmitted pollution," in effect he "totally discards" that key Calvinist tenet. Rand dismissed Finney's famous illustration of the man saved from Niagara Falls as a rhetorical cheap trick. It gave the impression "that the agency of the Spirit in conversion is a small matter." Finney did preach that the Holy Spirit always works through natural means. Rand countered that "if the Spirit *only* warns, alarms, and persuades, the awakened sinner is gone forever." Perhaps most tellingly, Rand went on to argue that by making conversion "simply an act of his own will," Finney degraded religion by giving it "the character of self-interest."

Benjamin Wisner answered this blast against Finney in another pamphlet, *Review of 'The New Divinity Tried'; or, An Examination of Rev. Mr. Rand's Stricture on a Sermon Delivered by the Rev. C. G. Finney, on Making a New Heart*, also published in Boston in 1832. He condemned the "vile tactic" of secretly taking sermon notes and then publishing them with negative commentary without the preacher's knowledge. He resented the fact that "other Orthodox Congregational ministers in the city are implicated in the charge" of holding Finney's allegedly "unscriptural and dangerous views." And he demonstrated the manner in which Rand's biased version of the sermon misconstrued some of Finney's points. Specifically, he supported Finney's orthodoxy on the grounds that, notwithstanding his view of human ability, not one sinner has ever chosen Christ, "or ever will do it, without the special and efficacious influence of the Holy Ghost." Wisner here regretted that Finney had not *"stated formally and distinctly"* what he "fully believes" and "what was plainly implied in this sermon." He did personally object to Finney's reduction of the work of the Holy Spirit to natural causes and "moral suasion," but he maintained that Finney did not forfeit his orthodoxy on this account. Joshua Leavitt in New York City wrote Finney in February 1832 on this very point, warning him to abandon the phrase "moral suasion" because of its "Arminian" tone. "You do not intend by it what heretics intend by moral suasion to the exclusion of the Holy Ghost." Wisner went on to defend Finney's "voluntarism" point by point against Rand's "strictures." He characterized Finney's view of original sin, his definition of "heart" as "the controlling or habitual preference or choice of the soul," his merging of affections and will, his linking of moral character with voluntary exercises, and·so on as valid developments in Reformed theology. Wisner introduced Charles Finney to the world as the heir of Augustine, Calvin, Edwards, Hopkins, "and the great majority of Orthodox divines in New England from Edwards to the present time."

Conservatives were far from convinced, and Rand and Wisner published two more pamphlets in their war over Finney. When the arch-orthodox Presbyterian Charles Hodge read the pamphlets, he seized the opportunity to launch a salvo of his own against Finney and the entire New School movement. Thanks to Finney, New School Presbyterianism could be exposed as corrupted with Taylor's New Haven Pelagianism. These shots were fired in rapid succession. In the April 1832 issue of his journal, *The Biblical Repertory and Theological Review*, Hodge argued that Finney both denigrated the operation of the Holy Spirit in conversion and ignored the work of Christ in salvation. Those who focus on the human decision to obey God as "the moral Governor of the universe," Hodge argued, make conversion "an act which has no reference to Christ." He went on to charge that in Finney's preaching "Christ and his cross are practically made of none effect." However it may stir people up, such a gospel "is fatal to religion and the souls of men." As the Presbyterians marched inexorably toward schism, the Old School began to fix its sights on Charles Finney as the heart of the New School problem.

With Albert Barnes still smarting from his heresy trials in Philadelphia and Boston having proven such a disappointment, where was Finney to go? Evangelical leaders in Philadelphia urged him to come and form a new "revival church" in their city, but that was now the last place he could imagine laboring. Invitations were coming in from the Midwest, from Louisville and from Cincinnati, where Lane Seminary was trying to lure Lyman Beecher as president. Friends in Ohio advanced the notion that America's future was not in Boston or Philadelphia but in "the Great Valley," and Finney began to think so too. Old upstate New York colleague Horatio Foote replied to a letter from Finney, "I am fully of your opinion . . . that either or both of us could do much more at the west." Foote envisioned "starting a *new order of things* there." He pressed Finney: "You speak of the Western Valley. What do you propose? What are your plans for future operations? One thing we want in this country and must have it somewhere — *a school* of the right stamp to bring forward young ministers who will be revival men and unshackled." Herman Norton's wife Amelia wrote Lydia in March 1832, "I long to see you, and cannot be reconciled to your going to Ohio — unless we go too."

In New York City, meanwhile, the Tappan brothers and other magnates were putting together a very appealing package for the evangelist. Lewis Tappan wrote, "Measures adopted here thrill the nation." He proposed setting Finney up in a converted theater on Chatham Street. He sent Finney maps, diagrams, good news on the financing, and elaborate details on the renovation. He even discussed what to call the building and the new church. He added enticingly, "there is a dwelling house, contiguous to the theater, *for the minister*." Lydia's sister had just recently written her, "O my dear Sister, I have often wished that you had a quiet little fireside of your own where you could sit down with your little ones." Finney went to New York City in March to view the Chatham Street property and to continue negotiations.

"The Valley is important," Tappan acknowledged, but "very soon Railroads will bring all the business men to this city twice a year." New York City was "the heart . . . the fountain" of the nation, "and if a good pulsation goes on there all the members will feel it and be made healthy." How could anything in Ohio compare with the "moral influence" that can be "exerted . . . in that thoroughfare where 30,000 walk daily?"

6 Not a Miracle

At some point in their careers, many popular or influential evangelical leaders in American history have sought to erect monuments more permanent than the legacy of their sermons — a megachurch, a college, a shelf of books, a new denomination or national institution. Charles Grandison Finney had little patience with institutions and no interest in denominational structures. People called themselves "Finneyites," but that was simply a description of their religious ethos; they belonged to no Finney-run organization. In a few years, Charles Finney would begin publishing transcriptions of his sermons and lectures in periodicals and in book form, and he would become identified with a college as well, first as its most notable professor and then as president. But the Tappan brothers and a few other New York City businessmen dreamed of creating a large revival-oriented church in the heart of the commercial capital of the United States. At the age of forty, Finney turned his attention to this project. When he returned to New York in 1832, his ministry centered in the Chatham Street Chapel (housed in the renovated Chatham Garden Theater); later he moved to a yet more eminent setting when his wealthy philanthropist friends built Broadway Tabernacle to the evangelist's own specifications.

George Washington Finney worried about the deleterious effects of stardom on his older brother. George himself had become a Presbyterian preacher who scratched out a living itinerating through upstate New York, on and off, for the Temperance Society or the American Sunday School Union or as a subscription agent for religious periodicals. Although his name was easily as grand as Charles's, George never made history. Still, he knew something about the Christian life. As Charles was hobnobbing with brahmins in Boston and being wooed by moguls in New York late in 1831, George wrote, "I know the platform on which you stand is verry far above my station ... but Charles, your unwerthy brother enjoys the same religion, loves the same God and I trust prays in the same Holy Ghost. ... If ever I did anything in my life from a sense of Duty it is writing this letter and must tell you that I tremble for you on account of your unbounded popularity. Yes, my brother, when I look at your elivation in society I allmost shudder." George had not learned to spell as consistently as his older brother, but he was able to press home his point with the same vigor. "I ... ask myself these questions — why is it that his enemies are becoming his friends and the opposition of the church and the world is dying away — is it because every body is becoming better — is it because the world are less inclined to hate and persecute a man that aims at a high tone of piety?" George pleaded with his brother that wherever he went, "May God keep you humble."

Some said the idea of fixing up a theater, and especially one like Chatham Garden, which had seen better days and was, as Finney put it, "in the heart of the most irreligious population of New York," was about as humble as you could get. The theater was near Five Points in lower Manhattan, where Chatham Street was intersected by three other streets between

Broadway and Bowery Lane. Finney painted the district in his *Memoirs* as "a place of resort highly discreditable to the city," and his description matches an 1827 cartoon-like lithograph showing Five Points filled with all manner of debauchery — liquor dealers on every corner; harlots looking down from second-story windows and soliciting on corners; several fistfights and a large mob; streets alive with hucksters, vendors, laborers, men and women falling down drunk. The illustration was a caricature, but a caricature of the truth. Chatham Street at Five Points in 1832 was the most densely occupied and ethnically mixed neighborhood in the city, and most of its buildings were owned by absentee landlords. Operators of the once-fashionable theater allowed prostitutes to work the galleries during performances and even brought in a circus to keep the business afloat. Evangelicals in the early 1830s who were committed to cleaning up the sleaziest sections of the city and making New York respectable once more saw Five Points as a prime target for reform. To bring in Finney and transform the theater into a church fit their moral reform agenda to a tee.

The principal owner of Chatham Garden Theater, ironically, was a minister who, along with some others, had inherited the property. He could not wait to see it used for a better purpose. The lease was held by William Blanchard, whom Lewis Tappan called "the great Circus man." When Tappan and his colleagues proposed to Blanchard their idea of using the building as a church, he was reported to have sputtered, "A w-h-a-t!" Tappan then preached to the hardened Blanchard businessman to businessman "until he wept and said he would aid us in converting the place into a church. He seemed to be under conviction of the Holy Spirit." Arrangements for the renovation and occupation of the building and for sharing the space with the Music Society fell into place in a way that confirmed Tappan's belief in providence.

With these arrangements complete in March 1832, Tappan then had to convince the evangelist to come and join the work. Finney did not warm easily to the idea of Chatham Street.

A caricature of Five Points, the tough New York neighborhood in which Charles Finney's Chatham Street Chapel was located. Finney's descriptions of the vice-ridden area, to which he was called in 1832, matches this 1827 lithograph from *Valentine's Manual* (1855). Reproduction from the collection of The New-York Historical Society

"Is not the location too filthy, etc. for decent people to go there?" he asked Tappan. His patron put the best light on it he could: "No. It is more decent than I had apprehended, and can be made quite so." He explained the plan to "raise and cover the pit with seats," so that, with the tiers of balconies, "2500 people can probably be seated." Finney persisted, "Can the place be made decent inside and out for the worship of God?" "Yes," Tappan replied, and "the *sensation* that will be produced by converting the place" would in itself draw a crowd. Tappan was not above being theatrical himself. "Curiosity will be excited." Moreover, he argued, Finney would be "rescuing from Satan one of his haunts. . . . A place admirably located for the destruction of souls [is] equally well located for conceiving them." Finally, he taunted Finney, "Have you lost your courage? Have you become 'prudent'?" Meanwhile, a new congregation with forty-one founding members had spun off from Joel Parker's Free Presbyterian Church and was meeting temporarily in the Masonic Hall. This Second Free Church was eager to welcome Finney as its pastor. The evangelist was not sure about becoming a settled pastor. A consummate negotiator, Lewis Tappan suggested that Finney not think of it as a permanent call. "You would be willing to remain while good was done and ought to go when you could do more good elsewhere." In the end, Finney wrote, "I concluded that I would accept the call from the Second Free Church, and labor for a time at least, in New York."

Upstate friends were unsure of Finney's wisdom. George Gale wrote to point out that in Boston his ministry "failed to produce to the same extent those soul-saving results as formerly" and warned that his new penchant for sermons on "abstract theological subjects" was to blame. "Oh! do not lose sight of dying sinners' souls." Another had heard that Finney's preaching had changed — "Not so much point. Not so much unction. More regard to niceness of diction." And yet another: "The people of Rochester are groaning that Brother Finney should become a settled minister." This one observed that "many evangelists have been shorn of their strength in cities." Alluding to the Samson story and perhaps also in wry comment on the fact that Finney was starting to bald in front, he wrote, "I warn him not to *lose his hair*." Friends cried out, "Do gird on the armour of 1824-7!" and lamented, "Oh *Revivals, Revivals, Revival Days*. Dear Brother! In those I was happy!" Charles Finney certainly remembered where he had come from, but his eyes were on the future.

Chatham Street Chapel opened its doors with Charles Finney in the pulpit on Sunday, May 6, 1832. The term "Chapel" was arrived at after negotiations with the Music Society, which rejected Finney's preference of "Tabernacle." He preached at the morning and evening services, and the two Free Churches gathered there for the Sacrament of the Lord's Supper in the afternoon. The house was packed, with more than two thousand people at every service. The Tappan brothers had arranged for the "anniversaries" — joint annual meetings — of the major Protestant mission and reform societies to convene at the new church the very next week. Representatives of the American Board of Commissioners for Foreign Missions, the American Home Missionary Society, the American Sunday School Union, the American Tract Society, the American Bible Society, the American Education Society, the American Temperance Society, and the American Colonization Society, among others, all showed up. Finney was not only host pastor of this major event but was featured as the keynote preacher. He rose to the occasion by delivering an enthusiastic endorsement of the Edwardsian doctrine of benevolence, on which they all agreed. The sort of social reform being promoted by the mission boards and charitable agencies he was addressing was the means by which evangelical Christians would soon usher in the kingdom of God. In June, Second Free Church officially called Finney as pastor, offering an annual salary of $1,500 and adding the proviso that he would continue to evangelize elsewhere as well. Chatham Street Chapel, in the notorious Five Points neighborhood, became the focal point of evangelical benevolence and evangelistic preaching in New York City.

At the end of June, Lewis Tappan and other supporters came up with a bonus of $700 to enable Charles Finney to rent a house on Grand Street near the church. Tappan advised his minister to furnish the home with "simplicity, only necessities," and not to "be afraid of meanness." Confessing (or feigning) embarrassment at the lavishness with which his wife had decked out his own home, and perhaps thinking of the ornate manse of the prominent Old School Presbyterian pastor Dr. Gardiner Spring, whose church was not far from Chatham Street, Tappan urged, "*Our* minister should set an example." Lydia Finney wrote home that for the first time "we are at housekeeping." Beaming like a newlywed after eight years of marriage, she wrote, "Had you been here my dear Mother a few of the first nights you would have smiled to see us. We slept on the floor without a blanket or bed quilt to cover us, but as the weather was warm we got along very well."

Coincidentally, Lydia's father, Nathaniel Andrews, sold the Whitesboro farm at just the time she and Charles were moving in. They were getting older, and "the more we cultivate it the more stony it grows and not so productive as formerly." In addition to her own possessions kept in the house, Lydia thought of a table that had belonged to her deceased sister which she would like to have "if there is no objection." Charles wrote, "I hope to be able to come up next month and get her things so that we can be comfortable in keeping house. . . . Whatever she has that can be safely boxed up and transported should not be sold." Charles and Lydia invited both their parents to come stay with them in New York over the winter. This was an extremely painful moment for the family. Charles wrote, "Lydia hesitates about coming up there, as she cannot go *home* as usual." Lydia herself wrote, "Although I am glad you have sold it, still when I reflect that that retired spot where I have spent so many of my days, days of childhood and peace, where I have received and enjoyed so much parental, brotherly, and sisterly affection, when I reflect that I can no longer call it *home*, my tears flow, and I cannot refrain from weeping bitterly." While Charles Finney made a half-hearted effort at comfort ("It is a great thing [for] persons of your age to be without a *home*"), he felt almost as strongly about the farm as Lydia, for it had been his annual summer retreat. The fact that Charles and Lydia underlined the word *home* each time they wrote it suggests a deep longing in the itinerant couple. Their new house in New York City would never be *home*.

During the summer, disaster struck with the arrival of a cholera epidemic in the city, and, as Finney wrote in the *Memoirs*, "it was especially fatal" in the densely populated area around Five Points. "The panic was great," with hearses constantly at neighbors' doors. Lydia wrote to her parents on July 15, "It is daily increasing, and deaths are fearfully multiplying. . . . The report from the board of health states 84 deaths and 133 near cases during the last 24 hours." Charles added in the margin, "People dying all around us. O that we may be also ready." Lydia reported: "As we were going to church in the morning, we saw a corpse just put into a coffin only a few doors from us. A little farther on we met a hearse followed by one carriage with only two or three individuals in it. Before we arrived at the Chapel, met a two-horse close carriage filled with coffins. The City is in great consternation, and multitudes are fleeing in every direction." Twice they packed up for Oneida County, then "concluded to remain for the present from a sense of duty." There was ministry for both Charles and Lydia to undertake, visiting, praying, offering comfort, presenting the way to salvation. "We may do good to a greater extent now than at any other time." Attendance at the Chapel naturally declined, and Finney felt acute fatigue set in, so in August the Finney family left the city and spent the rest of the summer with family and friends in Oneida County.

Charles and Lydia Finney returned to the city at the end of September in time for his service of installation as pastor of Second Free Church. During the service he fell ill, and it was soon apparent that he "was seized with the cholera." Finney lay sick in bed for weeks. He survived the illness but was debilitated not only by its effects but, he wrote, from "the means that were used for my recovery." By the end of October he was reported much improved and receiving visitors, but he was unable to resume his ministry on even a part-time basis until the spring of 1833. Supply preachers had to be called in to keep Chatham Street Chapel going from week to week. When Finney did return to the pulpit, he launched a series of meetings in cooperation with several colleagues, alternating the preaching responsibility. "Very little was accomplished," he recalled, and he concluded that that "was not the way to promote a revival there." Deciding that if the Chapel was going to experience a revival, he himself would have to be unequivocally at the center of it, Finney advertised that he would preach every evening for three weeks. The results were staggering, with upwards of 500 converts, many of whom joined the congregation.

Finney then directed his attention to training his members as lay evangelists. Once "instructed in regard to labors for the conversion of sinners," they became, he wrote, "a praying, working people . . . thoroughly united." Chapel members, both men and women, went "into the highways and hedges" and invited people to prayer meetings. They distributed printed announcements of meetings on "little slips of paper" along with "an oral invitation" to those they met, going "from house to house" and focusing on the rough Five Points neighborhood. "Our ladies were not afraid to go and gather in all classes from the neighborhood round about into our meetings," Finney boasted. He rejoiced that in the former saloon rooms at the rear of the galleries — which previously "it was said . . . had been used for very vile purposes" — lay men and women taught Sunday school classes and prayed with penitents after his sermons. For the first time in his career, Charles Finney relished the thought of reaching people other than the rich and powerful. At Chatham Street, members "were gathered from among the middle and lower classes of New York citizens. This was what we aimed to accomplish, to preach the Gospel especially to the poor." In 1832 and 1833, Charles Finney and Joel Parker were so successful at this that two additional Free Churches were established by the Third Presbytery of New York City.

Chatham Street Chapel also became a leader in church music with the arrival of Thomas Hastings as music director. In August 1832, Lewis Tappan had written Finney, vacationing upstate, that congregational singing and choral music needed to be "awakened" in New York's churches. A friend advised, "We must get Mr. Hastings here." Finney knew Thomas Hastings well, for he was a choir director in Utica and editor of the important pro-revival paper *The Western Recorder*. In addition to being a brilliant conductor, he was writing new hymns that were beginning to catch on, including the mission hymn "Hail to the Brightness of Zion's Glad Morning," the music for Toplady's "Rock of Ages," and one that was ideally suited for a Charles Finney revival —

> Come, ye disconsolate, where'er ye languish,
> Come to the mercy-seat, fervently kneel;
> Here bring your wounded hearts, here tell your
>   anguish;
> Earth has no sorrow that heaven cannot heal.

Finney went to the bookstore in Utica run by Thomas Hastings's brother before catching the canal boat for New York. Charles Hastings wrote on September 24, 1832, that Thomas had come to the store to see Finney just minutes after he left. "Your remark to me in conversation that you felt that it was a duty that Thomas owed the church to devote himself more exclusively to church music — this I have long felt and so has he, but how to let go of his present occupation and how to get himself located so as to afford him any reasonable prospect of usefulness has been his principal difficulty." Chatham Street Chapel gave Hastings that opportunity, and the city provided him with a national audience. The Finney-Hastings team proved an effective combination, both at Chatham Street and at Broadway Tabernacle a few years later.

Throughout the 1820s, Thomas Hastings's *Western Recorder* had been the most reliable source of news of "Finneyite" revivals and the most consistently available forum for pro-revival views. With Finney operating primarily in the large eastern cities, a periodical with a national circulation was needed. Frustrated at their inability to get sympathetic stories published in *The New York Observer*, the evangelical businessmen of New York created a new weekly paper in 1830, *The New York Evangelist*. Founding editor Noah C. Saxton, himself a former evangelist, was a friend and correspondent of Finney's. Joshua Leavitt, who assumed editorship in December 1831, became one of Finney's greatest promoters. All the favorable stories about the founding of Chatham Street Chapel and the revival and other public meetings that took place there were published in the *Evangelist*. In 1834 Leavitt helped devise the method by which Finney became an author, publishing his sermons and lectures in the *Evangelist* from Leavitt's own notes.

Following his recovery from cholera, Charles Finney preached the gospel of salvation to large crowds at Chatham Street Chapel from March through December 1833. During this period, the application of the gospel to the issue of the abolition of slavery increasingly commanded the attention of some leading church members. Finney wrote in his *Memoirs*, "When I first went to New York I had made up my mind on the subject of the slavery question, and was exceedingly anxious to arouse public attention to the subject." He had believed all along that slavery was a national sin, but by 1832 he had joined those who rejected the notion of colonization as the answer to the problem. Only the full emancipation of black slaves would do. The question was how soon. William Lloyd Garrison, who burst onto the national scene in 1830 as an abolitionist editor in Baltimore when he went to jail for libel, began publishing *The Liberator* in Boston in 1831. Garrison and his paper stood for immediate abolition of slavery. Arthur and Lewis Tappan were major financial supporters of Garrison and helped found the New York Anti-Slavery Society in 1833 and the American Anti-Slavery Society in May 1834. Even though they established *The Emancipator* as a less inflammatory paper, the name *Tappan* became synonymous in the popular mind with the cry for immediate freedom for blacks and, more threatening still, the "amalgamation" of the races.

For his part, Charles Finney refused to serve communion to slaveholders at the Chapel. He believed that this form of discipline exerted "a decidedly good influence" on those individuals and on the church as a whole. He preached against slavery in vivid terms: "Two millions of degraded heathen in our own land stretch forth their hands, all shackled and bleeding, and send forth to the church of God the agonizing cry for help." His revival call for rebirth from sin "here and now" provided a ready-made radical style and language for evangelical abolitionists, including his Utica convert Theodore D. Weld, who demanded immediate emancipation. Finney saw "that a considerable excitement came to exist among the people" at the Chapel when in his prayers and preaching he "often alluded to slavery and denounced it." But, as he stated succinctly in the *Memoirs*, "I did not . . . turn aside to make it a hobby, or divert the attention of the people from the work of converting souls." In fact, the idea of "amalgamation" made Finney squirm. He welcomed blacks to the Chapel but insisted that they sit in a special section. He told the Tappans he did not think "that it always is a wicked prejudice" if a person has a *"constitutional* taste" against associating too closely with blacks. In short, Charles Finney shared the conflicted emotions of most white Americans, evangelicals included, on the matter of racial justice in the 1830s.

A crisis loomed during the first few days of October 1833, when the organizational meeting of the New York Anti-Slavery Society was scheduled to take place in Clinton Hall. Some Colonization Society members, frustrated over their waning influence and angry at the rise of Garrisonian rhetoric, planned

to infiltrate the meeting posing as "Friends of Immediate Abolition" and then disrupt the proceedings. Two anti-abolitionist
New York City newspapers, the *Gazette* and the *Courier and
Enquirer*, meanwhile, called for a rally outside Clinton Hall to
protest "this most dangerous species of fanaticism." Posters
were put up throughout the city, printed in mock invitation
form as if it were to be a formal ball, requesting the presence
of "Southerners" and "all citizens who may feel disposed to
manifest the *true* feeling of the State on this subject." A mob of
fifteen hundred showed up at the Hall, demanding the blood
of Tappan and Garrison. The building was empty. Arthur and
Lewis Tappan, Joshua Leavitt, and the other organizers had
hastily changed the meeting site to Chatham Street Chapel. The
anti-abolition crowd reassembled at Tammany Hall, but when
word suddenly came that the Anti-Slavery Society meeting was
at the Chapel, the mob roared up the street and stormed Finney's church. They got there too late. The Society had held a
quick meeting to organize itself officially and elect Arthur Tappan president and then slipped out the back door as the mob
began beating on the gate. The men forced their way into the
empty building, carrying torches and dragging with them an
elderly black man they found on the street. They hung a sign
on him, "Arthur Tappan," and made him pretend to convene
the mob as the Anti-Slavery Society. They passed a number of
outrageous resolutions, including one for "immediate amalgamation."

Charles Finney was appalled at the entire debacle. As
much as he despised everything the anti-abolitionist mob stood
for, he also opposed the kind of activism by which the church
was so closely identified with a single reform issue that its
primary identity and mission became secondary. He saw nothing but more ideological strife on the horizon. By raising the
cause of abolition to such a pitch, Finney feared, his friends
had brought on a culture war that neither side could win.
Indeed, 1833 was only the beginning of a period of mob violence in America which peaked in the summer of 1835. The

intense anger of so many ordinary Americans, engendered by deep-seated racial phobia and high-stakes sectional politics, terrified many observers of the troubled society. Charles Finney's patrons were constantly in danger for their lives during this period, and Chatham Street Chapel, which one newspaper termed the "focus of pollution," was at extreme risk for arson.

Charles Finney reached a point of crisis in his own ministry late in the fall of 1833. Still suffering from lingering effects of his cholera and its treatment, he was not physically strong. It was two and a half years since his last unmitigated revival success in Rochester. He no sooner got started at Chatham Street than he had to take almost six months off for sickness. Then, just when membership was growing and evangelistic outreach among the residents of the Five Points area was becoming effective, the slavery issue consumed the passions of the city and threatened the church's very existence. For some time Finney had considered taking a long trip, something more than a summer vacation in Oneida County. He explored possible itineraries with several friends who might serve as travel companions — England, the Sandwich Islands, South America. His father, Sylvester Finney in Henderson, wrote on New Year's Day expressing his displeasure at the idea. "I had rather you would come into the country and get you a farm." Correspondence with his Philadelphia friend James Patterson in early January indicates that Argentina was Finney's first choice. But at the last minute he decided instead on a voyage to the Mediterranean to visit mission stations, with a destination of Smyrna in Asia Minor and after that Palestine. He would go all by himself. Lydia and the children would divide their time between the city and visits with family upstate. The Chapel called an associate pastor, the Rev. John Ingersoll, who would serve together with Jacob Helffenstein of First Free Church in Finney's absence. The evangelist would leave everything behind for six months, maybe more.

The New York Evangelist reported Finney's January 20, 1834, departure on board "the Brig Padang," explaining that "his health has been declining for several months." He had of late ventured out of doors only "in pleasant weather" and had "not preached for several weeks." Before he left, Finney gave one piece of advice to Joshua Leavitt at the *Evangelist*. He had "watched . . . with a good deal of attention and anxiety," Finney wrote in his *Memoirs*, as the paper gave an increasing amount of space in every issue to abolitionist news and editorials. Now he "admonished Brother Leavitt to be careful and not go too fast in the discussion of the Anti-slavery question, lest he should destroy his paper." With that he said farewell to his family and friends. Charles Finney set sail praying that when he returned his health would be restored and the church could once more go about its main business of winning souls.

Neither of these hopes was realized. The sea voyage was a miserable experience. It was winter, Finney recorded in his *Memoirs*, and "we had a very stormy passage." Cramped in a tiny stateroom, "I was on the whole very uncomfortable; and the voyage did not much improve my health." The small ship made it across the Atlantic and through the Straits of Gibraltar, but Finney reported getting only as far as the islands of Malta and Sicily, halfway across the Mediterranean Sea. Lewis Tappan wrote Lydia a kind letter on June 7, reporting information from shipping lists that the voyage had taken sixty-eight days. He noted, "We shall soon hear, probably, that Mr. Finney has arrived in Smyrna." But after several weeks on those islands off the boot of Italy, Finney decided he could go no further. He sailed to Messina and secured passage on the next ship returning to the United States.

While her husband was away, Lydia Finney carried on an active correspondence concerning family matters and, increasingly, in support of benevolent causes. A Sunday school superintendent from Rochester wrote asking advice on recruitment and funding. Reports arrived from New York City on the work of the Maternal Association and the Female Moral Reform Society. A New York City friend reported her excitement at attending "the Colored Convention," where she was one of only "a few white persons present." She expressed optimism that "the Abolition Cause . . . will soon triumph in the extinction of Slavery." She told Lydia, "We value your judgment." Lydia wrote another friend in the city urging more female leadership in social causes. The friend replied with delight, "I believe the day is coming, or has already come, when Young Ladies will shake off their sloth and repent. We have too long, already, depended on our Ministers and Elders, to take the lead of Benevolent enterprises and contented ourselves because we were females, supposing we were weak." Charles Finney's prospects for avoiding social issues and getting back to pure 1820s-style revivalism on his return were not good.

Chatham Street Chapel, meanwhile, continued to be a hotbed of abolitionist activity in Finney's absence. The mission and reform society annual meetings in May degenerated into a fight between the Colonization Society and the Anti-Slavery Society. The fourth of July had for some years been used by anti-slavery advocates of all persuasions as an occasion for promoting public awareness and fund-raising, but the 1834 observance fomented another riot. Arthur and Lewis Tappan planned the celebration at the Chapel to include a reading of Garrison's Declaration of Sentiments and an anthem by a racially mixed chorus. Newspapers decried the plan, and posters throughout the city urged "friends of the UNION and of the SOUTH" to crash the meeting and break it up. Protesters in the galleries hooted down speakers and threw hymnals and debris on the audience below.

On July 7, more violence erupted at the Chapel. The Music Society normally scheduled recitals on Monday evenings, but as none was planned the Chapel was rented to a black organization that wanted to hold a meeting on the meaning of American freedom. Several Music Society directors and some supporters, irate at the decision to allow the group in, arrived and ordered the blacks to disperse. When the blacks refused, a melee ensued in which canes, lamps, and chairs were employed as weapons and benches were heaved from the galleries. When the anti-abolitionist mob left the church, they went to the home of Lewis Tappan, where they jeered and shouted. Newspapers headlined the event as a "Negro Riot" fanned into flame by "Arthur Tappan and his troop of incendiaries." Lewis Tappan moved his family to the country the next day and returned to find his house ransacked and looted. A mob again broke into the Chapel on July 9, when another mixed-race meeting was rumored. On July 10 and 11, mobs attacked black churches and burned homes in black neighborhoods. Presbyterian pastor Samuel Cox received special attention for saying in a sermon that with his dark complexion Jesus would be denied free seating in an American church. An anti-abolition speaker, a New York merchant, cried out, "Would you believe it? He called *my Saviour* a n-----! God damn him!" Riots continued throughout August. Targets included the homes and churches of anti-slavery ministers, individual blacks on the street, black neighborhoods, and the Tappan brothers' warehouse and store, where clerks were issued rifles. Mayor Cornelius W. Lawrence struggled to restore order, but his sympathy was with the anti-abolitionists.

On board ship in early July, Finney's mind was in turmoil as he contemplated the dismal task of preaching in 1834 America. In his *Memoirs* he wrote, "On my homeward bound passage my mind became exceedingly exercised on the question of revivals. I feared that they would decline throughout the country." He despaired that his health "had nearly or quite broken down." He admitted that he had lost confidence in other pastors who might carry on as evangelists. The situation "distressed my mind," he wrote, and made sleep impossible. Finally, "my soul was in utter agony . . . such agony as to wring my hands, and almost to gnaw my tongue, as it were with pain. . . . In fact I felt *crushed* with the burden that was on my soul." There was no one on board with whom he could talk. Charles Finney turned to God in prayer, and he received an answer that day. "It was the Spirit of prayer that was upon me; that which I had often before experienced in *kind,* but perhaps never before to such a degree for so long a time." The message from God was one of comfort and assurance. "After a day of unspeakable wrestling and agony in my soul, just at night the subject cleared up to my mind. The Spirit led me to believe that all would come out right, and that God had yet a work for *me* to do." God would give Finney strength to do his work. "But I had not the least idea," he confessed, "of what the course of providence would be."

Charles Finney arrived back in New York two weeks after the July 4 riots, took one look around, and went on to Oneida County, where he reunited with his family. He did not return to the city until early November, making for a total absence from Chatham Street Chapel of about ten months. Charles and Lydia spent August through October on a farm in the Oneida County village of Western. It was no doubt a wonderfully pleasant time for the family, but the question of the Finneys' future remained unanswered. In the *Memoirs* there is no hint that his spiritual crisis on board ship was anything but resolved. He wrote, "The work of God immediately revived on my return." This statement obscured the real turmoil that continued to cloud his mind. The length of time he languished upstate suggests that a condition described in the nineteenth century as a spirit of melancholy may have descended upon him. After he finally returned to New York, he expressed a desire in a November 10 letter to Lydia, who remained at the farm, "to rest from preaching" for perhaps two more years and take up farming. He confessed to swinging between feeling strong and wanting to stay at Chatham Street and then "get[ting] fatigued" and thinking "I will not preach again but will leave immediately." Finally, he confided the reason behind his chronic indecision: it was not so much poor health as his ambivalence as a revivalist on the issue of emancipation. "Some think the church would scatter in every direction as soon as it has known that I was going on account of the abolition movements."

In November Charles Finney discovered how much rebuilding would be necessary if he was to work in New York.

The church had suffered under the ministry of John Ingersoll. Whenever Finney was away, the pews remained empty. When he was on vacation in July 1833, Lewis Tappan wrote, "attendance . . . falls off, particularly in the evening, but this can't be helped while you are absent." William Green, a lay leader of the Chapel, gave Finney a state-of-the-church report in September 1834, informing him that his extended leave was devastating and urging him to return. He focused on John Ingersoll's failings as an abrasive, ineffective, long-winded preacher. An abolitionist colleague of the Tappans, Green disagreed with Finney's assessment of the church's role in the recent riots. "I believe the Lord means to bless the Free Churches . . . *because* of the stand they have taken in defence of the rights of man, and for raising their voice against the oppressor." Others, however, insisted that "his sermons upon Anti-Slavery and moral reform . . . created dislike." Everyone was glad when Ingersoll accepted a call to the Free Church in New Haven. According to a member who recounted the tale many years later, when Finney surveyed "the remnant of a congregation" that was left, he gave Ingersoll "a withering look" and demanded, "Where is the church I left in your charge?" Ingersoll reportedly buried his face in his hands and wept. If Finney actually said this (the member vividly recalled that "the scene was fearful"), it certainly demonstrated nerve for someone who had avoided conflict by absenting himself for an entire year. Perhaps his resolve was growing strong once more.

The sad state of the church was matched by a precipitous decline in the circulation of *The New York Evangelist*. According to the *Memoirs*, Joshua Leavitt also came in November with his head in his hands, blurting out, "Brother Finney, I have ruined the Evangelist. I have not been as prudent as you cautioned me to be. . . . and we shall not be able to continue its publication beyond the first of January, unless *you* can do something to bring the paper back to public favor again." Leavitt proposed that Finney "write a series of articles on revivals," in hopes that their weekly appearance would attract subscribers and "restore

the paper immediately to public favor." Finney had never written much apart from his correspondence, and even that was
spotty at best; friends often complained, "Why do we not hear
from you?" He did not fancy the thought of trying to be an
author. "After considering it a day or two," Finney made a
slightly different suggestion. According to the *Memoirs*, the
editor "caught at this at once. Says he, 'That is the very thing!'"
As Finney wrote Lydia upstate on November 24, "You will
probably after this hear me preach once a week through the
Evangelist as I have consented to preach a course of lectures on
revivals and let Brother Leavitt take notes and publish them in
order to help the *Evangelist* as the abolitionism has greatly
infused it and unless something of the kind can sustain it he
says it must go down." He added pointedly when Lydia returned to New York, "I don't believe that it would do to say
much about abolition here in public."

Finney embarked on a similar publishing project during
the second week of November, using two stenographers. In his
letter to Lydia on the tenth he reported that "Emily Seely is
about commencing to write some sermons for me." At that
time, still seriously torn between trying to preach in New York
and returning to the farm, Finney wondered what Lydia would
think of his bringing Emily north with him. "I could dictate to
her an hour in the morning and have [my] mind off the subject
the rest of the day." On November 24 he informed Lydia, "I
have about made up my mind should my health continue as it
is to spend the winter here." Attendance at the Chapel was up
— "preached last night . . . house was crowded aisles and all."
He promised to meet her in Schenectady the following Tuesday
and finish the canal boat trip with her to New York. Work was
progressing on the sermon manuscripts, which were going to
be brought out monthly in pamphlet form by the publisher
John S. Taylor. William Green now alternated daily with Emily
Seely as amanuensis, and the notes were transcribed to produce
a manuscript suitable for the printer. Finney described his
method as being much easier than working at a desk. "I walk

about and dictate . . . which is a great relief to me." It would be intolerable "sitting and day after day keeping my mind heated with writing." He confessed that he had "not found a place for us to board yet" but promised to attend to it immediately. He tenderly added, "I am sorry you are so lonesome. I should nearly die were it not that my time is so completely taken up." As if it would make her feel better, he noted that "if you were here I cannot be in my study so much." Finney suddenly sounded like a classical pastor.

Publication of his sermons and lectures, together with gratifying crowds at the services, proved to be a tonic that restored Charles Finney's energy. He was ready once more to make himself public. He had had a portrait of himself painted earlier in the year, and now, he wrote Lydia, "I am sitting for my portrait again. . . . I wish you were here to have yours taken." No portrait of Lydia exists. The two 1834 portraits, the first by Frederick R. Spencer and the second by the famous New York studio of Samuel Lovett Waldo and William Jewett, are remarkably similar. The Waldo-Jewett portrait, commissioned by William Green, shows Finney with more of a smile and a sparkle in his eye. They both reveal him as a handsome gentleman and suggest the inner strength that enabled him to survive both the cholera epidemic and his personal ordeal. Sitting for the portraits was Finney's way of stating not only that he had achieved professional stature but that he would continue to make his mark in church and society in the future.

In December 1834, Taylor published the first sermon pamphlet and soon followed with the entire collection in book form, *Sermons on Various Subjects*. Another edition appeared in 1835 from another publisher, and in 1836 Taylor published an enlarged edition, containing twelve sermons, under the title *Sermons on Important Subjects*. It was also in December 1834 that Finney began the series of twenty-two Friday lectures on revivals that were to be compiled from Joshua Leavitt's notes for publication; they appeared weekly in the *Evangelist* from December 6, 1834, through May 2, 1835. As attendance at the

In his early forties, Charles Grandison Finney still displayed the raw intensity and natural charm that had contributed to his evangelistic success in upstate New York the decade before, softened now with a refinement befitting his station as pastor of a large New York City congregation. The books in Finney's hands and lap are conventional in clergy portraits but also suggest his emerging popularity as an author and perhaps his quest for intellectual respectability. This oil portrait by the studio of Samuel Lovett Waldo and William Jewett is one of two for which Finney sat in 1834. The portrait is in the collection of the Allen Memorial Art Museum, Oberlin College. Photo courtesy of the Oberlin College Archives

Chapel climbed, new subscriptions also came in daily to Leavitt at the *Evangelist* office. Finney's account of this entire period in New York in the *Memoirs* can be confusing, because the events are not treated in chronological order. But it was in reference to these new successes during the winter of 1834-1835 that he wrote, "I continued to labor thus in Chatham street, and the church continued to flourish and to extend its influence and its labors in every direction."

The published *Sermons* included newly prepared versions of some of his best-known, most frequently repeated, and most controversial sermons. The volume was the equivalent of a greatest hits album of the early C. G. Finney, complete with an iconographic engraved likeness of the evangelist over his signature as the frontispiece. Beginning with his trademark "Sinners Bound to Change Their Own Hearts" and its follow-up, "How to Change Your Heart," the compilation also included his famous Troy sermon "Can Two Walk Together?" (his only previous publication) under the new title "Christian Affinity." Bootleg versions of some of these sermons had been circulating for years, usually published by some adversary intent on exposing his heresy. Now Finney himself offered the public the authorized version of his homiletic reconstruction of the Calvinist tradition within which he operated. The very title of "Traditions of the Elders" was an ironic swipe at Presbyterian confessionalism. Finney preached in restorationist fashion that "the gospel had not yet its primitive effect," despite the Reformation, because "systems of mental philosophy" injected "contradiction, mystery, and absurdity into the gospel." His most serious criticism was always against "the doctrine of *physical depravity*," which "inculcates that depravity is *constitutional*," and its corollary, "physical regeneration." These "death-dealing" dogmatic "traditions" produced what Finney called "the waiting system," with its attitude of "cannotism." Traditional Calvinism, Finney argued, froze people in sin. His two sermons on "Total Depravity" made clear his position that every human being is a complete sinner. All people are sinful in their "whole character" and "universally destitute of love to God" — but their sin is "a voluntary state of mind," a "voluntary selfishness" that produces "voluntary action" which is evil.

In a sermon entitled "The Doctrine of Election," he denied that people are saved "irrespective of their moral character" and that Christ died only for the elect without regard to the whole human race. It was not that "Christ agreed to purchase a part of mankind . . . and paid so much suffering for so much sin, and took his choice from among them." Still, election for Finney did mean "that a part of the human family are chosen to eternal salvation" and that others will be lost in hell. Since every individual is a free agent in a world full of free human choices, it is inevitable that many will ignore God and live for themselves. "The conversion of all men," Finney believed, "would require a very different arrangement and administration of the divine government from that which we now experience." Positively speaking, the doctrine of election means that God saw that some sinners would indeed respond to divine grace and live in obedience. Thus, "foreknowledge and election are not inconsistent with free agency, but are founded upon it." How, then, can one know if one is among the elect? "Those of the elect that are already converted are known by their character and conduct." And, Finney preached, "Those that are unconverted may settle the question each one for himself whether he is elected or not. . . . If you will now submit yourselves to God, you may know that you are elected. But every hour you put off submission, increases the evidence that you are not elected."

Finney's sermons presented salvation as the voluntary choice of penitent sinners, by the power of the Holy Spirit, to embrace Jesus Christ as sovereign over their life. In a strikingly nonpartisan political analogy, Finney preached, "Let the President of the United States, appoint his greatest political enemy to the first office in his gift, and he makes him his friend. Suppose the greatest anti-Jackson man in this city . . . should be reduced to poverty. . . . Now suppose, when the news of his extremity should reach the president, he should appoint him to a post of high honour and emolument, would not this change his heart? Would he complain that he *could not* become the president's friend, until the Holy Ghost had changed his heart? No. . . . How, then, does it happen, that all the offers of heaven, and all the threatenings of hell, that all the boundless love, and compassion manifested in giving his only begotten, and well beloved Son to die for you . . . will never change your heart, unless made effectual by the Holy Ghost?" To resist conversion, to wait and wait for God to act, to believe one cannot repent, or that one is already good enough for heaven — all of this is to "hate God." "You see, how necessary it is, that there should be a hell," Finney concluded. "What shall be done with these enemies of God, if they die in their sins. Heaven is no place for you." Very soon, he preached, unless you repent now, "the knell of eternal death shall toll over your damned soul, and all the corners of despair will echo with your groans."

His book of sermons presented the substance of Finney's message as he had delivered it throughout the northeast for a decade. Likewise, his *Lectures on Revivals of Religion* set forth his description of the method he had employed so effectively. When the revival lectures began to appear as articles in the *Evangelist* in December 1834 and January 1835, the public response was overwhelming. *The New York Evangelist* was saved. Finney's brother-in-law Samuel P. Andrews, a subscriber who received the paper at his farm in Michigan, expressed the feelings of many when he wrote, "I can sometimes when reading them, almost see him and hear his voice." This was a tribute to the skill of Joshua Leavitt, whose accomplishment was all the more remarkable given the fact that, as Finney explained in his *Memoirs*, he "could not write shorthand" and so had to copy in longhand as Finney spoke. He must have written at a furious pace, because he consistently turned over the manuscript to the printer one day after Finney had dictated it. Leavitt modestly noted that he "aimed to preserve, as much as he could, the style of the speaker, and is thought to have been in some degree successful." Finney used the published version himself to prepare the next Friday's lecture. "They were wholly extemporaneous. I did not make up my mind, from time to time what the next lecture should be until I saw his report of my last. When I saw his report I could see what was the next question that would naturally need discussion." Finney was pleased with Leavitt's accuracy and stated in a preface that he saw fit to make only a few corrections here and there when it was made into a book.

The book was published on May 15, 1835, only a week after Finney delivered the final lecture. *Lectures on Revivals of Religion* gave Charles Finney an international reputation. He rejoiced in the *Memoirs* that the book did well in America (12,000 copies sold immediately), went through numerous editions in England (several hundred thousand copies were in print by the mid-1840s), and quickly achieved worldwide distribution. The Welsh translation sparked a notable revival in Wales, and it was soon translated into French as well. Throughout the remainder of his life and wherever he went, the evangelist received expressions of gratitude from individuals and groups for the deep and abiding spiritual impact of this book.

In his *Lectures on Revivals,* Charles Finney argued provocatively that just as "religion is the work of man" and "consists in obeying God," so a revival of religion is an essentially human activity. Contrary to the traditional Edwardsian view of them as a "surprising work of God" that could not be predicted or precipitated, Finney always believed that a revival was the "purely philosophical result of the right use of constituted means." In other words, if a preacher delivered the right gospel message, extemporaneously and with appropriate enthusiasm, and if the work was accompanied with faithful prayer, a revival could be expected. "A revival of religion is not a miracle," he wrote, in one of the most controversial sentences in American religious history; it is not "something above the powers of nature" but results from "the *right exercise* of the powers of nature." Old School and even moderate Presbyterian critics would have a field day with this, but Finney cared nothing for their opinion. In his view, he was simply updating the old doctrine of the "means of grace" with effective "new measures" and carrying on the spirit (if not the letter) of Jonathan Edwards's example, as his lengthy quotations from Edwards suggest.

In his earliest preaching and up through Rochester and Boston, Charles Finney had entered communities assuming that many church members and all nonmembers were still lost in sin. Here he argued that the very notion of revivalism "presupposes that the church is sunk down in a backslidden state." Nominal Christians and unbelievers alike needed one thing: plain preaching that demanded "deep searchings of heart." Revival preaching must be disruptive, he insisted, for "the fountains of sin need to be broken up." The first step was to produce in sinners "a deep repentance, a breaking down of heart, a getting down into the dust before God." When Finney came into a village, he would often ask if any praying women lived there, and he would use them as the spiritual center of the revival. He now taught that if churches could first be "awakened and reformed . . . the salvation of sinners will follow, going through the same stages of conviction, repentance, and reformation." Of those who wished for a revival, Finney asked, "Will you have one?" And if the answer was yes, he would push: "When shall it begin? Would you answer, Let it begin tonight — let it begin here — let it begin in my heart NOW?"

In the *Lectures* Finney describes "prevailing prayer," which he also called "agonizing prayer" and "effectual prayer," as "an essential link in the chain of causes that lead to a revival." Such prayer succeeds in "moving God," not in the sense that God's mind is changed but in the sense that it "produces such a change *in us* as renders it consistent for God" to bestow his grace most fully. "The prayer of faith" must always be specific — for individuals by name and for specific blessings — and made "in submission to the will of God" and in full expectation that it will be answered. Finney attacked the "absurdity" of using published prayers on the grounds that they "destroy the spirit" as readily as a manuscript in the pulpit. Prayer meetings should "exercise the gifts of every individual member of the church — male and female" — but they must not get too lengthy. Prayer and preaching constituted a Charles Finney revival. Although he often led the singing of a few verses of a hymn, promoted the introduction of choirs and organs, and in New York City worked with Thomas Hastings, on balance he did not place a great emphasis on music. "I never knew a singing revival [to] amount to much," he wrote. The point was not to uplift a congregation with song but to preach so that each individual felt the Spirit of God pressing hard to repent.

Finney called for a major change in the education of ministers, claiming that young men came out of seminaries "not worth half as much" as when they entered. The problem was that they were "shut up in their schools, confined to books and shut out from intercourse with the common people." Ministers must be trained, Finney argued, "to know how people think *now-a-days*" in order to bring them to their knees. The church needs "practical" and "direct" preaching, which for Finney included both doctrine and exhortation, with the emphasis on exhortation. Preaching must be "conversational," "repetitious," and "colloquial," using the "language of common life." Against high-minded critics he urged, "Tell stories! Why, that is the way Jesus Christ preached. And it is the only way to preach." He taught the wisdom of extemporaneous preaching and the use of gestures. "Mere words will never express the full meaning of the gospel. The *manner* of saying it is almost everything." And the aim of preaching was always to cause a response, to spark a decision for Christ, to bring penitent sinners to the next inquiry meeting, to move them to come forward to the anxious seat, to stir them to lives of benevolence and holiness. "We must have exciting, powerful preaching," Finney wrote, "or the devil will have the people, except what the Methodists can save."

A predictably biting Old School Presbyterian review of Charles Finney's two 1835 books was written by Princeton professor Albert Baldwin Dod and published in *The Biblical Repertory and Theological Review*. It amounted to a systematic condemnation of every point in Finney's "Pelagian" theology and a devastating attack on the "vulgarity" and "arrogance" of his "fanatical" brand of revivalism. Dod concluded his lengthy review, published in the July and October 1835 issues of the journal, by "pointing out to Mr. Finney his duty to leave our church. . . . Nor will we withdraw our charges against him, until he goes out from among us, for he is not of us." Princeton declared Charles Finney anathema. The attack convinced Finney that he had no future in the Presbyterian Church. Doctrinal conservatives who demanded strict adherence to the Westminster Confession had stepped up their assault on New School evangelicals whose links with progressive New England theology made them suspect. The 1831 Albert Barnes heresy trial in Philadelphia was only the beginning. Other heresy trials conducted from 1832 to 1834 focused on the errors of "Taylorism." Then in June 1835, just as Dod was writing his review of Finney's books, Old School leaders in Ohio charged Lyman Beecher with heresy before the presbytery. Beecher had moved to Cincinnati from Boston in 1833 to assume the presidency of Lane Seminary, a Tappan-financed Presbyterian institution. All those charged had thus far been acquitted, but Finney lacked interest in mounting a defense should he be brought to trial. He had other plans.

A new educational institution in the Western Reserve district of northeast Ohio, incorporating both a college and a seminary and designed along lines with which Charles Finney was in full agreement, was being born. The school, the Oberlin Institute, stood to receive a sudden boost in enrollment if a group of "Lane rebels" could be induced to transfer. Theodore

Dwight Weld and many other Lane Seminary students were "Finneyites" from central New York and had promoted the abolitionist agenda at the Cincinnati school. With Beecher languishing on the East Coast during the summer of 1834, the trustees disbanded the campus Anti-Slavery Society, clamped down on public debate, and fired John Morgan from the faculty for supporting the students. The Rev. Asa Mahan, a colleague of Finney's at Rochester and now a Cincinnati pastor and Lane trustee, was appalled by the behavior of both his fellow trustees and Lyman Beecher. Forty students formed a makeshift seminary-in-exile in Cumminsville, Ohio, where they met with Oberlin founder John Jay Shipherd to discuss transferring to the new school. Theodore Dwight Weld's proposal that Charles Finney be offered a professorship met with unanimous approval.

Finney was in the midst of his revival lectures at Chatham Street Chapel when he received a letter dated January 10, 1835, from some students at Cumminsville setting forth this bold new plan. "A proposition is about to be made to you by brothers Mahan and Shipherd to become a professor of theology in the Oberlin Institute." Among the arguments that persuaded Finney to come, perhaps the most cogent was that there was "no theological seminary west of the mountains from whose professors young men can catch that high tone and moral feeling and that practical energy which are so essential for ministers at this crisis." The students went on to say, "We think *Oberlin* a good location" and a "favorable point to affect the whole Valley." As negotiations began, Finney wrote, "My heart is set if God opens the way." The formal offer, dated February 12, 1835, came from John Keep, president of the board of trustees and pastor of Cleveland's First Congregational Church. Lydia Finney's parents had moved to Cleveland, where they were members of Keep's church, and several brothers and sisters also now lived in the area. Perhaps the evangelist began to think of the Western Reserve as a replacement for his old summer retreat at Whitesboro. There were many reasons why Oberlin looked good to Charles and Lydia Finney.

Charles and Lydia left New York for Oberlin in mid-May 1835 with the ambitious idea of establishing his ministry in both locations. As he wrote the Oberlin trustees on June 30, "I cannot leave my people in New York without returning and laboring with them a part of each year." He noted that only "with this condition they consent that I should go." It was not just that Finney loved New York. He believed that "unless a professor of theology spend a considerable portion of his time in the actual duties of the ministry he is wholly unqualified" to teach effectively. In his *Memoirs* Finney wrote, "I had never thought of having my labors at Oberlin interfere with my re-vival labors and preaching. It was therefore agreed between myself and my church that I should spend my winters there [in New York], and my summers here at Oberlin. That they would be at the expense of my going and coming; and that I would come out here in April, and return there in November of each year."

As he traveled with Lydia to Ohio to begin teaching in May 1835 — having completed his revival lectures at Chatham Street Chapel and the preparation of his two books for publi-cation — ground was broken in New York City for a new church for Charles G. Finney. Broadway Tabernacle, as it would be called, was in a more fashionable neighborhood than the Chapel and would be constructed on a grander scale as an evangelical cathedral, with an imposing entrance on Broadway and a domed ceiling with a skylight above the center of the sanctuary. The Tappans were putting their money into the Oberlin Collegiate Institute, so financing for the Tabernacle came from William Green, Isaac Dimond, and other wealthy supporters. The backers were so resolute that even when the partially built structure was set ablaze by anti-abolitionist ar-sonists ("a story was set in circulation that it was going to be 'An Amalgamation church,' in which colored and white people were to be compelled to sit together"), they "went forward and completed it." Joseph Ditto, who had worked on other Free Church construction projects including Chatham Street, was the architect and builder, but, as Finney wrote, "the plan of the interior of that house was my own." This was to be Finney's dream church, built with pews in the round, a vast gallery around the entire circle, and clear visibility from every seat. The design would allow the evangelist to address "a much larger congregation than any house would hold that I had ever seen" and it would be built so he could look every auditor in the eye. Ditto objected that the plan was impractical, but Finney insisted. When it was complete, he felt the Tabernacle was "the most spacious, commodious, and comfortable place to speak in that I have ever seen of its size." The auditorium, with a capacity of three thousand, could easily host the May "anniversaries" of the mission societies and other significant conventions.

Finney returned to New York in December 1835 after more than six months at Oberlin, but he preached at the Chapel as pastor of the Second Free Presbyterian Church only through February 1836. During this transition period, as construction proceeded on the new building, Finney made a crucial decision about his denominational affiliation. In the *Memoirs* he describes the turning point as a moment of frustration at the inconsistent and autocratic governance of New York City's Third Presbytery. Having been told once by the presbytery that Second Free Church had jurisdiction in a certain disciplinary case, it proceeded to discipline a member in a subsequent, apparently identical case, and then the presbytery contradicted itself by ruling that the local church had no jurisdiction. Finney threw up his hands. Broadway Tabernacle would not be a Presbyterian church. The deeper reasons for Finney's departure from Presbyterianism had to do with his fatigue with the Old School–New School conflict and the very real prospect of a heresy trial. "The leading members who formed the church there, built it with the understanding that I should be its pastor," Finney wrote, "and they formed a Congregational church.

I then took my dismission from the presbytery, and became pastor of that Congregational church." On March 2, 1836, Finney resigned from his pastorate of Second Free Church, and on March 13 from his membership in the presbytery. Broadway Tabernacle organized itself with 118 founding members along Congregational lines and called Finney as pastor, although worship continued at the Chapel for a few more weeks until the new building was ready.

Broadway Tabernacle opened its doors on April 10 with an impressive service of worship and music under the direction of Thomas Hastings. Finney was installed by Congregational church delegates, including some from Connecticut, in the evening. A month later, when the major reform and mission societies held their convention at the Tabernacle, the building received great acclaim. Finney wrote in the *Memoirs*, "The Spirit of the Lord was poured out on us, and we had a continuous precious revival as long as I continued to be pastor of that church." That was only for a few months, for in June he was back at Oberlin for the start of school. He returned to New York at the end of the year and preached there until April 1837. Then, complaining of ill health and convinced of the impracticality of carrying on his ministry in two states, he resigned from the pulpit of Broadway Tabernacle. He would become pastor of the church at Oberlin as well as professor — and as an evangelist remain free to preach as the Lord would lead.

Finney experienced both spiritual and physical renewal during 1835. It was an amazing year, involving the publication of two books, success in rebuilding both *The New York Evangelist* and the membership of Chatham Street Chapel, a faculty appointment at Oberlin Collegiate Institute, the decision to cut loose from Presbyterianism, and the construction and organization of Broadway Tabernacle. In describing these events, Finney admitted in his *Memoirs* (in a passage deleted by editor John Fairchild), "this looks egotistical." But, he went on, "let the reader remember my agony at sea, the long day of travail of soul that I spent in praying that God would do something

163

Interior of the Broadway Tabernacle, built according to Charles G. Finney's specifications in 1836. The circular design enabled him to look virtually every listener in the eye. The auditorium accommodated regular meetings of the major mission and reform societies as well as vast crowds eager to hear the evangelist. Finney resigned from his New York City pastorate only a year later, in 1837. Photo courtesy of the Oberlin College Archives

to forward the work of revival, and enable me, if He desired to do it, to take such a course as to help me forward the work. . . . Nobody but myself can appreciate the wonderful manner in which those agonizing throes of my soul on that occasion have met with the divine response. Indeed it was God the Holy Ghost making intercession in me. . . . He pressed my soul in prayer until I was enabled to prevail." Finney may have considered the conduct of a revival to be "not a miracle," but he spoke of the revival of his career as if it were just that.

7   Holiness to the Lord

Students erected a circular tent large enough to hold three thousand people in front of the small cluster of buildings that housed the Oberlin Collegiate Institute. Made in New York and paid for by Arthur Tappan and friends, the tent had arrived just in time for the fledgling school's convocation on the first Wednesday in July 1835. Before leaving New York, Finney had had to place the order twice, because Oberlin leaders had once asked him to cancel it out of fear that it would become so popular for revivals in outlying villages that it would siphon energy away from educational work. None of the early buildings would accommodate a crowd, however, and so the tent was reordered. From the top of the central pole flew a blue streamer, almost ten feet long, inscribed with the prophetic words "Holiness to the Lord." This biblical reference — from the description of the tabernacle or tent of meeting in Moses' time (Exod. 28:36; 39:30) and the vision of worship on the millennial day of the Lord (Zech. 14:20) — expressed a theme for which Oberlin and Charles Finney would become famous.

165

This sketch of the Oberlin Holiness Tent, with its famous banner and the overflow crowd, conveys something of the excitement of Finney's early years at Oberlin. Both the banner and the cupola on Tappan Hall are drawn disproportionately larger than their actual size. The homes of President Asa Mahan and Professor Finney flank Tappan Hall. The sketch is not contemporary: it was drawn by Professor Charles Henry Churchill (class of 1859) many years after the tent was abandoned. Reproduction courtesy of the Oberlin College Archives

Three hundred students in addition to trustees and Oberlin colonists (as the village's first settlers called themselves) — a thousand people at most — gathered that summer day for the inauguration of the school's three professors. Teachers in the preparatory, "infant," and female departments (the founders believed in education for young women) had been at work for over a year. The Rev. John Keep, who headed the board of trustees, opened the exercises, delivered the charge to the professors, and formally presented the charter from the State of Ohio. The Rev. Asa Mahan, the former Cincinnati pastor and Lane Seminary trustee who had sided with the student "rebels," was installed as president. Mahan was a Hamilton College graduate and a colleague of Finney's from the Rochester revival five years before. The Rev. John Morgan, also a Lane Seminary refugee, became professor of Bible and church history. He grew up in Utica, graduated from Williams College, and became acquainted with Finney in New York City as a ministerial student before he joined the Lane faculty. Charles G. Finney, who held no college degree but was a published author, became professor of theology. All three spoke at length on the common theme of America's need for educational reform. In his address, Finney echoed passages from his *Lectures on Revivals*, denouncing classical seminary education and calling for a more practical method of training gospel ministers. The next day, the colony's founder, John Jay Shipherd, was installed as pastor of the Oberlin church. A year later, when the first commencement was held under the tent for fifteen theology graduates on September 14, 1836, three more professors were inaugurated — James Dascomb in science, Henry Cowles in classical languages, and J. P. Cowles in Old Testament. It was an auspicious start. Students were pouring in, many from upstate New York, and the financing by evangelical philanthropists seemed generous and secure.

Visitors to Oberlin in 1835 such as New York businessman William Green and Finney's old mentor George W. Gale, who passed through on his way to Illinois, where he would establish a similar project at Knox College, were impressed with the physical progress the colony and school had made in just a few years. Appropriate college buildings were quickly going up, the centerpiece of which was Tappan Hall, a four-story brick building topped with a cupola. Substantial brick homes were constructed for Mahan and Finney. Only three years before, the area had been an inhospitable tract that not even land-hungry settlers were willing to grab up. But John Jay Shipherd, pastor of the Presbyterian church in the village of Elyria on Lake Erie west of Cleveland, was a man with a dream. A Vermonter, he came to admire Charles Finney during the 1827 Troy-area revivals. The feeling was mutual, and Finney proposed his name as settled pastor at Stephentown. When Shipherd stopped in Rochester on his way west in 1830, he heard Finney preach, and the evangelist asked him to stay and assist with the revival. Shipherd was committed to the evangelization of the west, however, and continued his journey to Lorain County, Ohio. After several years of preaching at Elyria, he secured five hundred acres in Russia Township, nine miles south, as the site for his ambitious communitarian experiment.

Shipherd envisioned a colony "of the Lord's peculiar people zealous of good works" and a school where learning, piety, virtue, social reform, and manual labor would be combined. Northeast Ohio was the ideal location for such a Puritan-like endeavor, for Connecticut's Western Reserve was being settled by Yankee Congregationalists and Presbyterians with a sense of themselves as latter-day Pilgrims. Aided in the foundation work by a ministerial student under his tutelage named Philo P. Stewart, Shipherd toured New York and New England to raise funds, recruit colonists, and hire teachers. As Finney wrote in his *Memoirs*, soon "the trees had been removed from the public square, some log houses had been built; and they had . . . opened the preparatory or academic department of the institution." Always the dreamer, Shipherd began to enlarge his vision to include a collegiate course and a theological seminary. While all this seemed unrealistic to many, and

Shipherd's fund-raising was far less successful than had been hoped, work progressed.

In the fall of 1833, the Institute was officially advertised: "The grand (but not exclusive) objects of the Oberlin Institute, are the education of gospel ministers and pious school-teachers. To fit them thoroughly for their important services, they will be furnished with academic, collegiate, and theological privileges." Emphasizing that manual labor was to be "systematized and incorporated" into the curriculum, the plan stated, "The system of education in this Institution will provide for the body and heart as well as the intellect; for it aims at the best education of the *whole man*." In the Female Department, the four hours of daily manual labor would include domestic and gardening tasks "suited to their sex, and conducive to their health, good habits, and support." Despite its humble beginnings, Shipherd asserted that "Oberlin will rise and the Devil cannot hinder it!"

The name of the colony and Institute was derived from the French Protestant pastor Jean Frederic Oberlin, who had founded religious communities and whose biography had recently been published. Significantly, the Finneys named their third child Frederic Norton in 1832, jointly honoring the French pastor and their friend Herman Norton. There were many ties between Oberlin and Charles Finney before he ever made the trip west.

The idea of "manual labor schools" employed by Shipherd at Oberlin had originated in 1825 and 1826 with George W. Gale as he farmed and served as pastor in the Oneida County village of Western. Others were founding schools based on similar principles both in America and Europe about the same time, but Gale was an innovator. He took in students for the ministry, just as he had Finney in Adams, but now believed that a combination of academic study and farm or mechanical work would build pastors who were healthier in body, mind, and spirit than those trained by the traditional method. It also seemed to him that if a school could produce its own income through farming and light manufacturing, then education would become affordable for all students. Gale founded the Oneida Institute in Whitesboro and required all students to engage in manual labor as part of the curriculum and as a means of paying tuition. In the late 1820s and early 1830s, Finney and his Mohawk Valley revivalist colleagues considered Oneida Institute the best place for pious youth to get an education. Oneida Institute students wrote Finney approving the idea of educating "the whole man" and education linked with moral reform. The school should "preach abolition — emancipation from sin and slavery." Theodore Dwight Weld, Finney's Utica convert and Rochester revival colleague, was a student there before enrolling at Lane Theological Seminary — where the manual-labor principle was also part of the curriculum in the institution's early years. Gale wrote Finney in May 1832 that of the one hundred Oneida Institute students, "34 . . . are pious and most of them have the ministry in view." Many of "our best fellows" went on "to complete their course at Cincinnati."

When Shipherd recruited the Lane rebels for his new school and Charles Finney's name was put at the top of the list for a faculty appointment, New York philanthropists shifted their support from Lane to Oberlin. The Tappan brothers and their practical-minded merchant friends believed in the manual labor system as the most promising movement in American educational reform. They were eager to fund Oberlin Collegiate Institute as a model for the rest of the nation to follow and as a place to prepare preachers and teachers with "the right stamp." Finney was persuaded to move to Oberlin in part by this promise of strong financial support. The other inducement was letters from Lane Rebels calling for "a theological seminary, established on high moral ground, correct in its theological sentiments, and decided in its revival spirit." They pleaded, "Our eyes have for a long time been turned towards you." Weld wrote that it was time to "pitch your tent" in the west. In a January 18, 1835, letter to the Rebels, Finney agreed that "without a new race of ministers we cannot possibly go much further." Most significantly, he agreed with them on the key issue that drove them from Lane Seminary: free speech in a school free of trustee control of student life, a school committed to human freedom through the abolition of slavery. When Western Reserve College in nearby Hudson, hoping to limit Oberlin's growth, made a bid for his attention, Arthur Tappan advised Finney to ignore the offer, and friends persuaded him conservative Presbyterian influences were at work there.

Abolition work was not an original part of the Oberlin plan, but it was engrafted after anguished debate. John Keep, president of Oberlin Institute's board of trustees, was a Finneyite pastor from central New York committed to temperance, abolition, education for females and African Americans, and new-measures revivalism. Like Finney, Keep was a Presbyterian in transition to the freer polity of Congregationalism. When Asa Mahan, John Morgan, and the Lane student rebels demanded as a condition of their transfer not only the right of free speech but also assurances "that students shall be received into this Institution irrespective of color," they had friends in Shipherd and Keep. But this endorsement of abolition produced a storm of protest. Philo Stewart called Shipherd "crazy," and many feared that Oberlin would become "a Negro School." Overall, students voted 32 to 26 to oppose the admission of blacks. The Oberlin trustees became mired in rancorous debate. Most of them did not want Oberlin to be a pioneer in this area, preferring to remain, as the board minutes put it, "on the same ground . . . with similar institutions of our land." It finally became clear, however, that Finney's professorship, the transfer of the Lane rebels, and Tappan money — which is to say, Oberlin's survival — all hinged on establishing racial freedom at the school.

Charles Finney, ever moderate on the race issue, offered a way out for the trustees. "We do not wish the Trustees to hold out an Abolition or an Anti-abolition flag but let the subject alone for the faculty to manage." Shipherd also wrote the trustees from New York that his intent was not that Oberlin "fill up with filthy stupid negroes" but simply that it admit "promising youth" regardless of their race. He supported Finney's proposal that the trustees "commit the internal management of the institute entirely to the Faculty, inclusive of the reception of students." When the board again deadlocked at its meetings on February 9 and 10, John Keep cast the deciding vote for the resolution establishing faculty control over admissions and student life. As it turned out, African Americans never made up more than 4 or 5 percent of the student body, but Oberlin Collegiate Institute established itself as a leading supporter of abolition nonetheless. Finney, Mahan, Morgan, former Lane students, and Tappan money all soon arrived in Oberlin. Finney in his *Memoirs* noted that within hours of hearing of the trustees' vote, "the friends in New York . . . had a subscription filled that endowed eight professorships." Arthur Tappan promised Finney privately, "I will pledge to give you my entire income, except what I need to provide for my family, till you are beyond pecuniary want." Finney replied, "That will do."

Charles Finney had already been teaching at Oberlin for over a month when he wrote out his official acceptance of the position of professor of theology on June 30, 1835. He reiterated his three conditions for accepting the post — that he be free for, evangelistic work every winter, that the school be financially secure, and that "the Trustees give the internal control of the school into the hands of the Faculty" to ensure that the admission of students would be "irrespective of color." That done, Finney became Oberlin's most promising fund-raiser. A week after the July inaugural ceremonies, William Green, one of his prime financial backers in New York, wrote, "What the Institute has done with respect to the sweeping away with the old course of studies suits me exactly." He also reported that Leavitt, Lord, and Company was "striking off the sixth edition" of *Lectures on Revivals* and that construction of the Tabernacle was proceeding well. In a letter sent a month later, he appended a postscript reminding Finney to "write to the church." When Finney did write, however, exhorting "the church to remain firm in the cause of Emancipation while the present storm is raging," he got a testy response from a deacon. " 'Firm!' I do not know of a single individual in the church who is not 'firm.' " This was the summer of the riots, and Americans were polarized over the race issue as never before. Many strong abolitionists, including some wealthy supporters, were growing impatient with Finney's moderation.

Lewis Tappan, more radical than his brother on the abolition issue, baldly accused Finney of being "a coward" and of hypocrisy. In letters to Theodore Dwight Weld at Oberlin, he charged Finney with "sinning against conviction." The falling out occurred as Finney was preparing to return to New York in the autumn of 1835 to make the move from Chatham Street Chapel to Broadway Tabernacle. Weld loyally defended Finney by reminding Tappan that the evangelist had always put social reform in second place. "The truth is Finney has always been in revivals of religion. It is his great business, aim and absorbing *passion* to promote them. He has never had hardly anything to do with Bible, Tract, missionary, Education, Temperance, moral Reform and anti-slavery societies." The rift between Finney and Lewis Tappan was obvious to everyone that winter in New York. Indeed, both Tappan brothers were galled that the evangelist who kept blacks separated in the gallery at Chatham Street now steadfastly refused to integrate seating at Broadway Tabernacle.

In his *Lectures on Revivals* Finney spoke strongly against slavery and told ministers that "their testimony *must* be given on this subject." Silence on the part of Christians implied "that they do not consider slavery a sin." Indeed, because of its complicity in the Southern institution, he thundered, "slavery is, pre-eminently, the *sin of the church*." If believers could but unite against this evil, he preached in progressive postmillennial fashion, "the millennium would have fully come in the United States before this day." But Finney believed the way to end slavery was through a national *spiritual* revival. He wrote Theodore D. Weld in July 1836 warning that ideological struggle was pushing the country "fast into a civil war" and expressing alarm that ministers were abandoning evangelism for political action. The primary work must be to save sinners, for, once saved, believers would reject slavery and every form of sin. Finney advocated making "abolition an appendage, just as we made temperance an appendage of the revival work at Rochester." This posture simply did not satisfy abolitionists, who saw slavery as the most compelling moral issue of the day.

Finney wrote to Arthur on April 30, 1836, a month before his scheduled return to Oberlin, in a vain attempt to make peace. "I think my Dear Brother that you err in supposing that the principles of Abolition and Amalgamation are identical." While slavery was "a question of flagrant and unblushing wrong" and an "outrageous violation of fundamental right," amalgamation of the races was merely "a question of prejudice that does not necessarily deprive any man of any positive right." Racial prejudice was not "wrong in itself," he said, and "to make these two questions identical is to give the opposers of Abolition a great advantage over us." To push for too much freedom too soon "would do infinite mischief to our cause." He conceded that "Brother Lewis, and I now fear yourself, think my views are the result of halfway Abolitionism." But Finney argued that the "question requires moderation" (a trait he candidly stated Lewis did not have) and that "violent measures are by all means to be avoided." Finney's position lost him some old friends. One wrote from Whitesboro warning him that if someone claiming to be for abolition should still "countenance the caste of colour . . . I say, to such a man, that he must repent or perish!"

At the same time the Tappan brothers began to lose confidence in Charles Finney, their fortunes took a downward turn. Their silk and dry goods business, like all of the great American fortunes, was built and depended upon a national market. For many, though, the Tappan name had come to

symbolize the Yankee threat to Southern liberty. Anti-abolitionists burned effigies of Arthur Tappan in cities north and south,
and a reward was offered to any who would capture and
transport the brothers to a Southern state. In New York City
threats against them were routine, and their property was repeatedly attacked. Southerners, and those with Southern sympathies, refused to deal with the Tappan company. By engaging
so zealously in sectional ideological conflict, the brothers
crippled their ability to do business in the national commercial
market. To make matters worse, in December 1835, shortly after
Finney had returned to New York for the winter, a fire broke
out in the city's business district. The brothers rushed to their
building to save their business records, and employees and
blacks worked to salvage merchandise, but below-freezing
temperatures hampered efforts to fight the fire, and hundreds
of structures — including the Tappan building — were destroyed. Even though they were at least partially insured and
managed to rebuild, the company was severely weakened. William Green informed Finney at Oberlin in September 1836 that
future support from the Tappans was questionable.

Then came the financial crash and national depression of
1837. Easy credit during the "Bank War" of Andrew Jackson's
second term helped produce a boom economy in the mid-1830s,
which contracted suddenly with the president's ill-advised
Specie Circular requiring payment in gold or silver for purchase of federal lands. The Bank of England, an important
player in the American economy, restricted credit. As interest
rates skyrocketed in New York, businesses collapsed, a bank
president committed suicide, and there was a run on the banks.
Among the hundreds of major companies that went bankrupt
were many of the firms that had supported Charles Finney's
New York City ministries and ensured the fiscal security of
Oberlin Collegiate Institute — including Phelps and Dodge,
Arthur Tappan and Company, and Finney's publisher Leavitt,
Lord, and Company. In his *Memoirs*, Finney recalled that with
"nearly all the men who had subscribed for the fund for the

support of the faculty" out of business, and with the school at least $30,000 in debt, "in human view it would seem as if the college must be a failure." Whether Charles Finney and the Tappans were inevitably coming to a parting of the ways over abolition and amalgamation became a moot question. No more funds could be expected from them.

Charles Finney resigned his short-lived pastorate of Broadway Tabernacle on April 6, 1837, citing health concerns as the reason. Numerous letters inquired about his waning strength. Two years later Finney was still complaining of "my present state of health, and especially the state of my throat." At least as important in Finney's mind was the fact that Lydia had given birth to their fourth child, Julia, back in Oberlin on March 16. Asa Mahan had been with him in New York during the winter, but he was otherwise alone, and he wanted to be with his family. The congregation's official "dissolution of the pastoral relation" referred to the move as a "painful necessity." Finney had purchased a house in New York City, which he now rented out. He and Lydia became permanent residents of Oberlin, Ohio. Beyond serving as pastor of the Oberlin church, Finney limited his revival work to the Cleveland area for the balance of the 1830s. He undertook this work during Oberlin's winter recess, when students went out to teach in village schools. During the summer, he made use of the huge tent for church services, convocation and commencement exercises, and occasionally for protracted meetings around the Western Reserve district. With his work thus focused at Oberlin, he wrote, "We . . . had a revival here continually. Very few students came here then without being converted."

Following the financial reverses of the institution's founders and a reduction in support from Finney's Mohawk Valley friends, who increasingly began to view him with suspicion, Oberlin's endowment fund failed, and the faculty had to work without regular salaries. But, Finney wrote in the *Memoirs*, "with the blessing of God we helped ourselves as best we could." When the family lost a cow, Finney resorted to selling his "travelling trunk," symbolic of his career as an itinerant evangelist, in order to replace it. The lean times did not last forever, though. Finney liked to tell the story of Thanksgiving Day 1837, when he had all but given up hope and prayed to God for a sign. At the worship service, he recalled, "I . . . enjoyed my own preaching as well, I think, as I ever did . . . and I could see that the people enjoyed it exceedingly." Lydia, who had walked home ahead of him, greeted Finney at the door with an open letter. As he approached, "she smilingly said, 'The answer has come, my dear.'" It was a check for two hundred dollars from Josiah Chapin of Providence, Rhode Island, with a promise of more to come. A businessman who had weathered the financial crisis, Chapin would pay Finney's salary of $600 a year until 1846, when Boston entrepreneur Willard Sears joined the Oberlin board and assumed that responsibility. In general, Oberlin began to garner financial support from new sources as the old ones dried up. When Finney's *Lectures on Revivals* became a best-seller in England, the school initiated a major fund-raising effort there, and the arrival of British gifts "very nearly canceled our indebtedness." People closer to home were not so generous. In Ohio itself, which Finney characterized as a state "then strongly democratic in politics" — under the control of Jacksonian Democrats — Oberlin was generally held in contempt "because of its Abolition character."

Charles Finney and Asa Mahan ensured that Oberlin was known not only for its abolitionism but more importantly for its holiness. It soon became apparent that their development of the traditional Calvinist doctrine of sanctification along Methodist lines was even more controversial than the school's stand on the slavery issue. In promoting the experience of "entire sanctification," they employed the language of "perfectionism." Oberlin was a community in which believers consciously sought to live in holiness. The manual-labor school movement, with its emphasis on educating the "whole man," was rooted in the Calvinist and American Puritan belief that all of life is to be sanctified, made holy, under the sovereignty of God. Oberlin's commitment to moral and social reform was based not on any secular ideology but on the doctrine of sanctification.

The founders pushed reform beyond a level where most Americans were comfortable, however. For example, in order to be consistent with its claim that all of life is under God, Oberlin was logically compelled to support coeducation for young women. But in January 1836 Amelia Norton wrote Lydia Finney, "I must tell you frankly my friend . . . there is something so revolting to the feelings of delicacy and propriety of conduct . . . in connecting a male and female seminary together, that I can never approve of it, and must join with those . . . condemning it in toto." In the fall of 1835, Charles Finney lectured at Oberlin on the concept of "retrenchment," by which he meant rejecting the American or Jacksonian spirit of acquisitive materialism and living more humbly. Instead of striving for more, holiness called the believer to "retrench" and do with less. Abstinence from alcohol and tobacco consumption was only the start. Stimulants devoid of nutritional value — tea, coffee, and spices — should also be eliminated. Simplicity in "dress, diet, furniture, carriages, and equipages" was embraced. The grain-fruit-and-vegetable-based diet promoted by health reformer Sylvester Graham became an essential part of student life at Oberlin, as at several other colleges, during the early years. Finney came to regret his endorsement of Grahamism, however. Anti-Oberlin sentiment, rooted in hostility to its position on racial justice and coeducation, gave birth to stories that students and residents striving for holiness were indulging in extreme behavior. Rumors of mass starvation began to circulate, and an 1837 poem by an enemy of Sylvester Graham's reforms referred to Finney and Graham as "starvation's monarchs." Some cases of religiously motivated compulsive fasting (a syndrome that has been termed "evangelical anorexia nervosa") probably did occur at Oberlin. Finney and the school soon backed away from any doctrinaire physiological reform programs and simply advocated moderation in diet and exercise.

Lydia Finney assumed a leadership position among the women of the church and college in the formation of reform societies beginning in 1835. She was an early member and officer of the Oberlin Maternal Association, which promoted godly family life and especially the Christian upbringing of children. Other organizations included the Oberlin Female Anti-Slavery Society, the Female Society of Oberlin for the Promotion of Health, and the Oberlin Female Moral Reform Society. These groups often met in the Finney home. Lydia corresponded with women throughout the northeast, offering advice on the administration of infant schools and maternal associations as well as on spiritual and family concerns. Along with her friend and fellow faculty wife Alice Welch Cowles, Lydia took a special interest in the Female Moral Reform Society, which dealt with issues of prostitution and female poverty. Beyond raising money for the cause, the women spoke out at public meetings advocating sexual propriety, moral guidance of children, and state laws against sexual exploitation. Lydia and her friends actively promoted the work of the Ohio Ladies' Anti-Slavery Society, and she attended state abolition conventions with her husband.

In histories of American evangelicalism, holiness has sometimes been reduced to a kind of pious legalism, an overweening concern for good behavior defined mostly in terms of what Christians must refrain from doing. But Charles G. Finney viewed sanctification as a positive spiritual experience. His move to Oberlin and his season at Broadway Tabernacle (November 1836 to April 1837) proved a turning point. After a career of preaching for conversion, he became intensely aware for the first time of the need to lead converted Christians into lives of holiness or sanctification. Of course, he had always characterized faith as obedience to God's law and preached that believers should engage in lives of benevolence. But now, he wrote in his *Memoirs*, "I was led earnestly to inquire whether there was not something higher and more enduring than the Christian church was aware of; whether there were not promises, and means provided in the Gospel, for the establishment of Christians in altogether a higher form of Christian life." In a letter dated January 30, 1839, published in the new periodical *The Oberlin Evangelist*, Finney briefly described his transition. At Broadway Tabernacle and at Oberlin, looking back on his earlier single-minded emphasis on converting sinners, he confessed that he had "overlooked in a great measure the fact that converts would not make one step of progress" without being guided into "sanctification and growth in grace." Charles Finney also came to a remarkable theological realization. Revivalism's tendency toward spiritual individualism had led evangelists "in a great measure to neglect the church." But it was in life within the church that believers could find "the truths of the gospel that constitute the food of Christians" that was "essential to their sanctification." Now was the time and Oberlin was the place to correct that deficit.

Finney was pushed in this direction by his experience in the self-consciously holy community of Oberlin, which was made up largely of strong believers who felt a need to progress in their faith. Christian students also wanted that "something higher," and during the summer and fall some students organized a missionary society, pledging first to eradicate sin from their own lives. Student discussion of entire sanctification raised the spiritual temperature of the revival at Oberlin during the summer of 1836. Finney recalled that once after an Asa Mahan sermon he rose to press Mahan's "distinction between desire and will" in such a way that listeners were challenged to consider "whether they were really consecrated persons." Soon "the Holy Spirit fell upon the congregation in a most remarkable manner." About this time, Asa Mahan reported experiencing what he called his "second conversion" and "baptism with the Holy Ghost." Then, at a prayer meeting, a theology student asked "whether there was not something better and higher than Christians had generally experienced . . .

180

whether sanctification was not attainable in this life." By this Finney remembered the student meant "that Christians could have unbroken peace, and not come into condemnation, or have the feeling of condemnation or a consciousness of sin." Mahan's quick affirmative answer left the faculty with the task of developing a theology of sanctification. Mahan began preaching the soul's liberation from "the thralldom of sin" and a "consequent change in the sensibility so that the balance of its tendencies shall always be in favor of holiness." Henry Cowles, John Morgan, and Charles Finney picked up these themes as well.

Postconversion Christian experience occupied Finney's mind. He was especially concerned that believers would often "fall back from a revival state," as he put it in his *Memoirs*. Speaking for himself, Finney confessed that, while God "did not suffer me to backslide" to any great extent, on many occasions he felt "weak in the presence of temptation." He also expressed dissatisfaction with his own lack of "stability in faith and love." Over his life, on many occasions he had spent days in fasting and prayer "in overhauling my own religious life in order to retain that communion with God, and that hold upon the divine strength" required for his work. To address these issues, Charles Finney determined to deliver in New York, after his first season at Oberlin, a series of lectures for those already converted and striving to live the Christian life. As he delivered them, they were published in the *Evangelist* in the same manner as his earlier *Lectures on Revivals* and then gathered and published as a book entitled *Lectures to Professing Christians.* The whole effort was prompted by a conjunction of pastoral concern and a personal quest for spiritual renewal.

Preparing his weekly lectures at the Tabernacle, Finney had met regularly in New York City with Asa Mahan to study the Bible and the literature of entire sanctification and perfectionism. John Wesley's classic *Plain Account of Christian Perfection,* recent issues of the periodical *The Perfectionist,* and spiritual biographies of believers who testified to experiences of the Holy Spirit provided a spectrum of opinion that Finney read with an eager but critical mind. He was especially influenced by Wesley's *Plain Account*, which he admitted he "never saw until lately" and judged "an admirable book." These books, and the ideal of living a perfectly sinless life, were being discussed at Oberlin in the summer and were much in the air. Small perfectionist and holiness groups were starting to gather here and there throughout evangelical America, coming out of churches in both Methodist and Calvinist traditions. Some of these were wildly idiosyncratic and hopelessly utopian. John Humphrey Noyes, who became America's best-known perfectionist after founding the Oneida Community in 1844, had been ejected in 1834 from Yale Divinity School after announcing that he was free from sin. At Oneida, Noyes practiced "Bible communism" and, rejecting monogamous marriage as a type of slavery, introduced a regulated form of free love that he called "complex marriage." Noyes had personal contact with Charles and Lydia Finney on at least two occasions. Finney certainly did not find everything in his perfectionist reading to his liking, and he vehemently objected to its tendency toward antinomianism. In general, he was appalled by the offbeat religion of Noyes and all those who spun out of the orbit of Christian orthodoxy, but his study of Scripture and perfectionist literature gripped him nonetheless. "My mind was satisfied that an altogether higher and more stable form of Christian life was attainable, and was the privilege of all Christians."

Charles Finney prayed for this higher blessing for himself as he prepared his Tabernacle lectures on postconversion Christian living. The weekly lectures "were very much the result of a searching that was going on in my own mind. I mean, that the Spirit of God was showing me many things in regard to the question of sanctification." Finney came to see entire sanctification, traditionally a Wesleyan doctrine, as the necessary theological outcome of his essentially Calvinist scheme of salvation. But his insight about the attainability of holiness was not only an intellectual breakthrough. In a January 1839 letter in *The Oberlin Evangelist* he confessed, "I found that I knew comparatively little about Christ. . . . What I did know of Christ was almost exclusively as an atoning and justifying Savior. But as a JESUS to save men from sin, or as a sanctifying Savior, I knew very little about Him." Charles Finney came to know this sanctifying Jesus. He recorded in the *Memoirs,* "After a season of great searching of heart [God] brought me, as he has often done, into a large place, and gave me much of that divine sweetness of my soul of which President Edwards speaks as an experience of his own soul. That winter I had a thorough breaking up, so much so that sometimes for a considerable period I could not refrain from loud weeping in view of my own sins, and of the love of God in Christ." The last phrase, and another in the *Memoir's* description, "the abundance of the grace of God," while not absent in Finney's earlier preaching, became for him a fresh emphasis. That winter in New York, he wrote, "the Lord was pleased to visit my soul with a great refreshing."

Charles Finney's lectures to professing Christians at Broadway Tabernacle were essentially an exposition of the Calvinist doctrine of the perseverance of the saints, which he defined quite simply as the consequence of genuine conversion. It was not a case of "once in grace, always in grace" but rather a confidence that believers who are truly converted "will continue to obey God." The eleven 1836 lectures encouraged believers to examine themselves to determine if theirs was an honest faith. Titles included "Self Deceivers," "False Professors," "Legal Religion," "Doubtful Actions," "Conformity to the World," and "True and False Repentance." The first two lectures in 1837 were entitled "True and False Conversion" and "True Submission." Preaching on justification by faith, Finney demanded, as he always had, a personal response. In a controversial distinction, he asserted that "justifying faith . . . does not consist in believing that your sins are forgiven," because "your sins are not forgiven *until* you believe." The penitent believer must "exercise" saving faith in "the atonement of

183

Christ." He concluded, "Sinner, you need not go home from this meeting under the wrath of Almighty God. You may be justified here, on the spot, now, if you will only believe in Christ. Your pardon is ready, made out and sealed with the broad seal of heaven; and the blank will be filled up, and the gracious pardon delivered, as soon as, by one act of faith, you receive Jesus Christ as he is offered in the gospel."

Only three of the lectures in the series addressed sanctification by faith and Christian perfection directly, and these were all delivered in 1837, but the topic was woven through many of the other lectures as well. In "Religion of the Law and Gospel," for example, Finney said, "I want you to distinguish between works of law and works of faith." While the believer is justified by faith apart from the law, he asserted, sanctification by faith fosters a life of voluntary obedience to God's law. "The gospel believer has an affectionate confidence in God, which leads him to obey out of love." This was quite different from the teaching of those "called Perfectionists, who held that they were not under obligation to obey the law." Like John Wesley a century earlier, Finney was keenly aware of the pitfalls of perfectionist language. In reference to Jesus' injunction "Be ye perfect, even as your Father which is in heaven is perfect" (Matt. 5:48), Wesley wrote, "There is scarce any expression in holy writ, which has given more offence than this." Finney similarly complained that "so much has been said within a few years about Christian Perfection" and misguided believers "have run into so many wild notions, that it seems as if the devil had anticipated the movements of the church . . . that the moment the doctrine of the Bible respecting sanctification is crowded on the church, one and another cries out, 'Why, this is Perfectionism.'" Finney outright rejected the wild theology, libertine behavior, and "peculiarities, whatever they be" of those he termed "modern Perfectionists."

Finney had in mind not only those like John H. Noyes whose theology had slipped into heterodoxy but also more extreme "prophets" such as Robert Matthews, who had taken

184

in some Finneyite evangelicals. The so-called Kingdom of Matthias in New York City, involving sexual promiscuity, financial swindle, and finally murder, became a newspaper sensation in 1834 and 1835. Yet Finney went on in *Lectures to Professing Christians* to advocate Christian perfection. If the term *perfection* was so tainted, why did Finney use it? For the same reason Wesley had: because it is in the Bible. In addition to many verses on the holiness of believers and Jesus' admonition to "be ye perfect," Paul offered the blessing "The God of peace sanctify you wholly" (1 Thess. 5:23).

Finney laid down his definition: "Sanctification is holiness, and holiness is nothing but obedience to the law." Christian perfection, then, was "perfect obedience to the law of God." Even in his earlier *Lectures on Revivals,* he had stated, "Sanctification *is obedience,* and, as a progressive thing, consists in obeying God more and more perfectly." Now he continued to integrate the Edwardsian-Hopkinsian theological language that had served him as an evangelist from the start, still insisting that believers turn from selfish goals in life to benevolent ones. "The law of God requires perfect, disinterested, impartial benevolence, love to God and love to our neighbour." People should not equate Christian perfection with perfect knowledge, freedom from temptation or mistakes, or exemption from "the Christian warfare." Nor should they equate it with "the *infinite* moral perfection which God has." For Finney perfect holiness meant simply full obedience to the law of God. He preached that when Jesus Christ enjoined believers to "be ye perfect," he was "command[ing] the very same thing that the law requires." God "has created us moral beings in his own image, capable of conforming to the same rule with himself . . . to love as impartially, with as perfect love — to seek the good of others with as single an eye as he does. This, and nothing less than this, is Christian Perfection." Each person's "natural ability" is thwarted by "a desperate unwillingness," though, which amounts to a "moral inability" on the part of sinners. Finney insisted that only faith in Jesus

Christ and the work of the Holy Spirit make sanctification "attainable in this life."

Earlier in his career, although he was constantly discounted by Calvinists for his Pelagianism, Finney had maintained at least a little distance from Wesleyan Arminianism with its doctrine of "gracious ability." In *Lectures to Professing Christians*, however, he forthrightly acknowledged his debt to "Mr. Wesley's 'Plain account of Christian Perfection.'" Still, as he explained in his *Memoirs*, he dissented from "the view of sanctification entertained by our Methodist brethren" on the grounds that Wesley had taught that "the privileges of Christians are in no wise to be measured by what the Old Testament records." He further criticized Wesleyan doctrine for its emphasis on purification of inner corruption and for relating "almost altogether to states of the sensibility," or feeling, rather than moral responsibility. If Asa Mahan tended in the Wesleyan direction, that mattered little at Oberlin in the late 1830s. Finney acknowledged that "many Christians regarded those lectures as rather an exhibition of the law than of the Gospel," but in his thought "the law and Gospel have but one rule of life."

Finney wrote in his *Memoirs* that "so far as I know [the lectures] did not startle the Christian church as anything heretical" at the time they were delivered. It was after he returned to Oberlin that it became apparent that the response to the lectures published in *The New York Evangelist* and the book when it came out in the spring of 1837 was quite mixed. William Green gushed, "You have expressed a correct definition of faith," and, "If I see straight, the doctrine of perfection will shake the Church yet, as much as Abolition" and become the "foundation of the new City" — that is, the millennial New Jerusalem. But, he warned, others were "alarmed at the ABC of truth that you preached in New York. . . . You will learn what it is to be persecuted and probably turned out of the Church." Finney's old friend William Wisner wrote in 1839 from Ithaca lamenting that though they had once been so close, "we have for many years been as the inhabitants of different planets." He professed to share Finney's belief in the higher Christian life — with one reservation: "If there is anything on earth for which my heart pants it is the state of mind which you so often describe. . . . But I do regret exceedingly that you have called it *perfection*." This language was "preventing your influence"; he might have "escaped all the alarm" if he had just substituted an Edwardsian phrase like "the assurance of faith" or "consecration to God." Finney acknowledged in the *Memoirs* that "the cry of Antinomian perfectionism was heard, and this charge brought against us."

The Oberlin faculty began publishing its own periodical in November 1838, in part to clarify the school's teaching on the doctrine of entire sanctification. *The Oberlin Evangelist* quickly became a significant vehicle by which professors Charles Finney, Asa Mahan, John Morgan, and Henry Cowles propagated their position on entire sanctification, so similar to that of the Wesleyan holiness movement. The paper created the impression of a single voice, but this was not fully the case. At the Oberlin Collegiate Institute, professors debated the finer points of sanctification and their similarity and distinction from other types of perfectionism. In a June 1839 private letter, Finney criticized with little mercy parts of a sermon by Henry Cowles that seemed to him theologically trite and other sermons that he said veered too close to Wesley. He also cautioned that the faculty must take care in public not to "preach against each other's views." He concluded, "If we really disagree in our views on sanctification, which I think we really do not in the great points, a candid, prayerful, and frank opening up of our views to each other, in conversation, will I trust bring us together." The views of the faculty were at least enough similar that they came to be known collectively as "Oberlin perfectionism."

Finney wrote a series of twenty-five lectures on Christian life and doctrine for the biweekly *Oberlin Evangelist* in 1839 and another series of nine in 1840 (which came out as a book, *Views of Sanctification*, the same year). These articles were actually the first major product of Finney's own pen, as distinct from his earlier publications, which had been transcriptions of his extemporaneous oral delivery. In addition, the *Oberlin Evangelist* published pastoral letters and occasional sermons by Finney. In all of these, as he explained in an opening letter, he aimed for his articles to serve as a substitute for his itinerant preaching. "My body is so far worn and especially my organs of speech so far exhausted that I cannot visit and preach to you orally the word of life. I therefore address you through the press." He stated, in typical Finney style, "I wish you to consider yourself as personally addressed by me. I wish you to read for *yourself* and feel that I mean *you*." He was not writing formal theology now so much as offering practical religious guidance heavy on theological content. He also wanted to make clear that while perfect holiness might be a new theme, it was fundamentally an extension of the Hopkinsian doctrine of "the moral government of God . . . and the influences of the Holy Ghost in the administration of that government."

Finney worked from the classic holiness text 1 Thessalonians 5:23: "And the very God of peace sanctify you wholly; and I pray God your whole spirit and soul and body be preserved blameless unto the coming of our Lord Jesus Christ." In his 1839-1840 *Oberlin Evangelist* lectures, he defined entire sanctification as "the consecration of the whole being to God." Although Finney had felt his soul lifted by the Holy Spirit, he argued that sanctification "does not imply any change in the substance of the soul or body." Rather, it was "the entire consecration of the powers, as they are, to God. It does not imply any change in them, but simply in the right use of them." In short, "all the powers of body and mind are to be held at the service and disposal of God." Finney explained that this did not mean thinking about God all the time, always feeling at peace, never making mistakes, being immune from conflict or temptation, or withdrawing from the world. It was necessary for wholly sanctified believers to "continue to grow in grace to all eternity." Individuals remained responsible for their own lives of obedience. Sanctification is an unconditional promise of God to the church, but its application in the lives of individuals is conditioned upon their faithful decision to love God and their neighbors. As always, Finney sought to balance the divine and human initiatives in salvation. On the one hand, he argued, in Wesleyan fashion, that just as believers embrace holiness freely, they can also lose this state of grace. On the other hand, he also used the Calvinist language of perseverance: "Both entire and permanent sanctification are based alone on the grace of God in Jesus Christ. And perseverance in holiness is to be ascribed alone to the influence of the indwelling Spirit of Christ, instead of being secured by any habits of holiness which we have or ever shall form."

Charles Finney took pains to disabuse readers of the idea that, as much as he emphasized obedience, his teaching on salvation and sanctification amounted to legalism. "How are this corrupt nature, this wicked[ness] and these sinful habits to be overcome?" asked Finney. "I answer, by faith alone. No works of the law have the least tendency to overcome our sins but rather confirm the soul in self-righteousness and unbelief." Religion that is based on right behavior is merely a form of bondage, like a slave who chooses to serve in submission rather than face the whip or like a woman who does not love her husband but chooses "to live with him rather than break up her family." True religion, the faith of the justified and sanctified Christian, is "genuine liberty." It entails choosing the will of God willingly and joyfully. Obedience is the free response of love. So far Finney sounded like his old fundamentally Edwardsian self. But at Oberlin he took another step beyond the classical orthodoxy of the Reformation when he rejected the notion that the believer is simultaneously a saint and a sinner.

Finney explained that, while he was once of the opinion "that a person may be partly *holy* and partly *sinful* in the same act and exercise," he was "now persuaded that this philosophy is false." Behavior results from "some *one* consideration" of the mind, either selfish and sinful or benevolent and holy. Again, it is not that "our constitutional susceptibilities" or temptations disappear but that "sanctification consists in subordinating all these to the will of God." The Christian will seek to glorify God in every aspect of daily life — "not a mere *desire* to do good but a *willing* good, a benevolence that controls the conduct, that is active, blessed, godlike." The goal of faith, then, is "universal reformation." Finney used Romans 6:14 — "sin shall not have dominion over you" — to advance his argument that a believer "under grace" can actually live in holiness. Such a life of obedience and benevolence is no mere ideal, he insisted: it is the promise of the gospel and a requirement of faith. The gospel, therefore, has "provided for the entire and permanent sanctification of the saints . . . in this life." Citing Galatians 3:14, Finney advanced the idea that this blessing comes when the believer "receive[s] the promise of the Spirit through faith." In this, he echoes Wesleyan "second blessing" theology. Faith he defined as "a yielding up of our voluntary powers to the guidance, instruction, influences and government of the Holy Spirit." He concluded by asserting that "this blessing of the Holy Spirit is to be received at once, by faith, irrespective of all works . . . at the present moment." The "something more" for which Charles Finney yearned, the "higher form of Christian life" that he had begun to preach, was thus to be received — not achieved — through the gift or baptism of the Holy Ghost.

"Professor Finney's Letters," as the column was headlined in the *Evangelist*, applied the Oberlin theology to practical situations in the church and to particular groups such as parents and youth. He asked converts from his previous revivals "why they have not grown more in grace." "Have you sought out young converts and . . . encouraged and strengthened them in the service of God?" He lamented the "sad state of division and sectarianism" and the "almost entire conformity to the world" in the American church. He argued that the future of the church depended "on the necessity of *ministers* having the baptism of the Holy Ghost" as a further blessing after conversion. He explained that most ministers, whatever their education, had never received this spiritual gift because they knew nothing of it and had never sought it. Until a preacher "knows what it is . . . 'to be endued with power from on high' . . . he is a mere child, and by no means qualified to be a leader of the Church of God." On the other hand, he advised "believers in the doctrine of entire and continued sanctification in this life" to "walk softly before the Lord." He warned against "spiritual pride" and "self-righteousness," against being "uncharitable" toward Christians who might be deemed less spiritual, and against the idea that "none are Christians except those who embrace" the holiness doctrine. Finney the pastor lamented, "I have had the opportunity to witness with pain, the developments of this principle of the mind for many years." And he begged zealous believers not to withdraw from their lukewarm churches but to stay and work for greater devotion.

Charles Finney put forth a higher ecclesiology in his *Oberlin Evangelist* articles than in his earlier preaching for individual conversion. He expressed genuine concern for the spiritual health of the whole "Church as a body," recognizing that it is in church life that individuals experience lifelong sanctification. In 1840 he admitted having "had almost nothing to do with the ecclesiastical janglings of any denomination of Christians, and never intend to have." But it was church politics that disgusted him and not the church as a spiritual fellowship. The Presbyterians split into two denominations along Old School and New School lines in 1837. Finney was unaffected, although he certainly had something to do with the chain of events leading to the schism. Still, it stung him that a number of New School presbyteries — Troy, Rochester, even Cleveland — began to condemn Oberlin perfectionism and that some of his former Mohawk Valley colleagues signed these resolutions. When he saw Nathan S. S. Beman's name at the bottom of the Troy action, Finney wrote in *The Oberlin Evangelist*, "I almost involuntarily exclaimed, 'Et Tu Brute!'" The predominantly

Congregationalist American Board of Commissioners for Foreign Missions began banning Oberlin-oriented missionaries. Promoters of evangelical higher education, including the American Education Society, Finney stated in his *Memoirs,* "shut out Oberlin brethren, and those that sympathized with Oberlin" from meetings and financial support. Finney was slow to join the Congregational Association after his move to Oberlin, hoping somehow to bridge Congregationalism and Presbyterianism in the Western Reserve. Ironically, at the very time Finney began to speak most strongly against sectarianism, he became a pariah in most Presbyterian and many Congregational circles.

Josiah Chapin wrote from Providence in November 1840 in a letter accompanying his regular check for Finney's salary, "Some *friends* of *The Oberlin Evangelist* here are of the opinion that the subject of 'Christian perfection' occupies too large a space in that paper — not that it should not have a *prominent* place, but so much is said, that it is calculated to impress the opinion, that it is a hobby at Oberlin, rather than a practical truth of God's Word." Finney responded in the *Evangelist* to such criticism by stating that entire sanctification is the gospel and must be preached. To some extent, Finney and Oberlin turned inward for a time. He wrote in his *Memoirs,* "We kept about our own business, and always had as many students as we knew what to do with. . . . The Lord was blessing us richly *within.*"

In 1836 the board of trustees reaffirmed "the plan of uniting a male and female department in the same Institute" after two years' experience with coeducation. In contrast to the typical all-male college campuses of the time, which were plagued by "irregularities, frivolities, and follies," their own coeducational setting was more natural and fostered "the cultivation of both mind and manners." They forbade students from marrying, however, while enrolled. The requirement of manual labor, another of Oberlin's distinguishing early traits, proved less successful. Early on, the student's workday was reduced to three hours and then in 1840 to two, but the college was unable to provide even that much work for many of them. In 1840 the board endorsed manual labor as "essential and indispensable" to the curriculum, but the "practical farmer" who guided the agricultural and mechanical side of college operations not only failed to produce income but actually cost the school money. By 1841 he had been fired, a new Manual Labor Department was established, and the college's farmland was rented out. The system gradually devolved into a program that coordinated part-time student employment, though the college continued to give lip service to the character-building quality of physical work. Students lived and studied in a cluster of buildings — Oberlin Hall, Ladies' Hall, Colonial Hall, and the more impressive Tappan Hall.

Worship services of the First Congregational Church of Oberlin were held in Colonial Hall in the 1830s and early 1840s, and the tent was used during the summer. Charles G. Finney served as pastor and primary preacher. Finney's duties as pastor of the church and professor of theology in the theological department, together with some evangelistic preaching in the region, occupied him almost exclusively through the late 1830s. Many had initially scoffed at the idea of the untutored evangelist teaching theology in a seminary. Students reported satisfaction, however, in letters to *The New York Evangelist* and in personal comments during their travels related to winter teaching jobs. Finney had the ability to impart both "a good practical knowledge of the whole field of theology" and practical training in ministry, one wrote. Indeed, Finney's two primary courses were systematic theology (didactic and polemic theology) for second-year students and pastoral theology for third-year seniors. The pastoral theology course was an introduction to church governance and the practice of ministry. Here Finney excelled as a storyteller, recounting illustrative conversions from his revivals and commonsense advice on preaching and pastoral care. He even included lectures on personal hygiene and etiquette. When visiting in homes, for example, a minister must have clean teeth and nails, wear fresh clothing and wipe his boots before entering, and must not tip back in his chair. Finney did his best to see that his graduates were adequately refined for the learned profession. He was a popular professor who engaged students in a participatory, give-and-take classroom manner quite different from the straight lectures of classical pedagogy. And he insisted that students eschew titles and call him Brother Finney, conveying the sense that the professor was learning along with the students.

After five years of teaching systematic theology, Finney compiled the first volume of *Skeletons of a Course of Theological Lectures,* published by James Steele at Oberlin in 1840, the same year his *Oberlin Evangelist* articles appeared in book form as *Views of Sanctification.* Finney's object at this point was not to produce a formal systematic theology. He designed *Skeletons of a Course* as a topical outline for classroom use and as a reference book for graduates. In the preface he worried that publication would hinder his teaching method, which was to present the topics of natural and revealed theology not as concrete truth to be memorized but as "a series of questions . . . for discussion." On each issue "every member of the class is required to make up his mind, and prepare a brief statement of his views, in writing." Finney would then call on each student to present his interpretation and "examination and discussion by the class, and by the Instructor" would ensue until "the views of the class are settled upon the point or points." Only after this process was complete would Finney sum up and present "the whole subject to the class in one or more lectures." Finney did not want his *Skeletons* to eliminate "original investigation" or "the necessity of much and close thought" by students. Students had to be acquainted with "Theology, as a science, so as not to be at a loss for an answer to almost any question," but he did not want them to fall "into the habit of following exactly in my track in their statements." Finney stressed that he provided definitions not to stop free inquiry but "to awaken thought . . . and lead the student to search for, and find out their answer" to the major questions of theology. He wrote the book, he said, for "those who think, and love to think."

In his famous introductory lecture at Oberlin, for which his own notes exist, Finney stated, "I have no sympathy with, or confidence in, that mode of theological instruction that merely reads lectures to a young man. . . . When you come here to study we . . . throw you upon your own resources, upon your reading and reflection and study to find out the truth . . . and then to make such suggestions as to stimulate and guide your investigations to a right result." In the Oberlin classroom, Finney stated, "utmost liberty should be given for the expression of opinion." He told new students that if they were to graduate and "go away and live upon our thoughts instead of thinking for yourselves — why this will be your ruin!" He pointed out the practical advantage of what he called Oberlin's "Socratic method." Requiring students to stand, speak, and debate would "beget the habit of rapid, correct, and consecutive thinking," thus preparing them to preach extemporaneously.

Skeletons of a Course was identified as a first volume, and the final page carries a footnote stating, "The remaining volumes will be issued as soon as they can be prepared for the press." No further *Skeletons* appeared, but in 1846 and 1847 Finney published two volumes of *Lectures on Systematic Theology*, which were identified as volumes two and three, and no first volume ever appeared. The topics covered in the 1840 *Skeletons* and the later *Systematic Theology* overlap: moral government, moral law, human government, and the doctrine of the atonement are covered in both. If Finney had produced a first volume of the *Systematic Theology*, it would have been on the topics addressed in the first twenty-one of the forty-two lectures in the *Skeletons:* the nature of theology, the doctrine of God, Christology and the doctrine of the Holy Spirit, and the authority of the Bible.

The evidence in these books and in Finney's surviving lecture notes helps us understand the reports that his theology lectures were remarkable for their ability to stimulate a love for "the science of God and of divine things" in his students. He insisted that seminary study not be dispassionately academic. "The first and indispensable qualification for the study of theology is sympathy with God, devotion to the same end to which he is devoted, and a heart set upon promoting it by means of holiness." He warned students to "avoid impatience at the ignorance or stupidity of your classmates" and to "avoid an ambition to excell them in study and argument." Rather, he advised, "regard yourselves as a band of brothers and as soldiers of Jesus Christ." Individual prayer must accompany studies. Students who later commented on their Oberlin experience uniformly cited class prayer as an unforgettable part of Finney's theology courses.

Finney concluded his introductory lectures by connecting theological study with other academic disciplines and with all of human experience. "A theological student will make but little progress unless he views *everything* in a theological light. All truth is symmetrical, all truth emanates from one common center. . . . God the infinite and perfect, the First Cause, the Supreme Ruler, the great natural and spiritual center of all being, is the object of our study. Every truth has a sacredness about it; every question a solemnity and meaning; every line of theological instruction has an importance and a sacredness to awe and stimulate and sanctify." Finney may have moved beyond Jonathan Edwards on such issues as free will and sanctification, but this spirit of inquiry certainly echoed the great theologian's almost mystical desire to comprehend all of life under the sovereignty of God. In an age when biblical and confessional restorationism of various sorts dominated American theology, Charles Finney freely admitted that his thought was in progress. He had come to believe that theology was not the study of a fixed set of ideas but a process of discovery.

William Wisner advised Charles Finney in 1839 that "there is something revolting to my feelings in having a man profess to keep the law of God perfectly." Finney was careful never to lapse into such arrogance regarding his own spiritual status. His references to his own religious experience always balance undeniable self-confidence with a certain humility. Nevertheless, at Broadway Tabernacle and at Oberlin, Finney preached that perfect obedience and entire sanctification were the duty of every believer. He used the term *Christian perfection* knowing full well that it was fraught with controversy. With unwitting irony, in April 1836, before the summer holiness revival took hold at Oberlin, Theodore D. Weld wrote Lewis Tappan, who was at that time upset with Finney's reticence on matters of racial justice, "I know that Finney is not a perfect man . . . but yet take him for all in all, when shall we look on his like again?" In the 1840s, despite the controversy over holiness and Christian perfection, many American evangelicals with both Reformed and Wesleyan backgrounds would still agree with Weld on that score.

8 Rebuke the National Sins

"Let no man say, that ministers are out of their place in exposing and reproving the sins of this nation," Charles G. Finney thundered. It was May 14, 1841, a national day of prayer and fasting called when William Henry Harrison died just a month after assuming the office of president of the United States. Oberlin's pastor and professor employed the conventional image of the nation as a troubled vessel on stormy seas — "We are all on board the same ship." To argue that Christians should "not be diverted from the work of saving souls, to intermeddle with human governments" would be like arguing that passengers on a ship in the Atlantic should not seek to meddle with the efforts of a saboteur attempting to sink their vessel. "The fact is, that ministers, and all other men, not only have a right but are bound to expose and rebuke the national sins."

The Oberlin pulpit was an ideal setting from which Charles Finney could address national issues as a pastor, abhorring as he did ideological conflict and politically motivated violence. In his *Memoirs*, he reflected on the early years in which

Oberlin was reviled as Ohio's beacon of abolitionism. The town was well known as a stop on the Underground Railroad for fugitive slaves on their way to Canada. Finney recalled "several cases . . . in which they were pursued by slaveholders, and the hue and cry was raised" in the surrounding area. "We had reason . . . to be seriously apprehensive that a mob from a neighboring town would come and destroy our buildings." Racial integration of dormitories and tables in the dining hall was at first coolly received by some even at the college, but faculty members took the lead in breaking down barriers. When a few white students asked that blacks be seated separately, the faculty shamed them by offering the whites their own table. Finney credited this plan, which he himself presented at the faculty meeting, with eliminating segregation among students. Faculty also set an example by boarding students in their homes with "no distinction on account of color." Charles Finney had matured on this question, overcoming his earlier aversion to mixed seating. And in time, personal contact with residents and leaders produced a modicum of respect for the town of Oberlin from neighboring communities. Farmers and political leaders came to see that Oberlin's effort to produce racial equality did not involve the encouragement of interracial marriage, as was rumored. Finney used the famous case of the 1840 "Oberlin lynching" — in which student vigilantes, who had trapped and whipped a fellow student who made lewd sexual advances toward a coed, were brought to trial — to educate the public about Oberlin's Christian character. Finney's testimony in court influenced some Democratic legislators to drop their scheme to revoke Oberlin's charter, and when he preached in Cleveland about the same time as the trial, he even converted the presiding judge. According to Finney, Oberlin succeeded in making its evangelical and reformist message heard because "we kept still, and kept about our own business, and let the smoke and dust clear away in God's own best time." If Finney was a reformer, he pressed reforms in the role of pastor and teacher. At Oberlin, Finney wrote in the *Memoirs*, "in our preaching and public instruction we aimed to correct this feeling . . . of prejudice against color."

The 1841 national day of fasting provided an occasion for explicit social analysis and exhortation. Finney denied that humanity's root problem of sin was limited to individual self-ishness. God also "deals with nations. . . . Each nation is regarded by God as a unit. Nations are regarded as public persons." The real reason for national observances such as the fast, he argued, was to "give ministers an opportunity to expose and rebuke national vices" and for churches and communities to bow in "public confession of national sins." Finney identified several sins of Jacksonian-era American society as especially egregious. Number one was "the outrageous injustice with which this nation has treated the aborigines of this country." The nation was guilty of "shameless wickedness" in the way it had "duped" Native Americans into signing treaties that it subsequently violated anyway in a "disgraceful" manner. Finney was referring specifically to President Andrew Jackson's violent uprooting of Cherokees from Georgia after the discovery of gold there and his policy of driving them west of the Mississippi. Of the Congregational and Baptist missionaries who fought for Native American rights in Georgia, some went to jail and some accompanied the Cherokees on the Trail of Tears. Finney applauded their heroic witness.

The second national sin that Finney cited was the "hy-pocrisy . . . upon which the Revolution was based" when liberty was simultaneously trumpeted for "all men" and systematically denied to whole groups of people. "The nation that proclaimed these truths, as an excuse for revolution and war, stood with their unsanctified feet upon the necks of prostrate slaves!" He went on to decry slavery itself and the very notion of a federal government that required the protection of slavery. In this, "the union was a league against God." If it could not exist with complete freedom for all, Finney demanded, "let it be given up." Among the "numerous other sins of this nation," Finney limited his jeremiad to five more: national desecration of the Sabbath, "especially by the Post Office Department"; materialism, or "the national love of money"; the "disgusting licentiousness and intemperance" of congressmen and the moral decay of the city of Washington; the legal sanctioning of duels by national leaders; and the "wickedness of political contests, and especially the great sins that were committed during the election of the late President."

Many evangelical preachers remembered Harrison that May 14 as a fallen hero who had fought not just of yore at Tippecanoe but for righteousness against the corrupt Jackson–Van Buren machine. The crash and depression of 1837 had rendered President Martin Van Buren vulnerable in his run for reelection, and the new national Whig political party made the most of the economic issues of credit and currency. But it was the apparent irreligion of the Democrats — their support of slavery and Indian "removal," for example, and their neglect of public prayer in times of national crisis — that brought evangelicals into Whig ranks in great force. Sixty-eight-year-old Harrison was a resident of Ohio, at that time the nation's fourth largest state. Although he had been born into a wealthy Virginia family, it was not hard for the spin doctors of the day to transform the plantation mansion into a "buckeye log cabin." Not only did the Whig media portray the candidate as a great Common Man in contrast to the effete Van Buren, but they consolidated the old Anti-Masons and sought to build the Whig coalition as the "Christian Party." The campaign included much out-and-out mythmaking about the nominal Episcopalian Harrison's personal religious devotion and many acts of charity. Publicists saluted Harrison the temperance advocate who as a general had opposed drinking in the military and as a farmer would not sell his corn for the making of whiskey. They transformed the old Indian fighter into a peace-loving "friend of the Aborigines." And they conveniently glossed over the fact that his running mate, John Tyler, was a ticket-balancing Southerner who cared nothing for abolition. Evangelicals joined other Americans to sweep Harrison into

201

office. With 80 percent of eligible voters going to the polls, Harrison defeated Van Buren with 53 percent of the popular vote and 234 of the 294 electoral college votes.

Charles G. Finney did not buy any of this political hucksterism. The "Tippecanoe and Tyler Too" campaign was, to his mind, as defiled as anything Andrew Jackson had ever attempted. Harrison was the first presidential candidate to conduct a campaign in person, and it was in Columbus, Cleveland, Cincinnati, and Dayton that the first presidential campaign speeches in American history were delivered. Whig newspapers reported that 100,000 "Old Tip" supporters turned out to hear the hero in Dayton. The rowdiness of revivalistic electioneering, with programmed hurrahs from "Log-cabin boys" planted in the audience, appalled Finney. The "Hard Cider" slogan of the Harrison campaign was even worse.

> Let Van from his coolers of silver drink wine,
> And lounge on his cushioned settee,
> Our man on a buckeye bench can recline,
> Content with hard cider is he.

Log cabins built as campaign headquarters in cities dispensed free hard cider in an effective effort to secure votes. Handbill cartoons of Harrison as the great Common Man depicted him at his mythical log cabin birthplace flanked with cider barrels. Party workers gave out campaign buttons and log cabin–shaped bottles of whiskey. Many evangelicals were willing to believe other, more sober party workers who explained that the candidate did not approve everything that was done in his name. But in Charles Finney's view, the campaign made a mockery of the temperance movement and of evangelical Christianity.

"We are assembled to celebrate a fast appointed in view of the recent death of that President," Finney preached at the Oberlin memorial service for Harrison. "Now who can wonder that he was taken away by a stroke of Divine Providence. . . . Who ever witnessed such disgraceful and bacchanalian scenes as very generally disgusted the eyes and grieved the hearts of the friends of virtue during that political struggle? What low, vulgar, indecent, and in many instances, profane measures were resorted to?" In 1840, as so often in American elections, Finney complained, Christians had surrendered any attempt to influence the political process in a meaningful way, allowing self-serving politicians to control the nominations. "Instead of choosing the best of two good men, they consent to vote for the least immoral of two bad men." Finney voiced despair that party politics was the answer. A "Christian Party" was essentially impossible, because the party system itself was inherently corrupt. As he had recognized during the election of 1828, there was a connection between evangelical revivalism's competitive nature and political ballyhoo. "As Christians, we ought to confess and lament the sectarianism and divisions of the Church, as lying at the foundation of, and as giving countenance to the strivings, slang and slander of party politics."

Finney's proposal was modest, apolitical, and no doubt naive. "Reformation must be brought about and may be brought about by promoting union among Christians, and by extending correct views on the subject of Christian responsibility in regard to their relation to government." Like many Oberliners, Finney supported the new third-force evangelical-abolitionist Liberty Party of Theodore D. Weld and Arthur and Lewis Tappan in 1840 and 1844 — with James G. Birney as their candidate — as a step in that direction. It was reported in 1844 that "after a sermon by Mr. Finney, about every Whig vote was given to the Liberty Party." Oberliners would line up for the Free Soil Party in 1848, although the selection of Martin Van Buren as the party's candidate must have been hard for many to swallow. Everyone knew that a third-party vote was a wasted vote except as a statement of principle. But for Finney, principle was everything. Still the evangelist, he believed that the ultimate answer to the sins of the United States was moral suasion, not the false god of direct political action. Spiritual revival was what the country required. If men who knew and followed Christ would run for office, no matter what their party, then government could truly serve the people rather than special interests. If the church would speak out against social sin and promote personal salvation, as it had in the Rochester revival of 1830-1831, then there would be hope for the nation.

By the time Charles G. Finney approached his fiftieth birthday in 1842, he had reinvented himself with remarkable success as a pastor and community leader, professor, theologian and author, and advocate of entire sanctification or holiness. For half a decade he had traveled as an evangelist very little, largely retiring from the work that had brought him fame. He contented himself that other evangelists were carrying on the revivals. Now Finney rededicated himself to revivalism, and he was not the only one to do so. After the death of President Harrison, when his successor, the ineffectual compromiser John Tylor, moved from Williamsburg to Washington, the revival spirit surged through the northern states with fresh energy in the early 1840s. It was thus not true that the movement usually thought of as the Second Great Awakening died in the mid-1830s. In fact, American evangelical revivalism ebbed and flowed without any decisive breaks throughout the century. Finney's extended career demonstrates the problem with the notion that the period termed the Second Awakening had a discrete beginning and end. It is more useful to think of the Second Great Awakening as the renewal of the evangelical spirit in American society after the Revolution. Finney's entire career, starting with his experience of being born again in 1821 and continuing through his evangelistic tours of the 1840s and 1850s, was the product of that turn-of-the-century Awakening.

In the fall of 1841, Willard Sears invited the evangelist east again to preach at Boston's Free Congregational Church. Sears was Charles Finney's Bostonian "friend and brother" who in 1845 would join the Oberlin board of trustees and in 1846 would begin supplying his salary. In the late 1830s, a group of abolitionist businessmen had purchased the Marlborough Hotel on Washington Street and renovated it as a

Christian hotel and chapel. During this period, Boston churches were generally closed to both abolition meetings and revival preachers, but the Marlborough chapel's pulpit remained "open to the free discussion of all great questions of reform." The Free Church met at the Marlborough. Finney arrived in Boston in October 1841 alone. Lydia remained in Oberlin, in poor health after the birth of their fifth child, Sarah.

Finney lived at the Marlborough Hotel and preached there until December. Unlike his previous Boston campaign ten years before, this time the evangelist found no clergy extending the hand of fellowship. His old colleague Edward N. Kirk was preaching at Park Street and would soon be settled at Mount Vernon Church, but Finney and he did not join forces. Nevertheless, members of many of the Congregational churches closed to Finney came to hear him at the Marlborough. As Finney told it, "I . . . preached with all my might for two months. The Spirit of the Lord was immediately poured out, and there became a general agitation among the dry bones. I was visited at my room almost constantly every day of the week by inquirers from various congregations in all parts of the city, and many were obtaining hopes from day to day." Among the visitors was a woman who converted from Unitarianism under Finney's preaching. She reported to the evangelist that her former pastor, the renowned but now ailing William Ellery Channing, had asked her to visit him and give an account of "her Christian experience, and the circumstances of her conversion." The woman reported that Channing expressed a lively interest in Finney's work and borrowed a copy of *Views of Sanctification* from her. When she returned for the book in a week, Channing expressed a desire to meet Finney and discuss the holiness doctrine. The woman reported his wonderment at the orthodox criticism of Finney. Channing reportedly affirmed that "if Christ is really God, I cannot see why people might not be sanctified by him in this life." The Finney-Channing conversation never took place, because the evangelist had just moved on to Providence, and by the time he returned to Boston the

205

great Unitarian founder had died. In the *Memoirs*, Finney acknowledged that he could not "vouch for the truth of what this lady said," except to say that she was "a true convert." The challenge in Boston was to "break the ice and overcome the stagnation" of "fastidious" Christians and churches bound "in a strait jacket" of formality. Because Finney enjoyed such limited success there, he felt especially gratified as he imagined Channing's deathbed conversion.

Finney encountered another major religious figure in Boston during this visit. William Miller, the self-taught Adventist who revolutionized the way Americans think about the second coming of Christ, came to Boston in 1839 under the auspices of his publicist the Rev. Joshua V. Himes. Miller had even lectured at Marlborough Chapel before moving his prophecy conferences to Himes's church. Through his study of Daniel and other apocalyptic books of the Bible, and with the help of elaborate charts that intrigued an astonishingly large following, Miller predicted that Christ's return and the last judgment would occur in 1843. Miller's significance outstripped that of other oddball prophets of the day in that his interpretive scheme constituted the first convincing premillennialist challenge to American Protestantism's bland postmillennialism. Finney and most other evangelicals believed Christ would return at the end of the Christian era to crown the benevolent work of the church during that period. Miller taught that the world was lost in sin and would be destroyed at Christ's second coming, after which a thousand-year reign of the saints would be inaugurated. By the turn of the century, vast numbers of conservative evangelicals and fundamentalists had adopted Miller's premillennial view on the end time.

"There was tremendous movement in the public mind on that subject at that time," Finney wrote in his *Memoirs*. The evangelist was dismayed by the "wild and irrational" excitement surrounding Miller's predictions. He attended several of the lectures and invited Miller to his rooms at the Marlborough "to convince him that he was in error." When Miller and Finney met, the discussion centered on Daniel 2:34, "A stone was cut out without hands, which smote the image upon his feet that were of iron and clay, and brake them to pieces." Miller used the text to argue "that Christ would come personally and destroy his enemies in 1843." Finney stated "that the stone was, not Christ, but the kingdom of God; and that the prophet there represented the church . . . as demolishing the image." In typical postmillennialist fashion, Finney held that "it was not Christ that was going to destroy those nations" but the church that would "overthrow" nations "by the influence of the church of God in enlightening their minds by the Gospel." Miller treated Charles Finney with great respect but remained firm in his more radical interpretation of the end-time texts.

Finney's relations with other Congregational ministers were cool on this visit, but he did enter an informal partnership with the fiery Baptist revivalist Elder Jacob Knapp, who was preaching in Providence, Rhode Island, that fall. When Knapp moved on to Boston, Finney's financial supporter Josiah Chapin induced him to come and fill the void in Providence. Finney explained in the *Memoirs*, "It was a great trial for me to leave Boston at this time. However, after seeing Brother Knapp and informing him of the state of things in Boston, and assuring him that a great work was begun and was spreading throughout the city, and that things were in a most hopeful way, I left and went to Providence." Finney rejoiced that "this was the time of the great revival in Boston" among both Baptists and Congregationalists. Church membership did in fact climb in Boston during the early 1840s.

At Providence in early 1842, Charles Finney preached at High Street Congregational Church, where Josiah Chapin was a member and the pastor was a graduate of the Oberlin theology department. The congregation was a more radically evangelical offshoot of Beneficent Church, which had welcomed Finney a decade before. As in Boston, his efforts were now limited to this one pulpit. The conversion of an elderly gentleman from a prominent legal family set the tone for the revival, and the church was filled almost nightly for two months. Because of crowding in the sanctuary, Finney did not call inquirers forward but instead invited them to "descend, after the blessing was pronounced, to the basement or lecture room of the church below." There, "from night to night," the hall was "filled with rejoicing young converts and trembling, inquiring, anxious sinners." Charles Finney was back in his old form. It was time to prepare for the spring semester at school, however, and, "being very weary with labor and travel," he needed some rest.

The old pattern repeated itself on the evangelist's return trip to Oberlin when he stopped for the night at an old friend's home in Rochester. Judge Addison Gardiner, who had resisted conversion during Finney's great 1830-1831 revival, implored him to stay and preach for a few days. The Rev. George S. Boardman of Washington Street Church, his wife Sarah, and at least one other Presbyterian minister, James B. Shaw, joined their voices to the appeal. The Boardmans went back to Finney's earliest days as a Christian and an evangelist. George Boardman was the pastor at Watertown when Finney was converted at Adams and was assigned as his tutor along with George Gale. Sarah was the daughter of prominent evangelical leaders in Oneida County, George and Sarah Brayton, and had experienced conversion in Finney's 1825 revival. He described her as "one of my spiritual daughters," and her correspondence with the Finneys over the years indicates that she was a special friend. The original plan was for meetings to alternate between "the Bethel," as Washington Street Church was known, and Shaw's Brick Church. When the crowds exceeded the capacity of either building, Shaw drafted veteran upstate New York revivalist Jedediah Burchard to preach at his church, and the protracted meetings continued in both locations.

If Finney's gentrification had gone unnoticed by some until now, it became obvious in Rochester in the winter of 1842, when his sermons were on display side by side with those of the more wildly emotional Burchard. Burchard had read theology briefly with George Gale just before Finney began his studies, and he went on to a colorful and controversial evangelistic career. The two made a good team. As Finney wrote, "Brother Burchard's labors were better calculated to attract the more excitable ones of the community than mine were." Finney's own work at Brick Church "made room for the lawyers and for the more sober and intelligent class in the house where I was preaching." Finney was not just an evangelist, after all, but a seminary professor as well, and he felt very much at home among the leading citizens of Rochester.

At the urging of Judge Gardiner, Finney preached a special "course of sermons to lawyers" from the Bethel pulpit, "a course adapted to their ways of thinking" that "logically presented" the entire scope of the Christian theology of salvation. After having delivered some of the sermons in the series, Finney learned through conversations with Gardiner that he was making headway with the intended auditors. Finally, Finney wrote in his *Memoirs*, "I had arrived at a point where I thought it was time to draw the net ashore. I had been carefully laying it around the whole mass of lawyers, and hedging them in, as I supposed, by a train of reasoning that they could not resist." As he came to the conclusion of this sermon, however, Finney was dismayed that Judge Gardiner was nowhere in sight. Suddenly the judge was at the evangelist's elbow whispering, "Mr. Finney, won't you pray for me *by name?* and I will take the anxious seat?" Finney announced what the judge had said, and "there was a great gush of feeling in every part of the house." Masses of penitents surged forward or knelt where they could "to accept Christ and his salvation." Finney added special midday inquiry meetings in order to give seekers adequate attention. The revival spread, as it had in 1830, among the business and professional people of the city and resulted in a number of young men entering the ministry, some of whom came to Oberlin to study. It also "took powerful hold in one of the Episcopal churches" where mill owner William Atkinson and his wife Elizabeth were members. Elizabeth operated Atkinson Female Seminary and was a leader in benevolent causes, an advocate of Oberlin perfectionism, and an organizer and promoter of Finney's 1842 Rochester revival.

Charles Finney finally arrived back at Oberlin in April 1842 to resume his teaching responsibilities. He reported in the *Memoirs* that in the church "there occurred a considerable number of conversions every week, and almost daily through the summer." In both 1841 and 1842, Finney also made brief midsummer trips to Rochester by stagecoach and railroad to attend holiness conventions and to preach. In 1842 Lydia and the baby accompanied him, for she wrote to the other children from there on July 19. Lydia's sensibilities as an evangelical mother are revealed in the letter, which admonishes the children to "live near the Lord" and ends with the hope "that when we return we shall be made happy by your good conduct." To Julia she spoke of seeing a little girl with a "calm, sweet, heavenly little countenance" who had but one hand. With shocking abruptness she inquired, "Dear Julia, will you love the Lord with both your hands? or will he have to take one or both of them away to make you think about Jesus Christ?" She advised Helen and Charles, fourteen and twelve, respectively, "Be wise, discreet, get all the knowledge you can upon every subject and lay it up for present and future use." She wrote the practical-minded Norton especially about the geology of the trip. She added her wish that Helen, the eldest, would "try to make everyone around you happy" and assist the housesitters with the smaller children. To all she concluded, "I ardently desire you should all be pure holy children" and "live wholly for the Lord." Charles and Lydia and the older Finney children received a blow on March 9, 1843, when two-year-old Sarah died.

New York City was Finney's destination for the winter of 1842-1843. Although Broadway Tabernacle had been constructed expressly for his preaching, Finney's pulpit from mid-November through mid-February was Niblo's Theatre at Prince Street and Broadway. The building had been refurbished as a Congregational church by Lewis Tappan, who had both recovered financially and overcome his annoyance at Finney. The pastor was the Rev. Samuel Cochran, a graduate of the Oberlin theology department. During this season, in addition to a regular course of evangelistic services, Finney delivered two lecture series. The content of one, "Holiness of Christians in the Present Life," was transcribed by Cochran and published in *The Oberlin Evangelist;* the text of the other, "Moral Government of God," was privately printed by Lewis Tappan. Although Finney wrote in his *Memoirs* that many "interesting cases of conversions occurred," he again experienced the frustration of working in "a great city" where it was "often impossible to form any judgment of the extent of a revival."

One case Finney could never forget was that of his future son-in-law Jacob Dolson Cox. One night when he invited seekers to the anxious bench, the evangelist suddenly "observed a young man" with "a very earnest look" who came forward "from a remote part of the house . . . stepping upon the backs of the seats." Since his relationship with Dolson Cox after he came to Oberlin as a student was somewhat troubled, Finney worded his description with some care here: "He appeared exceedingly well as a young convert, and I had no doubt then that he was truly converted to Christ. Indeed, I have not seriously doubted it since."

The great revivals of 1841-1844 extended from New England west across New York and Ohio, and Finney participated in the movement as an itinerant each year during winter break. Invitations to preach now came primarily from Congregationalists, but often in cooperation with Methodist and Freewill Baptist colleagues. But the Congregational church at Oberlin was the primary focus of Finney's evangelistic work. The construction of the Oberlin church's meetinghouse greatly enhanced worship in the town, as the congregation had outgrown Oberlin Hall. Willard Sears of Boston contributed the plans, and a local carpenter who was a member of the church supervised construction. Although the building is rectangular rather

211

This drawing by Henry Lowe shows Tappan Square in 1846, with the church's newly constructed meetinghouse and Tappan Hall. The Oberlin Collegiate Institute buildings shown are, from left to right, Oberlin Hall, Ladies' Hall, and Colonial Hall. Reproduction courtesy of the Oberlin College Archives than square, the design incorporated some features of Broadway Tabernacle, most notably affording Finney the ability to look every congregant in the eye from the pulpit. When the cornerstone was laid on June 17, 1842, Finney offered the prayer and a new hymn was sung:

> May the presence of thy love
> Rest upon us from above;
> May thy glory and thy grace
> Shadow o'er this holy place;
> Shield us by thy power divine
> O thou God of Oberlin.

Construction proceeded slowly due to financial constraints, but the large brick church building, with a seating capacity of more than a thousand, was finally complete in 1844. The tower was added a year later. Here Charles G. Finney and his fellow professor and associate pastor John Morgan preached year after year to large congregations. The music director, George Nelson Allen, likewise combined a professorship with service to the church. By the end of the 1840s, Allen, a disciple of America's leading church musician, Lowell Mason, was directing a powerful choir of over a hundred voices. With its grand meetinghouse and impressive services, the Oberlin church was a pilgrimage destination for many revival-minded mid-century American evangelicals.

Revivals in one city after another made Charles G. Finney famous, but it must not be forgotten that he also served as pastor of a local congregation for thirty-five years. His towering presence in the pulpit, his voice and piercing eye, and his familiar figure walking across the square from home to the meetinghouse or classroom were essential to the soul of the community. Finney made himself regularly available for spiritual counsel. He advised civic leaders on local issues and involved himself in the work of the board of education. He could be stunningly explicit in the way he spoke his mind. A former student wrote, "I heard you once, at family-prayers, pray God to 'annihilate the Democratic Party.'" Oberlin people remembered the flourishes of oratory in his sermons, such as the one that concluded with a warning that angels would toll a great bell in heaven over the doom of lost souls (at which point he pulled mightily on an imaginary rope). His prayers were plain and practical. Legends grew up concerning his petitions for rain in time of drought, some of which, by all accounts, God speedily answered. Once he prayed, "O Lord, the long looked-for clouds are at last over our heads, and we pray that they may now burst and deluge the parched earth. Do not let them pass by and discharge their water upon the lake, as the clouds have done so often of late; for thou knowest that there is already water enough in the lake." When Finney was absent from Oberlin, friends would often write of how they longed to hear him once more from that pulpit.

Finney was back in Boston in October of 1843. He noted that the Millerite "excitement had blown over" after the predicted date of the second coming had come and gone, but he found the people still susceptible to religious error. He was especially concerned with a young man from within the Marlborough Chapel congregation itself who suddenly claimed to be a prophet. Although it was easy for Finney to demonstrate that his predictions were fallacious, the confusion had weakened the church and "really neutralized their efforts as Christians." Finney blamed Boston's gullibility on the pervasive influence of rationalistic Unitarianism. "Their system is one of denials" that "call[s] in question all the principal doctrines of the Bible." With no solid spiritual and theological foundation, he wrote, "it is extremely difficult to make religious truths lodge in their minds." Even at the Chapel, believers went in many directions; some were "extreme Non-resistants" (pacifists), and all were "reformers" of one sort or another. Finney did his best, feeling that "upon the whole . . . they were a praying, earnest, Christian people," but he was frustrated that they were not "a *united* people" and "not at all in a prosperous state as a church." In fact, the congregation dissolved itself while Finney was preaching in December 1843 and early 1844, some members drifting away and others attempting to regather as a new church.

The religious confusion of the city of Boston echoed in Charles Finney's soul and brought him through another spiritual "overhauling" that winter. Alone in his hotel rooms, he would awaken at four each morning to read the Bible and pray until breakfast. He came to a deeper sense of the Bible as "ablaze with light" and as "the very *life* of God." Many weeks of such intense devotional activity brought Finney to question his own consecration to God. After years of teaching and preaching, had he merely deluded himself as to his own salvation? His resolution brought him to a point where much earlier in his career he had disagreed with Hopkinsianism. He now affirmed that if God's wisdom demanded he should "go down to hell, I accepted His will." Finney's mind turned to Lydia at Oberlin, in very poor health and expecting another child. He dreamed about her. In the morning, although he had often placed his family on God's altar, the act of "giving up my wife to the will of God" gripped Finney with anguish. "I struggled and prayed until I was exhausted, and found myself entirely unable to give her up altogether to God's will." He wrote Lydia describing his experience. Descent into "discouragement and bitterness" — in which Finney confessed, "I could not get hold of my former hope" — led him to a new and complete submission to God. Early in the morning, he wrote, "My mind settled into a perfect stillness." Throughout the day, he recalled, "Holiness to the Lord seemed to be inscribed on all the exercises of my mind."

In the *Memoirs,* Charles Finney wrote of his Boston experience as "a fresh baptism of His Holy Spirit." He had been preaching this second blessing of Holy Ghost baptism since 1836 and 1837 and had in fact experienced it for himself at that time. The Boston experience was a renewed infusion of that blessing, an "enlarged experience," "a fresh baptism." He described it, however, in superlative terms: "So deep and perfect a resting in the will of God I had never before known. . . . My soul was wedded to Christ in a sense in which I had never had any thought or conception of before." Nor was it an ephemeral spiritual high, for it "sprung a vein of joy in my mind that kept developing more and more for weeks and months, and indeed I may say for years." Finney's prayers were now expressions of spiritual delight. "The language of the Song of Solomon was as natural to me as my breath," and "I often found myself smiling, as it were, in the face of God." With God now he enjoyed "the freedom of a child with a loving parent." He professed to be able at almost any time to "find God *within* me in such a sense that I can . . . lay my heart in His hand, and nestle down in His perfect will." Others noticed a change in Finney and asked him about the source of his joy. But when he began to preach at Marlborough Chapel about the experience of "full and present salvation in the Lord Jesus Christ," he sensed that he was preaching "over the heads of the masses of the people." It was something new for the evangelist who took pride in speaking the language of the people to admit that "they did not understand me."

Finney's message of a sanctified "higher Christian life" appealed to enough believers that a remnant at the Chapel formed a new church and offered him a call as their pastor. The idea of dividing his time again between Oberlin and an East Coast congregation, however, struck him as impractical. Finney returned to Oberlin and brought with him the "sweet frame of love to the brethren and love to all mankind" of the holiness revival, as an *Oberlin Evangelist* report put it. Although he had hoped to preach in northern New York State during the fall of 1844, Lydia's health deteriorated alarmingly after the birth of their sixth child, Delia, who was born mentally handicapped. On one occasion he held Lydia as she vomited blood violently. It seemed as if her end was near, but she recovered. Travel was now out of the question. Charles Finney devoted himself to his teaching and pastoral work and found satisfaction in the continuous state of revival in the Oberlin church.

Finney remained at Oberlin for two and a half years, from

the spring of 1844 until the fall of 1846. He finally felt confident enough to leave Lydia in order to preach for the winter at Congregational churches in Detroit and Pontiac, Michigan. One moment of joy came in May 1846 when the Finneys' eighteen-year-old daughter Helen Finney married William Cochran, a professor of logic and one of Oberlin's most popular and able teachers. In addition to duties at school, church, and home, Finney busied himself with writing. His sermons and letters had been a regular feature in *The Oberlin Evangelist* from its inception. In the sermons, transcriptions of those delivered to the Oberlin church, he repeatedly worked over his basic themes of sin and salvation, human responsibility, the ability to repent and turn to the Savior, faith as "an active principle," and "entire consecration" or sanctification by the power of the Holy Spirit. On January 29, 1845, Finney began a major new series, "Letters on Revivals," which ran until June 24, 1846. These writings supplemented his famous *Lectures on Revivals* from ten years before. He updated his observations on the nature of evangelistic work with what he had learned from the revivals of the early 1840s and from his "ripened experience."

Finney began the "Letters on Revivals" series in *The Oberlin Evangelist* by confessing that "in some things I erred in manner and spirit" in the early revivals. He stressed the importance of preventing protracted meetings from "degenerating into a spirit of fanaticism and misrule" and urged evangelists to work closely with "stated or settled pastors." He warned that in recent years revivals had become "more superficial" than in "1830 and 1831 and for some time previous." As preachers probed less deeply into "the horrible guilt of . . . depravity," Finney argued, converts were "not so deeply humbled and quickened and thoroughly baptized with the Holy Ghost as they were formerly." Rejecting both antinomianism and legalism in traditional Calvinist fashion, he pleaded for the centrality of Jesus Christ and the Bible in evangelical preaching. Religion has to do not with excited feelings but with a holy will and benevolent action, and the excitement of a revival must stem from "perceived truth" and "the healthful operation of the intellectual powers." New believers "will be excited," Finney insisted, but not just for the sake of excitement. Enthusiasm produced by the Holy Spirit is "not a spasm, or explosion of the nervous sensibility, but is a calm, deep, sacred flow of the soul in view of the clear, infinitely important and impressive truths of God." Fanaticism and "a censorious spirit," Finney complained, had damaged not only revivalism but evangelicalism's associated movements — temperance, dietary reform, peace, abolition, and the rest. Evangelism must be motivated by joy and love, not by sectarian anger, he argued. Finney called for a new day of revivals led by ministers "anointed with the Holy Spirit" in which sinners would be converted and believers would be taught "entire holiness of heart and life, as a practical attainment in this world."

Finney called evangelicals to repent of the great sin of individualism, for in revivalism "the *Church has been neglected.*" To leave converts without regular teaching and fellowship, he warned, was to expect them to "grow without food." Finney envisioned a grand partnership of settled pastors, lay men and women, and evangelists working to develop mature congregations of Christians committed to serving God and doing good in the world — congregations like the one he served at Oberlin. There can be no doubt that the evangelist's second important statement on revivalism was based as much on his experience as a pastor as on his experiences as an itinerant.

The "Letters on Revivals" could almost have been written as an answer to German Reformed theologian John W. Nevin's churchly critique of new measures revivalism, *The Anxious Bench,* published in 1843 (and in an enlarged edition in 1844), although there is no evidence that Finney had seen it. In his thoughtful analysis, Nevin held that "the system of the bench" was undermined by Pelagian or humanistic subjectivity, and he endorsed instead the "system of the catechism," with the work of Christ and the long-term teaching of the church as the only firm grounding for the spiritual life. In one of his more colorful passages, Nevin excoriated "Finneyism and Winebrennerism, the anxious bench, revival machinery, solemn tricks for effect, decision displays at the bidding of the preacher, genuflections and prostrations in the aisle or around the altar, noise and disorder, extravagance and rant, mechanical conversions, justification by feeling rather than faith, and encouragement ministered to all fanatical impressions." He went on to say, "If these things . . . have no connection in fact with . . . the cause of revivals, but tend only to bring them into discredit, let the fact be openly proclaimed. Only in this way may it be hoped that the reproach put upon revivals and other evangelical interests by some . . . will be in due time fairly rolled away." By 1845 Charles G. Finney sympathized with much of what Nevin had to say and, whether he was conscious of Nevin's challenge or not, he addressed the issues in his *Oberlin Evangelist* "Letters."

During this period Finney also began writing his *Systematic Theology*, the first volume of which (designated volume two) was published in July 1846. The second (designated volume three) he completed after returning from Detroit and brought out in August 1847. Finney had learned to write with speed, no doubt aided by the mental rigor of twenty years of extemporaneous preaching. In his *Memoirs* he noted that he wrote the second volume "at the rate of a lecture a day, and sent it to the printers." He "would correct the proof of one lecture, and write another and send it to the press the same day." He passed over topics covered in *Skeletons of a Course of Theological Lectures* that he planned to incorporate in an eventual volume one: his introduction to theology, the authority and inspiration of Scripture, evidences for the existence of God, the attributes of God, the humanity and divinity of Christ, and the doctrine of the Holy Spirit. With these included, Finney addressed in his *Systematic Theology* most of the major areas of theology. The 1846 volume presented his views on moral depravity, moral government and moral obligation, the atonement and regeneration, and benevolence and evidences of regeneration; the 1847 volume discussed human ability, repentance and impenitence, faith and unbelief, justification, sanctification, election and reprobation, divine purpose and sovereignty, and perseverance. While much of his thought remained within the bounds of the modified Calvinism of New England theology and New School Presbyterianism, the Oberlin doctrine of entire sanctification cast the hues of the holiness movement on many sections.

In his preface, Finney states, "What I have said on the 'Foundation of Moral Obligation' is the key to the whole subject." Building on the doctrine of human beings as free moral agents, which had guided his preaching from its earliest days, he explained, "The well-being of God and the universe of sentient existences is intrinsically important or valuable, and all moral agents are under obligation to choose it for its own sake. . . . All obligation resolves itself into an obligation to choose the highest good of God and of being in general for its own sake, and to choose all the known conditions and means of this end for the sake of the end." This doctrine constituted for Charles Finney the foundation for sanctified human life, including both social reform and personal holiness. Finney went on to apply the concept of "the simplicity of moral action," adopted from New England theologian Nathaniel Emmons, as especially helpful to the holiness doctrine of perfect love. An actor is moved either by love for God or by some lesser loyalty, by disinterested benevolence or by selfishness. "Sin and holiness, then, both consist in supreme, ultimate, and opposite choices, or intentions, and can not, by any possibility, co-exist." If believers are indeed dead to sin and alive to God, Finney argued, then, because they are in Christ, they will not sin. Charles Finney transformed the standard Hopkinsian doctrine of disinterested benevolence with an emphasis on holiness that he now characterized as "moral harmony of character." He thus wove the notion of entire sanctification, or holiness, like a golden thread through his *Systematic Theology*.

Finney maintained, as he did throughout his career, that "regeneration is always induced and effected by the personal agency of the Holy Spirit." The Spirit works through natural means and human agency, most especially through "truth, argument, and persuasion," to cause the saved to conform their wills to God. Finney shared the governmental theory of atonement with many New England and New School Presbyterian divines but went beyond them with his doctrine of the "entire consecration of the heart." He used "the term entire sanctification to designate a state of confirmed, and entire consecration of body, soul, and spirit, or of the whole being to God." It was not that "a soul entirely sanctified cannot sin" but rather that it will not sin. The redeemed will love Christ perfectly at every moment even though they continue to be assailed with temptation and so will grow in grace. Reflecting on his own experience, he wrote, "When tried from time to time, a new revelation of Christ to the soul, corresponding to the temptation, or as the help of the soul in such circumstances, is a condition of its remaining steadfast. This gracious aid or revelation is abundantly promised in the Bible, and will be made in time, so that, by laying hold on Christ in the present revealed relation, the soul may be preserved blameless. . . . Sanctification is by faith as opposed to works."

The perseverance of the saints, which Calvinists deduced from the doctrine of the sovereignty of God, bothered Finney because it was susceptible to abuse by the spiritually lazy. He preferred to think of perseverance in terms of the tightrope walker poised over Niagara Falls. Because we have free will, Finney believed, we *can* fall from grace and lose our salvation. Nevertheless, he believed that the hope of eternal salvation is rooted in the "persevering, and sin-overcoming, and hell-subduing grace of God in Christ Jesus," not in human effort. No Christian could "stand and persevere without the drawings, and inward teachings, and over-persuading influences of the Holy Spirit. . . . This doctrine, though liable to abuse by hypocrites, is nevertheless the sheet anchor of the saints in the hours of conflict."

Critics of Finney's *Systematic Theology* appeared immediately upon publication. In the fall of 1846, when the evangelist

221

went to preach in Michigan for the first time, opposition was waiting for him. Some members of Lydia's family lived there, including a sister and her mother (her father, Nathaniel Andrews, had died in Flint in September 1845). Prior to Finney's trip north, a niece of Lydia's wrote warning that "a spirit of heresy hunting, and . . . an effort to put down the Oberlin heresy" had gripped "the different Ecclesiastical bodies throughout the land." It was difficult for Oberlin graduates to "get access to the churches belonging to the different presbyteries and associations of the country." Finney managed to secure an invitation from the First Congregational Church of Detroit, the pastor of which, Henry L. Hammond, was from Oberlin, but even here Finney encountered a hornet's nest. In the *Memoirs* he supplies examples of how internal conflict brought revivals to a standstill. "I never in any meeting in my life saw so manifest a quenching of the Holy Spirit's influences as was manifest" at Pontiac, for example. Overt opposition to Finney also developed when Hammond's Presbyterian counterpart in Detroit, George Duffield, organized his denomination against the evangelist. Duffield had himself been tried for heresy in 1833 for his New School views, and in 1837 he succeeded Finney as copastor (with Jacob Helffenstein) of Broadway Tabernacle, but he had since turned against him. Duffield not only objected vehemently to Oberlin perfectionism but had himself adopted — and become a vocal early Presbyterian proponent of — a distinctly premillennialist theology. As Finney put it, in Michigan he "arrayed himself strongly against my preaching." Finney believed that Duffield's "influence no doubt greatly circumscribed the work there that winter." In 1847 Duffield formally censured Finney's theology in a statement adopted by the Detroit presbytery and the Synod of Michigan, published as *A Warning against Error*.

Charles Hodge, the leading Old School Presbyterian theologian at Princeton Seminary, took Finney to task in a lengthy review of his 1846 volume published in *The Biblical Repertory and Princeton Review* in April 1847. It appears from the fact that

Hodge simply repeated his criticisms with no revisions in later publications that he never read Finney's published rebuttal of the charges or Finney's final volume, about half of which had to do with sanctification and holiness. But it is scarcely likely that reading them would have persuaded Hodge to modify his views of Finney in any event, for his Westminster Confession–based Calvinism was fully at odds with Finney's more progressive theology. Hodge fundamentally disagreed with Finney and with his Yale Divinity School counterpart Nathaniel W. Taylor concerning original sin, freedom of the will, and the human ability to choose to obey God's will. If virtue comes down to nothing more than godly intentions, Hodge argued, Finney must be lumped with the Jesuits. Hodge charged Finney, in essence, with promoting humanism — replacing the work of Christ with human work and deifying the human will. Hodge accused Finney (as J. Gresham Machen would accuse theological liberals two generations later) of abandoning Christianity for something new. By turning Calvinism on its head, he wrote, Finney changed "the whole nature of religion."

Finney answered Hodge in the August 1847 issue of Oberlin's short-lived scholarly journal *The Oberlin Quarterly Review* and followed with a reply to Duffield's *Warning against Error* in the May 1848 issue. He presented a point-by-point defense of his own orthodoxy, insisting that he had not abandoned the sovereignty of God or the centrality of the work of Christ. He added this parting shot at Duffield: "All I need to say in reply to such a production is, that if he has enlightened anyone by what he has written, I shall be happy to know it."

Charles Finney had things other than theological debate on his mind after handing the last chapters of his *Systematic Theology* over to the Oberlin publisher in the summer of 1847. Oberlin Collegiate Institute was in the depths of a financial crisis, and professors' salaries were not being paid. Dissatisfaction with Asa Mahan's presidency had begun to build. Lewis Tappan wrote, "The devil is at Oberlin sure enough." Finney and other faculty members had threatened to resign. Helen's husband, Professor William Cochran, did resign and then suddenly died in August, at the age of thirty-three. They had been married only a little more than a year, and Helen, only nineteen, was expecting a child. Finney wrote in *The Oberlin Evangelist,* "The first intelligence we had of his death was the return of our dear, stricken daughter Helen with the corpse of her departed husband for interment. In the weak state of my wife, this was a severe shock to her as well as to myself." Within days Finney had to prepare himself for graduation exercises. Following months of overexertion, he suffered physical collapse after delivering the commencement address. "I was taken with the typhus fever," he wrote in his *Memoirs,* and, bedridden for eight weeks, "came very, very near the gates of the grave." The Finneys' sons Charles and Norton and a young woman boarding in their home also became sick. Lydia attempted to care for the family, but before the end of September, Finney wrote, "my precious wife was failing of consumption." In addition to grieving for her husband, Helen shouldered responsibility for her three-year-old sister Delia while her parents and brothers were ill. It was an overwhelmingly dreadful period.

Lydia Finney lay near death as autumn turned to winter. In preparation for her passage to the next life, she had spoken with each of the children, bestowing upon them her last maternal and spiritual admonitions. Charles Finney had perhaps thought that he would be prepared for losing his "beloved wife," as he always called her, for he had often placed her on God's altar in his devotions, most especially during the spiritual ordeal in Boston that led to his renewed baptism in the Holy Spirit. At that time, when he found himself "exclaiming, 'Wonderful!' 'Wonderful!' 'Wonderful!'" he felt that his "religious buoyancy" and "steadiness of faith" would see him through any trial. Moreover, Lydia had not been well for some years, and, although she was only forty-three, no one expected her to enjoy a long life. Her pregnancy and delivery of Delia at age forty took its toll. Throughout the fall of 1847, Finney sensed that her end was near. She died on December 17, 1847, "in a heavenly frame of mind."

Charles experienced Lydia's death as "a great affliction." It was not that he rebuked God or felt "the least resistance to the will of God." But as he released her, he recalled in his *Memoirs*, "it was to me a great sorrow." Nevertheless, amid this darkness the Spirit of God intervened once more in Charles Finney's life. "The night after she died I was lying in my lonely bed," with her body laid out in its casket on the first floor, "and some Christian friends were sitting up in the parlor and watching out the night." He slept fitfully and suddenly awakened as "the thought of my bereavement flashed over my mind with such power! My wife was gone! I should never hear her speak again, nor see her face! Her children were motherless! What should I do? My brain seemed to reel, as if my mind would swing from its pivot." Finney sprung from his bed and cried out, "I shall be deranged if I cannot rest in God!" Soon, through prayer, the Spirit of the Lord descended and "calmed my mind for that night." In the days following, however, he confessed, "at times seasons of sorrow would come over me that were almost overwhelming."

Charles Finney could not work. Not fully recovered from his own illness, and with his strength sapped by grief, he wrote in his *Memoirs*, "I stayed at home that winter, and did not perform much ministerial labor here or elsewhere." He published a lovely eulogy for Lydia in the January 5, 1848, *Oberlin Evangelist*, in which he recalled how she had "accompanied me in my labors as an evangelist" and "participated in my labors . . . through many of the most searching and powerful revivals of religion." He revealed pride in her work at Oberlin "in lecturing to the classes of young ladies as they have passed through this Institution." He used the language of partnership in describing her deep spirituality "in view of the great success God was pleased to give us in our labors." At Oberlin, he wrote, "our eyes were opened . . . more distinctly *to the way of life of faith,* and we began to preach *Christ* as a *present sanctification.*"

Finney deeply appreciated her management of the family, which included "frequent prayer meetings with her children." He rejoiced that throughout her illness "she often said, 'My soul enjoys perfect peace.'" Now, Finney wrote, grieving over the loss of "my precious help-meet . . . my sensibility bleeds at every pore," and he asked for the prayers of his friends.

Condolence letters began to arrive daily. Finney's grief finally abated when one day he was "communing with God upon the subject." God seemed to speak to him directly, saying, "You loved your wife?" Finney replied, "Yes." The Lord challenged him then, "Well, did you love her for her own sake, or for your sake? Did you love her, or yourself? If you loved her for her own sake, why do you sorrow that she is with me? Should not her happiness with me make you rejoice instead of mourn, if you loved her for her own sake?" Finney reflected that God was telling him that loving his wife for her own sake meant loving her for God's own sake. The Lord thus preached to the grieving pastor a Charles G. Finney sermon on disinterested benevolence, and the message hit its mark. Finney reported experiencing once more the blessing of God's gracious love. "The feelings that came over me . . . produced an instantaneous change in the whole state of my mind in regard to the loss of my wife."

Still, Finney's strength returned only very slowly, and he admitted hindering his recovery by resuming some teaching and preaching too soon. He prepared a collection of his sermons on entire sanctification for the press, and Oberlin publisher James M. Fitch came out with *Guide to the Savior; or, Conditions of Attaining to and Abiding in Entire Holiness of Heart and Life* in that year of 1848. He was beginning to think of the future, too. He may have begun considering the possibility of remarriage as early as the summer following Lydia's death. Elizabeth Atkinson of Rochester, whose husband had died in 1843, came to mind as an ideal candidate. A committed, prominent, and financially well-off evangelical, she was a longtime supporter of Finney's preaching and herself operated a female academy. She would not only be a good wife and devoted stepmother but would also be useful as a leader in Oberlin's female department. The story of the courtship of Charles and Elizabeth is unknown — no letters between them are preserved — but the relationship developed quickly. On November 13, 1848, the couple was married by Oberlin president Asa Mahan in Akron, Ohio. Elizabeth brought another daughter, about Julia's age, into the Finney family.

Charles Finney and his new wife remained at Oberlin during the winter of 1848-1849. They wanted to be available to support Helen, who gave birth to a baby in March 1848, and Elizabeth wanted to establish herself in her new home and community. After several years with the shades drawn and the rooms hushed with illness, the Finney home was once again alive with activity. Willard Sears, Finney's Boston patron, wrote, "I rejoice with you in your new family relations, and hope they may long be continued."

The evangelist had not paid much direct attention to the sins of the nation for several years. The presidential elections of 1844 and 1848 gave him little reason to hope that Christians were uniting effectively for political change. Both major parties wooed Protestant believers. Democrats paraded the religious family background of James K. Polk while the Whig party chose "the Christian Statesman" Theodore Frelinghuysen as Henry Clay's running mate. Many Oberliners shunned these choices and rallied to the Free Soil party's cause. Charles G. Finney, meanwhile, attempted to communicate the power of the second blessing, with mixed results at best. He devoted his energy to publishing two volumes of his *Systematic Theology*, and he did his best to keep up his work as pastor and professor while his health failed and his wife suffered her final illness. In 1849, his personal life reassembled with his remarriage, he found that the invitations he had been receiving from across the Atlantic Ocean were beginning to sound increasingly attractive.

9 Whitefield Redivivus

However integral evangelicalism was to the culture of the United States, and whatever distinctively American traits it had acquired by the antebellum period, it remained in a significant sense an international phenomenon. During the awakenings of the eighteenth century, transatlantic revivalism was conducted by such individuals as John Wesley, Nikolaus Ludwig von Zinzendorf, and, especially, "the grand itinerant" George Whitefield, who made seven trips to America and died in Massachusetts. Most American evangelicals regarded members of British denominations independent of the Church of England as their spiritual cousins. These included dissenting Congregationalist and Baptist churches, which had refused to be absorbed into the Church of England after the restoration of the monarchy in 1660, and the Methodist fellowship, which had gained popularity in the eighteenth century. Barred from most opportunities for higher education and public service by the Anglican establishment, members of these churches founded their own system of schools, academies, and philanthropic institutions. By the Victorian era, the number of these heirs of the Puritans and of the eighteenth-century evangelical awakening rivaled the number of members of the Church of England regularly attending worship nationwide. American evangelicalism in the time of Finney was still a piece of a larger whole that included this popular Protestantism of Great Britain and the Continent. The influence of his books among believers across the Atlantic Ocean served to remind Charles Finney of this fact.

Ten clerics calling themselves "Ministers of the Congregational Denomination in North Wales" wrote Charles Finney a letter of appreciation dated February 27, 1840. The Annual Assembly of Independent Ministers in three counties of South Wales followed suit on July 13, 1840. *Lectures on Revivals of Religion* in its Welsh translation, they wrote, "under the blessing of God, has been the means of rousing the dormant energy of our churches." They believed the recent awakening in their country, commonly referred to as "Finney's Revival," could be "attributed in great measure to the reading of your works." They informed Finney that his " 'Sermons on Important Subjects' is also in the course of translation and will shortly issue from the press." From time to time, the evangelist received similar expressions of gratitude and warm invitations from the British Isles. Other American evangelists and pastors were making preaching tours of England, financial support for Oberlin had been forthcoming, and President Asa Mahan was planning a brief trip.

Finney was keenly aware that his works were reaching a much larger market in Britain than in the United States. This provided him with some comfort, for his first American publisher, John S. Taylor, had gone bankrupt by 1840, and, according to Finney's financial agent in New York, "never expected to be able to pay [him] anything more." While English publishers were coming out with huge printing runs of *Lectures on Revivals* and his other works, Taylor "persist[ed] in saying that he printed only 2000 copies of 'Sermons on Important Subjects' — that the first, second, and third edition was inserted [on the title page] as a 'trick of the trade' to induce the public to believe that they sold well." Throughout the 1840s, Charles Finney's influence in the United States had definitely been circumscribed by his endorsement of the doctrine of Christian holiness and by Oberlin's reputation as a radical abolitionist community. In 1849, England offered an attractive opportunity — and something of a refuge — for the evangelist.

Elizabeth Atkins Finney, an ambitious and energetic woman who wanted the best for her new husband, encouraged Charles to plan a British tour. Capping a flurry of correspondence, less than two months after their November 1848 wedding a pastor wrote, "I am rejoiced to hear of your visit to England" and offered a preaching engagement. Then a February 13, 1849, letter arrived from Potto Brown at Houghton, a village near Huntingdon and St. Ives about sixty miles north of London. Brown was an important Nonconformist lay leader and philanthropist. The fact that his wealth derived from substantial flour-milling enterprises provided a point of contact between him and Charles and Elizabeth Finney in addition to their shared evangelical faith. Potto Brown appeared to be the English counterpart of the evangelical mill owners in Rochester, which had included Elizabeth's first husband, and the philanthropic businessmen of New York City. The Browns and the Finneys would become close friends. On behalf of both Congregational and Baptist missionary societies, he expressed the hope that a Finney-led revival would be "a great national mercy" and that "God who has greatly blessed you in America may make you as extensive a blessing in England." Potto Brown suggested to Finney that November would be the best time to begin evangelistic work and offered to organize his preaching schedule.

On October 20, 1849, Charles and Elizabeth Finney departed by steamer from New York. They left twenty-one-year-old Helen, whose son William had been born in March 1848, to supervise the house and care for five-year-old Delia. Finney's son Charles, then a nineteen-year-old Oberlin student with a life of his own, would not have been much help. Willard Sears in Boston promised he would see to the training of Finney's other son, Norton, now seventeen, "with an Architect, or an Engineer, or some place to which his class of talent would be adapted" during Finney's absence. Julia, who was twelve, and her stepsister, Angelina, accompanied their parents to New York City, where they were going to live in Brooklyn with "Uncle Hobart" and "Aunt Sarah" Ford, Elizabeth's brother and sister-in-law. (Before departing for England, Finney preached at Henry Ward Beecher's church in Brooklyn.) Everyone was taken care of. What the Finneys did not know was that Helen had plans of her own. She and J. Dolson Cox, who came to Oberlin as a preministry student in 1846 after being converted during Finney's most recent campaign in New York City, had been courting. They would marry — against the faculty's rules on student life — two months after her father and stepmother left Oberlin. Furthermore, Dolson was not altogether happy with the demanding piety at Oberlin and was telling people that he planned to quit school and go home to New York to study law. Charles and Elizabeth received this news not long after they arrived in England.

After what Elizabeth described in a letter to her sister as a "tempestuous voyage," the Finneys received a "cordial welcome" in "our Fatherland." Potto Brown's pastor, the Rev. James Harcourt, met the Finneys at Southampton and escorted them to Houghton. Finney was impressed with Harcourt, an "open-communion Baptist" whom Brown had hand-picked to preach at the Independent (Congregational) chapel he sponsored in the village. Brown had grown up a Quaker but as an adult became a zealous evangelical who "was entirely catholic in his views." He was a member of the outreach-minded Independent congregation at St. Ives, a few miles away, which was engaged in operating schools, Sunday schools, and mission chapels in the surrounding villages. Harcourt, "a rousing preacher, and an earnest laborer for souls," as Finney described him in the *Memoirs*, was successful at reaching "the poorer and

231

lower classes" but could not convert "the class of people that Mr. Brown had more particularly on his own heart." The inspiration for calling Finney derived from his ability, so evident in all they had read by him and about him, to speak to the middle class of business and professional people. Brown was especially concerned for the salvation of the Goodman family, the grown children of his deceased business partner.

Charles and Elizabeth Finney moved into the bustling home of Potto and Mary Brown, where friends were invited to dine with the evangelist "nearly every meal." After resting for several days, Finney began to preach on November 11. Elizabeth wrote, "His first text was, 'Thou shalt not tempt the Lord thy God.' It was a fearfully searching sermon." As Finney recalled in the *Memoirs*, "a revival immediately commenced," and among the converts were members of the Goodman family and other business associates of Potto Brown. The chapel, with a seating capacity of four hundred, was inadequate to hold the crowds, and Brown erected a tent that could hold perhaps three times that number. After a week of preaching, Finney called the anxious forward, and they came in large numbers so that, Elizabeth wrote, "a large vestry room . . . could not hold them." Elizabeth Finney, who herself proved to be an extraordinarily effective evangelistic worker in England, immediately began organizing women's prayer meetings in the village. Charles Finney wrote Julia and Angelina, "Your dear mother has been greatly useful at Houghton."

Charles and Elizabeth made two excursions to London during their three-week sojourn at Houghton, to preach at a Baptist chapel and to enjoy some sightseeing. "This country is a world of novelties to us," he wrote the girls. "We spent a day . . . riding about London to visit its wonders." While Asa Mahan was in London, he encouraged some of his patrons there to schedule Finney for their pulpits. Meanwhile, Finney was receiving invitations from many other Congregational and General Baptist leaders, the most promising of which came from the Rev. Charles Hill Roe, a well-known Baptist pastor in

Birmingham. In early December the Finneys traveled west to that large industrial city, where the evangelist undertook his customarily rigorous schedule of preaching twice on Sundays and three or four times on weekdays at Heanage Street Chapel.

C. H. Roe had alerted Finney in letters that he was trying to gain the support of his Congregationalist colleague in Birmingham, John Angell James, pastor of the huge Carr's Lane Church and one of the most influential dissenting clergymen in England. James was an early supporter of Finney and wrote a preface to the English edition of *Lectures on Revivals*. Later, persuaded by Finney's American critics that his revivals were in reality ineffectual and his theology heterodox, he had retracted his endorsement. Elizabeth alluded to the situation in her Christmas Day letter from Birmingham, in which she wrote, "We find there has been a great effort on the part of some of our American ministers to prejudice the minds of the ministers over here against revivals, saying all the pretended revivals in America have been a failure, and things are only the worse there for what has been done." James was eager to find out the truth about Charles G. Finney. He hosted a clergy breakfast at which he and his Congregationalist colleagues could inspect Finney's manner and his views on how to revive their lukewarm congregations. According to the *Memoirs,* by the end of the discussion there was general agreement to schedule Finney, as soon as he completed his commitment to Roe's congregation, "alternately in the different Independent churches, preaching around in a circle among them." James was still not convinced of Finney's soundness, however, and he and Finney carried on a lively correspondence on the matter. Reports were coming in from other pastors that Mahan and Finney made an "unfavorable impression" when they appeared to preach that "faith was *not* the gift of God." George Duffield's scathing review of Finney's theology was being reprinted in English periodicals.

Finney described in his *Memoirs* how he challenged James, "You hear my preaching every night, and whenever I preach. . . .

Have you heard me preach anything that is not Gospel?" James replied, "No, not anything at all." Finney handed him his two-volume *Systematic Theology*, saying, "I want you to take it and read it" and come back with any points of disagreement. James involved a prominent pastor-theologian, Dr. George Redford of Worcester, in the discussions as well, and the two men began to read Finney's volumes. They sat down with Finney and went through the doctrinal statement of the Congregational Union with him. According to Finney, Redford concluded that he had "his own way of stating theological propositions; but I cannot see that he differs, on any essential point from us." For his part, Finney "was satisfied there was a substantial agreement between us." The discussions continued, however, as James still pressed Finney to modify the way he expressed his views on original sin, freedom of the will, and divine sovereignty. Redford invited Finney to preach at his church in Worcester and envisioned an English edition of the *Systematic Theology* — if Finney would make some revisions.

Elizabeth Finney wrote to her sister on April 22, 1850, with a detailed summary of their activities. "After preaching around for four or five weeks Mr. Finney's labors were confined to Ebenezer Chapel, the second largest in Birmingham. The house [was] full on week evenings, and so crowded on Sunday evenings that hundreds went away for want of room. The inquiries were so numerous that a school room which would hold five hundred would be filled." Even allowing for slight exaggeration, it was an impressive effort. Finney received "a very gratifying letter" from George Redford expressing approval of his theology and urging his visit to Worcester, but the evangelist undertook a new cycle among the Birmingham churches until finally "he found his strength exhausted and left Birmingham unexpectedly." Finney resisted further invitations, insisting, "I must rest." He went to Worcester for that purpose in the middle of March, intending to stay with "an old friend and spiritual child" from New York City who now lived there. Finney took with him copies of his replies to George

Charles Finney and his second wife, Elizabeth, sat for this daguerrotype portrait in 1850, during their first sojourn in England. Elizabeth was more than just a helpmate; she became a partner, organizing women's prayer groups, counseling both men and women, and teaching large groups.
Photo courtesy of the Oberlin College Archives

Duffield's and Charles Hodge's reviews of his *Systematic Theology*. Redford found these to be convincing and useful additions to the books themselves. Both he and leaders of a Baptist congregation encouraged Finney to preach in Worcester after he had rested for a few days.

Although Finney was planning to return to America in April, Redford insisted that he stay at least long enough to attend the annual meeting of the Congregational Union with him in London in early May. Redford wanted to enlist the evangelist in a concerted effort "to revive religion throughout the Kingdom." Finney rededicated himself to preaching in England. Elizabeth reported that at Worcester, although her husband was greatly fatigued, when he appeared in the pulpit "the house was crowded aisles and every place . . . and every doorway was filled." Charles Finney "preached two hours — all was solemnly still" — and "it was manifested that God was there with great power." Some businessmen, noticing that none of the dissenting chapels was large enough for the crowds the evangelist was drawing, proposed constructing a kind of "movable tabernacle" that could be taken down and transported by railroad. Finney dismissed the idea as impractical, but he must have been flattered. In a postscript to his wife's letter, Finney added a note regarding Elizabeth's contribution to the work — of which, he wrote, "she has said nothing." Whatever part convenience, utility, and mutual respect may have played in bringing the couple together, it is obvious that Finney genuinely loved his second wife. As Elizabeth entered "a wonderful field of usefulness" in England, she became "truly a help meet for me," he wrote. "Her sweet temper, her engaging manner, her ladylike address and polished manners . . . her great faith . . . her ability as a lecturer to the females and as a conducter of female prayer meeting" all helped to "forward this work." In her next letter, Elizabeth wrote, "My husband rejoices that I can make myself . . . so useful as not to be considered a mere apendage for his comfort." And in the summer she displayed evident pride, writing, "Many say, Mrs.

Finney, *your mission* to England is *almost,* if not *quite* as important as that of your husband's. . . . I know God can work
without *me,* but I love the work." She organized women's
prayer groups, afternoon "mothers' meetings," and special
"tea meetings." In her talks she combined homey wisdom and
spiritual advice with conversion preaching, the call to
benevolent service, and a plea for the emancipation of women.
When men began attending Elizabeth's female prayer meetings
to hear her speak, her husband was pleased and encouraged
her to continue. Charles Finney thanked God and proclaimed
that it was "Providence that made her my wife." And Elizabeth
constantly referred to Charles in her letters as "my precious
husband." Charles and Elizabeth Finney enjoyed being in England together.

Finney's participation in the meeting of the Congregational Union was enormously rewarding. Redford delivered
one of the major addresses, in which he reported on the recent
revival in Worcester and highlighted, in Elizabeth's words,
Finney's "honesty and *orthodoxy*" and "the success attending
his preaching." Finney spoke at an afternoon session, making
an impression favorable enough to generate a flood of preaching invitations. John Campbell, a significant Congregational
pastor in London and editor of *The British Banner,* had helped
prepare for Finney's appearance on this national platform by
publishing favorable articles about his work in Houghton,
Birmingham, and Worcester. In a series of letters exchanged
with the evangelist, Campbell also expressed his eagerness to
attract Charles Finney to his two churches for a prolonged
London engagement. He suggested that September, not summer, was the best time to begin work in the capital. Finney
wrote a postscript to his wife's April 22 letter that revealed their
thinking: "My purpose is to remain at London, *at this visit*" —
that is, for the meeting of the Congregational Union — "only
a short time and then retire to some place and get a little rest,
God willing, and return to London early in the fall for more
protracted labors." He added that it was "altogether uncertain

when we shall return to America. The Lord will take care of all. . . . The breath of the Spirit is reviving dry bones."

Finney's decision to remain in England came as bad news at Oberlin. John Morgan wrote on January 7, 1850, to inform Finney that the faculty had met and "agreed to draw up and subscribe a paper expressing to Brother Mahan the opinion that the interests of the Institution would be promoted by his resignation." Resentment had been growing for years. Not only did Mahan's version of "Oberlin Perfectionism" have a far more Wesleyan cast than that of the others, but the president's heavy-handed administrative style alienated almost everyone. Most recently, at the very time Finney was ill and Lydia was dying, Mahan had taken sides in a disciplinary case at the Oberlin church in such a way that the church teetered on the verge of schism. Even Finney's long friendship with Mahan soured on that occasion. Morgan suggested that Finney could help the school and avoid embarrassment on all sides by intervening with Mahan in England. "If Brother Mahan should before he leaves England conclude to resign and express to you that determination," the faculty would not feel compelled to issue its demand. Morgan asked his colleague to "tell him your whole heart and what you know of the views of others" and warned him not to "allow him to suppose that you do not concur with the rest of the Faculty in the expediency of his resignation." Further, Morgan stated, Finney was desperately needed at Oberlin. If he would not return in the spring, there was a danger that the "theological department shall become extinct."

Asa Mahan in England also wrote several times to Finney in January, and he, too, voiced the "great concern among the theological students about your return to them." If Finney were to return soon, he wrote, "the theological department will not go down." Whatever Finney may have communicated to Mahan by return mail, it is clear from subsequent correspondence that he never discussed resignation with the embattled president. Indeed, that was precisely the kind of conflict Finney had crossed the Atlantic to avoid. When Finney confided in

Potto Brown that he was needed back at Oberlin, his English friend continued to urge him to stay. If England offered "an open door of usefulness," Oberlin would be "an open grave to swallow you up." Finney did write John Morgan expressing his criticisms of Mahan. Morgan wrote back, "I have not thought it best to read it to Brother Mahan, nor was I sure that you meant I should." Meanwhile, Lewis Tappan had met Mahan in New York on his arrival back in the United States and, after discussing the situation at Oberlin, "advised him to resign." Joab Seely, an Oberlin fund-raising agent, in another effort to save face for Mahan, had somehow arranged for a prestigious church in Newark to call him as pastor. Mahan waffled for a bit but then renewed his resolve to fight for his position. Students got up petitions for and against, and suddenly the campus was divided as never before. Morgan wrote, "I do not think he will leave unless the Trustees tell him he must. What the Faculty will ultimately do I do not know."

The Oberlin faculty — "with much trembling," as John Morgan said in a letter to Finney — presented their complaint against Asa Mahan to the trustees at the board's April 18, 1850, meeting. According to the minutes of the meeting, the professors stated that the president's "self-esteem has amounted to self-conceit," that he denigrated others while boasting of his own accomplishments, that he misrepresented facts in arguments, that he used "language unbecoming to a Christian minister and the president of a religious institution," that he represented the institution as holding views (presumably on perfectionism) peculiar to himself, and that he disturbed the harmony of the Oberlin church. Mahan supporters protested that the charges were vague and unsubstantiated, but Morgan and the faculty explained that they simply could no longer work with Mahan. A "very full and free conversation and discussion" took place over the course of an entire day, but no resolution was achieved. The board did vote to change the name of the school to Oberlin College, however, having received prior approval from the state legislature to do so.

John Morgan wrote Finney on May 7 to say that the Oberlin faculty had agreed that "your aid in this enterprise is indispensable." Not only were students clamoring for his return to the classroom, but, Morgan candidly explained, the college desperately needed "your rich friends" and "their funds." The junior theology class had dwindled to five or six students, but if Finney would return there would be "from 12 to 14." He warned again, "If you leave things in the wind, I fear the theology department will vanish." Meanwhile, Morgan, who had been carrying on alone as pastor of the church, was tired. "If you conclude to remain over till next spring," he said, "I must resign and give them a chance to make another selection." Morgan made it clear too that he had to know what Finney was planning so he could make his own career decisions. He concluded affectionately, "All the faculty long to see your face once more and to hear your voice."

In June Finney heard from another Oberlin friend that the situation with Mahan was much improved and "the whole community seemed relieved." Concerning Finney's return, however, no one knew quite what to think; "the anxiety is wide and intense." Still another correspondent, in July, confirmed that "Brother Morgan is nearly worn out with his work and quite discouraged." He also reported that Mahan's good behavior had not lasted and he was now talking of resigning to take a position in Cleveland as president of a newly proposed "National University." Finney's son Charles wrote that Mahan's announcement "has made quite a stir here," and in a letter that summer Dolson Cox also reflected on the uncertainty of whether Mahan would stay or leave. Meanwhile, the Oberlin congregation had voted that Asa Mahan should join John Morgan as a copastor of the church. Dolson wrote that the church was split, locked in "a quarrel as to which party shall have the meeting house." As the College's annual meeting approached, the trustees felt they had to "do something within a fortnight" about Mahan's presidency. "All is gloomy — gloomy!" Cox wrote. "Considering all things I am glad you have determined to stay till spring."

"The President sent in his resignation" to the trustees at their board meeting August 26, 1850, John Keep informed Charles Finney in an excited letter. Mahan cited his call to the presidency of "a National University now in contemplation" as the reason, and, according to the minutes, "after mature deliberation and a season of prayer it was Resolved that said resignation be accepted." The faculty was discussing who would pick up Mahan's courses and wondered if Finney would teach moral philosophy. Now more than ever, the future of Oberlin was in his hands. If Finney had been present, he would easily have been elected president, Keep insisted. "But you are not here."

Charles Finney received disquieting family news from Oberlin during the summer of 1850 as well. His oldest son, Charles, then twenty, confided in a July 9 letter that he was thinking of transferring to Yale. One of the professors refused to treat him as an adult, and he felt "it would lower my self-respect" to continue under him. He also confessed that he was often "lonesome and would like to have someone whom I could love with all my heart and who would love me." All in all, he wrote, "I do not care to stay here another year." Charles reported that Norton, by contrast, now staying with the Braytons in Oneida County, had written and "wants to come home very much, and I told him to come and make a visit. . . . Did I do right?" Charles Finney was not personally available to his anguished son on the brink of adulthood.

Then came a letter from Helen dated July 31 conveying the news that she had had a baby the first week in July. She stated that "Dolson wrote you immediately after the birth of our babe, stating the circumstances, etc.," but if the letter arrived, it is not among the extant papers. Dolson did add a postscript to Helen's letter in which he apologized, "We should have mailed our letters long ago, but thought every mail would bring us news from you and have thus delayed." Helen wrote, "Our feelings have of course been varied and at times most unpleasant when thinking of this unexpected development of our married life." The baby was born nine months after Charles and Elizabeth had left Helen in charge of the house and only seven months after she and Dolson were married. She wrote that for the most part "we have been treated very kindly so far and hope for the best." But with "so much party feeling in town" — the church and community were torn over the issue of Asa Mahan's leadership — "it necessarily produces some gossip, and we have been told that there is a good deal being said." Helen insisted that she and Dolson would "spend no time or breath in contradicting stories or running after suspicions, but go right on our way with quiet dignity, trusting in the Lord to defend our reputation." By August 19, when Helen and Dolson wrote again, their daughter was still unnamed.

The good news was that Dolson was planning to continue his theological studies at Oberlin. In the August 19 letter, he affirmed Finney's intention to remain in England so his reputation would be "fixed, not merely as a preacher, but as a theologian." If the English edition of his *Systematic Theology* was well received and its "orthodoxy fully admitted in an authoritative manner," Dolson prophesied, "the reflex influence upon the Church of this country will be immense." He assured his father-in-law that if he returned to teach, "I shall endeavor to remain and have your instruction." And he was urging his brother-in-law Charles not to drop out on the grounds that his presence at the school had symbolic importance. J. Dolson Cox may have been the only person at Oberlin who was not eager for the professor to come home. Charles Finney was in accord with Dolson on that one matter at least; he would remain in England for the time being.

Finney began preaching for John Campbell in London on May 12, 1850, the first Sunday after the meeting of the Congregational Union, and continued there except for a break in the fall until April 1851. The two London churches served by Campbell — the Tabernacle in Moorfields, Finsbury, and Tottenham Court Road Chapel — had both been built for the greatest evangelist of the eighteenth century, George Whitefield. As Finney wrote in his *Memoirs*, Campbell "lived in the house in which Whitfield resided, which was the parsonage; and used the same library, I believe, that Whitfield had used. Whitfield's portrait hung up in his study in the Tabernacle. The savor of his name was still there." Ironically, Whitefield's successor was not a preacher. He served as pastor and administrator of the congregations and as editor of *The British Banner* and several other religious periodicals, and he engaged "the most popular ministers that could be employed, to preach to his people." For almost a year, that would be Charles G. Finney.

George Whitefield's name still had "savor" in the United States as well. His enormous abilities as "the grand itinerant" were inflated even more by legend. His seven American visits, amplified to thirteen by John Campbell in the *British Banner* article announcing Finney's preaching schedule at the Tabernacle, ballooned to sixteen in Elizabeth Finney's letter to her sister in Rochester, New York. As a broadly evangelical Anglican who would preach from any pulpit open to him and, in order to reach the entire community, in the fields and public squares of the cities, Whitefield was a fitting symbol of the noncreedal revivalism that characterized much of the religion of the early Republic. Whitefield's name was also emblematic of the dramatic, extemporaneous style of preaching — culminating in the call for repentance and faith in Christ — that marked Methodist, Baptist, and evangelical Presbyterian-Congregational evangelistic services. Whitefield's persona had entered the popular religious culture. An Ohio woman who was a friend of Oberlin in 1846 wrote the Finneys with her views on female education and to share family news. She had named her baby after the evangelist who was famous for his ability to be heard by an outdoor crowd of thirty thousand people, and sure enough, "George Whitfield weighs twenty pounds and although he is but six months old sits on the carpet and screams so loud that no one can think." Elizabeth Finney wrote to Julia and Angelina with a sense of awe after moving into "Tabernacle House" in London, "I am pleasantly situated

in the family of Dr. Campbell in the very house where good
Mr. Whitfield used to live."

From the earliest days of his ministry, Charles Finney and
his "new measures" revival colleagues had drawn connections
between the leaders of the transatlantic Great Awakening of
the 1740s and themselves. The evangelists of the 1820s and
1830s were conscious of following in the footsteps of Jonathan
Edwards and George Whitefield and invoked their names often
in their letters. Every one of the numerous American pastors
and evangelists who made preaching tours of England no
doubt cherished the feeling of mirroring Whitefield's campaigns in the colonies. With Finney the comparison was made
explicitly and often. Joab Seely wrote from Auburn, New York,
"We pray that God may do by you for England what he did
for America by Whitefield." John Campbell told the American
evangelist that "it is my honour to succeed George Whitefield,
who, had he been on earth . . . would have had you in his
pulpits." Campbell went on with his flattery, "You are aware
that it pleased God, now a century ago, through the instrumentality of an Englishman to bless America; who can tell but it
may please him, by means of an American, to bless England?"
Campbell trumpeted the comparison publicly in the *British
Banner* articles announcing Finney's meetings on Sundays and
weekday evenings. "It is meet that Mr. Finney should commence his labours in this Metropolis in an edifice reared by
George Whitefield, the most eminent Evangelist that England
ever produced."

Whitefield's Tabernacle was a square, hulking, un-
churchly edifice that could hold more than three thousand
people on the main floor and in its immense gallery. Finney
wanted to replicate in London what he had achieved in some
American cities. As he stated in the *Memoirs*, "I put in in earnest
for a revival. . . . I preached a course of sermons designed to
convict the people of sin as deeply and as universally as
possible." Preaching on a grueling weekly schedule similar to
ones he had so often adopted before — twice on Sunday, and

Whitefield's Tabernacle in Moorfields, London, was the site of Charles Finney's preaching fom May 1850 to April 1851. The huge stone chapel was built as headquarters for the ministry of the great Anglican evangelist George Whitefield in 1741, after his first visit to the American colonies. Reproduction courtesy of the British Library every evening from Tuesday through Friday, with a "general prayer meeting" on Monday evening and a session for "inquirers and converts" in his study on Saturday evenings — Finney began to see results. "Always on Sabbath and Sabbath evenings the house was crowded to its utmost capacity," and attendance was excellent at the weekday services as well. "The Word was taking great effect." When Finney determined that it was time for an inquiry meeting, however, he found that Campbell did not fully comprehend what he intended. On every other Sunday evening the service was dismissed early and the Lord's Supper was served to members in good standing who "had tickets for the Communion service." Finney proposed to conduct his inquiry meeting during Communion but in another location. Campbell, who, as Finney had learned, could adopt a "belligerent" attitude, scoffed at the evangelist's idea of using a lecture room in an auxiliary building that would hold over fifteen hundred people. When the evening arrived, after rushing through his Communion service, Campbell was astonished to find that room full to overflowing with penitent seekers "anxious for the salvation of their souls."

Finney implies in the *Memoirs* that John Campbell never really understood the nature of revivalism, but the evangelist did not do his host justice on that score. Campbell managed a special media campaign to promote Finney's meetings. As he informed Finney in a letter in November 1850, "no other man in England" had the power "to open up your way and to offer you the aids which the Press alone can bring." In addition to articles in *The British Banner* and his other periodicals, Campbell printed tens of thousands of advertising flyers and handbills and arranged for young men and women from the Tabernacle to distribute them house to house. Posters advertising Finney's meetings were put up throughout London and carried on sandwich boards through the streets. Campbell also arranged for the transcription and publication of many of Finney's sermons in a weekly magazine, *The Penny Pulpit*, and elsewhere. The effort paid off, for, as Finney noted, "the masses who were thronging there were as much unknown to [Campbell] as they were to me." When the British government conducted a census of national church attendance on Sunday, March 30, 1851, Finney's services at the Tabernacle made a very strong showing, with a capacity crowd both morning and evening. The publicity blitz, unprecedented in urban evangelism for its scope, was both reminiscent of George Whitefield's shrewd pioneering use of the media and anticipatory of some of the elaborate methods employed by modern-day mass evangelists. Finney failed to credit Campbell properly either at the time or later in the *Memoirs* for his contribution to the evangelist's success in London.

As always, Finney confronted the anxious in London with the need for an immediate decision for Christ. It was necessary to "do away [with] their idea of *waiting God's time*" for conversion. Assuming that most of those he was addressing had imbibed some religious influence from the Church of England, Finney wrote, "I tried . . . to guard them on the one hand against hyper-Calvinism, and on the other against that low Arminianism in which I supposed many of them had been educated." Struck by what he saw as "the moral desolation of that vast city," Finney focused his preaching less on the second blessing of holiness — which he knew could alienate him from some of his supporters — than on the primary human need for salvation from sin. He was thoroughly at home, and the responses along the Thames River seemed almost to echo those throughout the valleys of the St. Lawrence and the Mohawk.

At the first inquiry meeting, he recalled, "after I had laid the Gospel net thoroughly around them" and "prepared to draw it ashore," Finney was about to have them "kneel down and commit themselves entirely and forever to Christ." Suddenly a man cried out in "the greatest distress of mind, that he had sinned away his day of grace." Seeing there was "danger of an uproar," Finney hushed the crowd and "called on the people to kneel down" and "hear every word of the prayer that I was about to offer." As he prayed, "there was a great sobbing and weeping in every part of the house." Elizabeth wrote in a letter home, "I never witnessed such a scene in my life, though Mr. Finney has often done so." She said that Finney stayed for an hour after the dismissal to "talk with distressed souls" and that "even after *he left*, I was obliged to stay for some time."

The response to Finney's call for "unqualified and present surrender of all to Christ," he wrote in the *Memoirs*, increased dramatically. Soon the lecture room was too small, and he began inviting the anxious simply to stand in the congregation "while we offered them in prayer." Hundreds would stand, and "on some occasions . . . not less than two thousand people have arisen when an appeal was made." Contemporary critics observed that Finney sometimes inflated his numbers regarding the London campaign (though Henry Ward Beecher saw Finney in action and attested to their general accuracy), and his narratives of evangelistic success there at times seem unduly sanguine. Finney clearly considered the English tour of 1849-1851, and especially his revival at Whitefield's Tabernacle, one of the most satisfying campaigns of his career.

Charles Finney complained about the London air, which was "unfit for respiration," with its "smoke and dirt and the suffocating gases generated by millions of coal fires." He charged that "men in high places" showed no concern for the environment or human welfare. After several months of constant preaching in this "miserable atmosphere," both he and Elizabeth suffered from hoarse throats. At Potto Brown's insistence, and at his expense, the couple enjoyed a two-week holiday in Paris. Finney spoke in a letter to Julia of "our pleasant excursion to France," which was followed by a month's rest at Brown's home. Finney was absent from the Tabernacle from mid-September until the first of December. Although he recovered his health during the break, the hoarseness soon returned in sooty London, and the evangelist decided to bring his work in England to a close. In January 1851, he completed his final corrections for the English edition of his *Systematic Theology* and saw it published in a handsome format, complete with a fine introduction by Dr. George Redford. It was time to return to Oberlin. Asa Mahan had vacated his house and moved to Cleveland. Finney's son Charles wrote that "the President's house and ours being vacant makes the village look lonely." John Morgan had survived discouragement and fatigue and was serving as the interim president of the college. The professors signed a statement on December 10, 1850, acknowledging receipt of Finney's letter "informing us of your full intention to return in the spring." They assured Finney that "cordial feelings towards you are universal in the Faculty" and that "you are our natural head and leader." A new fund-raising program was also under way. Finney knew that his son Charles at Oberlin was feeling lonely, but he had not heard from his other son, Norton, for some months. The college, the church, and their family all needed Charles and Elizabeth Finney's attention.

Six hundred guests attended a reception for Charles Grandison and Elizabeth Finney at the Royal British Institution March 31, 1851, after which they all joined a full house at Whitefield's Tabernacle for a farewell service. Amidst sincere sharing of affection and lighthearted reminiscing, Charles and Elizabeth received gifts and good wishes from their friends. John Campbell read George Redford's laudatory introduction to Finney's *Systematic Theology* and expressed his feeling that it was "certainly a pity that a man so singularly endowed for evangelic labour should be chained down by the dull routine of College duties." When the couple boarded their ship on April 7, another "great multitude of people who had been interested in our labors, gathered upon the wharf." Finney reflected in his *Memoirs* that "I left England with great reluctance," having "become greatly interested in the people" and committed to his work there. Elizabeth had an even harder time leaving. "Tearing away as we did from such a multitude of loving hearts, completely overcame the strength of my wife," wrote Finney. "As soon as the ship was clear of the dock she retired to our state-room with a violent headache." The evangelist stayed on the deck "and watched the waving of their handkerchiefs and the holding up of their hats" until the crowd was out of sight.

In the United States, Finney remained a controversial figure. In 1850, *The Presbyterian* of Philadelphia and *The Puritan Recorder*, a Boston paper, launched new attacks on Finney's orthodoxy and spiritual integrity aimed at undermining his ministry in London. But an upstate New York friend wrote Finney before his return indicating that others among the American religious press had begun to "speak very kindly of you" and reprinted favorable extracts from British periodicals. He speculated that the evangelist could be entering a period of greater influence in his own country. "But do not infer that I am desirous that you should again be popular in America. I am not. I do not covet popularity for you, for Oberlin, or for myself." He advised Finney upon his return simply to rededicate himself to "winning souls." Meanwhile, John Keep wrote that on the national scene Oberlin's stock had risen as a result of reaction to the passage of the Fugitive Slave Law of 1850. "The diabolical legislation of Congress has greatly aroused the North and sympathy for the black man never ran so deep and broad as now." That, too, was something of an overstatement, but it may have contributed to Finney's willingness to undertake the presidency of the college.

The Finneys arrived in New York on April 26, 1851. They remained in the city long enough for him to preach two Sundays, at Broadway Tabernacle and at Henry Ward Beecher's Plymouth Church in Brooklyn, and to address the American Antislavery Society at its annual meeting. Reports of his work in England had to some extent restored Finney's reputation among mainstream evangelicals and reform activists. Upon arriving, Finney also discovered that a letter he had written to two New York papers, *The Independent* and *The Evangelist*, protesting the vitriolic attacks he had received in *The Presbyterian* and *The Puritan Recorder* during his absence, had just been published. Several letters reflecting positively on Finney's earlier revivals were also published. His earlier pattern had been largely to ignore his critics, but now he determined that he would protest more vigorously. For the first time Finney worked hard to create a positive public image of his evangelistic career.

The two and a half weeks in New York also gave the Finneys time in Brooklyn with Hobart and Sarah Ford, Elizabeth's brother and sister-in-law, who had taken care of Julia and Angelina. After another stop in Rochester to visit friends and more of Elizabeth's relatives, the family proceeded to Oberlin. There a festive reception welcomed them on May 20. Charles and Elizabeth Finney gathered around them Julia, Angelina, Charles, Norton, Helen, and Dolson. After hugs and kisses for Delia and Helen's son, Willie, they no doubt took turns holding the baby. They were ready to settle back into their home on Professor Street.

On August 26, the third day of the Oberlin College trustees' meeting that summer, Charles Finney and the rest of the faculty came in and "an interlocutory meeting" commenced. According to the minutes of the board, "the subject of filling the vacant office of the President was taken up and fully discussed." The vote was unanimous and enthusiastic. Charles G. Finney was elected president of the college and assumed the chair. The financial report was also brightly optimistic, as $80,000 had been raised toward the goal of $100,000 for the endowment. In another vote, the board named Elizabeth Finney to the Ladies' Board, which administered the female department of the college. Commencement exercises began immediately after the meeting adjourned. Charles Grandison Finney Jr. (he had dropped Beman as his middle name and assumed his father's full name) was among the graduates. The community had enjoyed its first major spiritual awakening in several years the previous summer. Now, as Charles Finney threw himself into the work of preaching on Sundays and most evenings during the week, the excitement of witnessing large numbers of conversions returned. Finney wrote in his *Memoirs*

251

that Oberlin "had a very interesting revival, especially among our Students, that lasted all summer." Three days after he was elected president, Charles G. Finney turned fifty-nine years old.

For seven years, from the fall of 1851 through the end of 1858, Finney devoted himself to his work at Oberlin as professor of theology, pastor of the church, and president of the college. He also resumed his pattern of preaching as an evangelist in various eastern cities during the winter each year. The Finneys exchanged letters regularly with English friends, sharing family and church news and always expressing the mutual hope of another visit. John Campbell, for example, wrote in November 1853, "I see from the public prints how things are proceeding at Oberlin. Truly, you have got an immense concern! . . . Blessings rest upon you, and all success attend your efforts to enlighten the world and to liberate the slave!" He paid Finney's "excellent wife" Elizabeth a high compliment: "We often think of her — talk of her — and always with respect and pleasure." Quoting St. Paul on the office of deacon, he wrote, "She earned herself amongst us 'a good degree and great boldness in the faith' [1 Tim. 3:13]. She would make a glorious Deaconess, and might do more good than all the wives of all the Bishops of the land." He went on to report, however, that "one of the Scotch Reviews" had attacked his *Systematic Theology* as heterodox and Finney as a "dangerous theologian." Potto Brown wrote that same month, regretting to say that he had "not had much co-operation of many ministers in promoting your return." Nevertheless, he insisted that another Finney campaign was precisely what England needed.

Letters sailed back and forth across the Atlantic in 1855 and 1856. An English Methodist pastor sent Finney a copy of his defense of his orthodoxy in the face of the calumny of Scottish Presbyterians. John Campbell always told how Finney's letters were "much prized" and passed from hand to hand. And Potto Brown continued to try to tip the scales in favor of another visit from his friend. Elizabeth Finney was so determined to return to England that she constantly badgered her wavering husband on the subject. Some members of the Oberlin community chided Finney for being under his wife's thumb, but she was unrelenting in her conviction that God was calling them overseas. Finally, in November 1858, the Finneys let it be known that the time had come for their second trip to England. In preparation, the evangelist gathered a number of letters of commendation from church leaders with whom he had labored since the last visit, including one from Horace Bushnell expressing gratitude for the revival under Finney's preaching in Hartford during the winter of 1852. When the couple stopped in Rochester on their way to New York in mid-December 1858, the pastors of the city gave Finney a letter of support addressed to the churches of England. It stated that any reports claiming that Finney's revivals in Rochester had been injurious to the churches were utterly false. To the contrary, William Wisner and the other pastors wrote, many of the city's leading citizens were Finney converts, and the churches had grown strong thanks to Finney's evangelism. Charles Finney was more than a little defensive, especially in light of the negative public relations campaign waged against him in the press during his first English tour.

The Finneys' ship docked at Liverpool on New Year's Day 1859. Elizabeth Finney had begun keeping a journal of their daily affairs and would record her husband's sermon texts and the results of his preaching. After spending the next day with a prominent merchant whom Finney had known in New York, they went on to Potto Brown's home in Houghton in Huntingdonshire. Their good friend, who arrived only later that evening after having missed a connection with them in Liverpool, laid out his plan that Finney commence his work with pulpit engagements in Houghton and St. Ives. "Precious revivals" quickly began in both towns, much to the consternation of the St. Ives pastor, who left town and eventually resigned in reaction to the evangelical awakening.

Invitations from many parts of the British Isles — from Methodists as well as Congregationalists and Baptists — arrived at Houghton daily. John Campbell wrote on January 5, "Is it possible? My very dear friends once more in England! Well, may you 'come in the fulness of the blessing of the gospel of Christ.'" This citation of Romans 15:29 appropriately enough referred to Paul's intended European journey to Rome via Spain. John Campbell was not in a position to promote Finney's campaign as he had a decade before, however. He had retired from Whitefield's Tabernacle in order to devote himself to the editorship of religious periodicals. The new pastor, Finney wrote, "was very much prejudiced against me, and did not invite me to preach to his people."

Finney's London contact in 1859 was James Harcourt, the former pastor at Houghton who now served the Baptist Burough Road Chapel in Southwark. The church building was large, but the congregation was deeply troubled, as Finney put it, having been "torn to pieces by most ultra and fanatical views on the subject of Temperance." The previous minister had resigned in despair over the people's "feuds on that subject," and Harcourt was attempting to rebuild the congregation. Finney wrote, "We went to work, my wife among the ladies of the Congregation; and I went to preaching, and searching them, to the utmost of my strength." For two months, from the end of February through the third week of April, Charles and Elizabeth both led daily prayer meetings, and the evangelist adopted his customarily rigorous preaching schedule. Finney focused his sermons on sin, repentance, and the urgent need for salvation. The response was overwhelming, as penitents emotionally confessed to "terrible things," many of which "had been covered up for a long time." The crowds swelled, people sat in the aisles and stood in the back, and it became common for fifty or more inquirers to come forward at the invitation. Harcourt and Finney were gratified that the revival touched "every household belonging to that congregation" in addition to seekers from the community. As Finney recalled, "His people were reconverted and cemented in love, and they learned to take hold of the work themselves."

At the same time, opponents of revivalist Christianity surrounded Finney, challenging him in print and in personal correspondence. The evangelist responded to one such critic, who had assumed that an earlier note from Finney was nothing but an attempt to "gain access to [his] pulpit." In a letter from St. Ives dated February 5, 1859, Finney assured him that invitations were "always . . . far more numerous than I could favorably respond to" and went on to defend revivalism against the charge that it damaged the Christian church by churning out large numbers of superficial believers. He admitted the method could be abused and offered his own objection to "that class" of "frothy efforts" as "counterfeit" revivals. Writing from "nearly 40 years" of experience as an evangelist and as "pastor of a church of some 1400 to 1600 members," Finney insisted that "if there be any true religion in the world, I have not the slightest doubt, it is found in its most unequivocal form as the fruits of the great revivals in America."

Finney's theology was subjected to as much scrutiny as his methods. Some English Christians thanked Finney for his "truly intelligent discourses," which, if given the opportunity, would "convince every rational mind" and make believers "weep for joy." One April 1859 correspondent had been in despair that he must abandon Christianity and "become an infidel" until he read Finney's *Systematic Theology*. "Your volume under God was the means of satisfying me as to the former and saving me from the latter alternative." This writer took note of recent attacks on Finney's orthodoxy, saying he "read with intense pain the criticisms which have appeared in *The British Standard*, on your views of Theology."

On the other side, prominent biblical scholar Samuel P. Tragelles wrote a piece for *The British Standard* criticizing Finney's doctrine of the atonement, specifically his rejection of the substitutionary theory in favor of the moral-influence theory. Then John Campbell turned against Charles Finney, as so many former friends had done in America. The perennially bellicose Campbell, who purported to have no more than skimmed the

Systematic Theology previously, in March 1851 suddenly found himself agreeing with Tragelles. Campbell made his paper into the battleground on which both sides engaged in the skirmish. He himself wrote several articles condemning Finney's deviations from traditional Calvinism, reprinted George Redford's preface to the *Systematic Theology* (which approved Finney's views), published Finney's replies to the criticisms, and encouraged readers to send in their responses for publication. Finney based his assessment of why Campbell and Tragelles "strangely misunderstood my position" on his experience with the American Presbyterian controversy back in the 1820s and early 1830s. It was because Campbell "had been educated in Scotland," he wrote, that "my New School statements of doctrine puzzled him." It was what he had said about a Princeton education many times before. Finney added in his *Memoirs* that many of Campbell's readers "impute[d] to him other motives than concern for orthodoxy," suggesting perhaps that the media wizard simply manufactured the controversy as a way to boost circulation, just as he had used his craft in 1850 to boost attendance at the Tabernacle.

Eventually, the work and the strife wore Charles Finney out. At the end of March, Potto Brown advised him to "come and stay a month at my house without preaching" and urged him to heed the "advice you give to others, you cannot constantly neglect yourself, that is, you must take care of your health." On April 21, Finney returned to Houghton with Elizabeth to recuperate. He even considered leaving England altogether and discouraged their daughter Julia from coming to join them. Elizabeth Finney wrote Julia, "You know these seasons are always seasons of great unrest to your Father. He is always sick and as he has nothing in particular to deeply interest his mind he feels the lassitude and I may say innui of one who has always lived intensely exciting scenes." Finney's mind was fully engaged a few days later when he discovered that *The Oberlin Evangelist* had reprinted one of Campbell's negative reviews of Finney's theology. Livid with rage, he wrote Julia on May 5, "If you are at Oberlin when this reaches you will you call on one of the editors of the *O. Evangelist* and ask who committed the blunder" of printing the piece and of referring to "Dr. Campbell as so great a theologian." In shaky handwriting Finney went on, "Dr. Campbell is anything but a great theologian."

Finney's health had not improved after several weeks in the Brown home, and so he and Elizabeth accepted an invitation from a physician, Dr. Michael Foster, to complete his recovery — with "no medicine," Finney stipulated — in his home in Huntingdon. Finney confided to Julia at the end of May, "My health is precarious. My spine and bowels are in a very complaining state." But the recuperation was effective, and his energy began to return. He engaged to preach at Huntingdon, first at the Baptist chapel and then at the much larger Temperance Hall. It was the town's first revival, and among the converts were the rationalist skeptic son of their host and other family members. In his *Memoirs* Finney reflected, "The revival greatly changed the religious aspect of things in that town." Testimony in local church records echoed with the gratitude of members from all the congregations. Finney also reported to Julia in an optimistic tone, "Calls for our labors are constantly multiplying" from London, Wales, and Scotland.

The Finneys returned to London at the end of June 1859 under agreement with the Free Methodist churches in the northeastern sector of the city. "All is ready for your reception," their representative Thomas Jones wrote the evangelist. Finney preached through the circuit at a different chapel every night of the week. Although he had certainly been influenced by Wesleyan theology and enthusiastic, down-to-earth Methodist preaching from the beginning of his career, he had not preached very often in Methodist churches. Finney had no difficulty adapting his invitation to anxious inquirers to their very similar altar call, but what he remembered most from those weeks was two "very striking providences" that occurred. "One Sabbath evening I had invited them 'to come forward around the altar,' as the Methodists express it," he wrote in the *Memoirs*, when he noticed a woman who was very much affected but resisted coming forward — even when Finney warned them "as I frequently did" that this "might be their last opportunity." She died the next day on a train. The very next Sunday evening the same thing happened. A man "in great distress of mind . . . refused to give his heart to God," although "the brethren remained and prayed for him." The next day "he died in an apoplectic fit." Finney always made effective use of extreme examples like these, which easily "made a great impression upon the people that attended worship there."

Even though Scotland had been the source of much criticism of Finney's theology during both British visits, Charles and Elizabeth made it their base of operation from mid-August until the end of 1859. The evangelist would have been no more welcome in the churches of the Calvinist Presbyterian Church of Scotland than in the pulpit at Princeton, New Jersey, but an independent movement called the Evangelical Union had long admired Finney's books for their progressive theology and his reputation for revivalism and social reform. James Morrison, whom Finney rightly termed "their leading theologian," had been expelled from the national church for teaching the doctrine of universal atonement. He founded the Evangelical Union and an academy in Glasgow in 1843. John Kirk of Edinburgh joined the Union a few years later, having begun as an Independent but split with the Congregational Union over the same issue and over his views on the work of the Holy Spirit. Finney became aware of the group during his 1850 visit and had corresponded at that time with Morrison on points of theological agreement and difference.

Finney preached at Kirk's substantial Brighton Street Church, which he described as "one of the largest places of worship in Edinburgh." Kirk and Finney made a good team, and, as he wrote in his *Memoirs*, they "had a very interesting revival in that place, and many souls were converted." Elizabeth Finney joined Helen Kirk in leading women's prayer meetings, and Mrs. Kirk presented their work as a model in her influential book *Woman and Prayer; or, The History of the Ladies' Union Prayer Meeting, Held in Bristo Place Hall, Edinburgh* (1861). Finney asserted that the congregation, not previously very large, soon swelled to fill the sanctuary. But a citywide revival was impossible because the Evangelical Union "was surrounded by a wall of prejudice" in Scotland's overwhelmingly orthodox environment. Moreover, theological differences between Finney and the Evangelical Union finally drove a wedge between them. Specifically, Finney wrote, they differed on the doctrine of election, and "their views of faith as a mere intellectual state I could not receive." In November James Morrison had to write an embarrassing letter to Finney retracting an impulsive invitation from his elders to preach in his absence. Because of differences "on important doctrines," Morrison said, he could not give his consent.

Charles Finney was not at all comfortable in Scotland. He accepted the invitation of Fergus Ferguson, another Evangelical Union pastor, to preach at Aberdeen but "felt uneasy" allying himself with an idiosyncratic group shunned by Presbyterians and Congregationalists alike. He liked the men personally, respected their vital piety, enjoyed witnessing many conversions in their churches, and delighted in the enthusiasm with which they received his reports of American revivals, such as his lecture during a brief visit to Glasgow which was published as *The Prevailing Prayer-Meeting* (London, 1859). But in the end he was "unwilling to continue my labors longer with that denomination" and declined an invitation to Glasgow. The reputation of the Evangelical Union, he felt, was "like a wall" keeping people from his preaching. It is probably also true that he would have had, as Kirk put it in a letter, "no opening" anywhere else in Scotland but in those churches. So Finney responded eagerly to an urgent request from William Hope Davidson, the Congregational pastor at Bolton near Manchester in Lancashire, to assist him with a revival that was already in progress.

The Finneys took the train to Bolton, a midsize factory city, arriving there before Christmas 1859. The Methodists were strong in this industrial part of the country. James Barlow, one of the Methodist pastors, welcomed the Finneys into his home. The revival began there the next evening, when some neighbors dropped in "for religious conversation and prayer." One woman became anxious for her soul while Elizabeth Finney knelt in prayer. When Finney encouraged her to submit to Christ *"then* and *there,"* she did so, and she and her pious husband "seemed spontaneously to clasp each other in their arms and melt down before the Lord." The servants in the kitchen were suddenly converted as well, and "the report of what the Lord was doing was soon spread abroad." In January 1860, the Congregational and Methodist churches joined forces with protracted union prayer meetings, at which Finney focused his preaching on the efficacy of "the prayer of faith." He recalled in the *Memoirs,* "The Word seemed to thrill through the hearts of Christians" with extraordinary power. When he "called for inquirers," the "vestry was thronged with them." After Scotland — which Finney dismissed in a letter to George Redford as "cold, formal, unloving" — the evangelist was himself revived by his ministry at Bolton.

The Methodist-Congregational "Bolton Evangelical Revival Committee" secured the vast Temperance Hall for nightly meetings. Under Finney's direction, they organized "to canvass the whole city" with personal visits, "bills, tracts, posters, and all sorts of [printed] invitations." Soon, three thousand and more were packing the hall at every meeting, and when the evangelist called the anxious, "great numbers would come forward and crowd as best they could through the dense masses that stood in every nook and corner of the house." Finney was put off, however, by Methodists who became too "noisy and demonstrative" during the prayers. He complained, "They . . . would pound the benches, pray exceedingly loud, and sometimes more than one at a time." He insisted that penitents needed to be "intelligently converted" and persuaded the

Methodists to restrain themselves, although it meant they were then "a little in bondage when they attempted to pray." As the excitement mounted, Finney wrote in his *Memoirs*, "I kept cool myself" and strove to keep the revival from descending into mere emotionalism. Criminals confessed to unsolved crimes, businessmen made financial restitution to people they had cheated, and mill owners repented of their "love of money." Elizabeth Finney nearly filled the Temperance Hall with her daytime women's meetings. Her ministry in Bolton was extensive, involving visitation, personal counseling, and continuous meetings. The broadly evangelical revival effort in Bolton spread into the mills and factories and, Finney was proud to say, through "all classes of persons, high and low, rich and poor, male and female." And soon it spread to the larger city of Manchester.

As was often the case for Finney in larger cities, Manchester came as a disappointment after his Rochester-like success at Bolton. Congregationalists seemed unwilling to enter into the work with Methodists to the extent he had expected, and some of the ministers were reluctant to participate in the revival fully. He felt it "grieved the Spirit" that men who had agreed "to engineer the work, — to get out the bills, do the necessary printing, and provide for carrying on the general movement" — failed to accomplish their tasks. Still, large crowds gathered, and Elizabeth Finney, as always, shone brightly in her ministry. She wrote her sister in June 1860, "Our Ladies' meetings were wonderful — we began with 30 and before we closed had from six to seven hundred. Our last meeting [had] 1000 women." As Finney recalled, by this time "the strength of both myself and my wife had become exhausted." More than a few who came to hear Finney preach went home unimpressed. The promoters of the revival urged them to go to Wales for a rest. In a rare moment of professional humility, Finney wrote in his *Memoirs*, "There was not a good spirit manifested at that time by the leading men in that movement. I did not learn the cause — perhaps it was something in me."

Some of what Charles Finney learned during this British visit became significant in the urban revivalism of later generations. He observed, "I found it to be true in England wherever I tried it, that the best way to promote revivals of religion was to hold independent meetings; that is, meetings in large halls, where they can be obtained, to which all denominations may come." Finney believed that in the United States members would generally attend protracted meetings in the churches of other denominations, but in England he was "persuaded that the true way to labor for souls there is to have no particular connection with any distinct denomination; but to preach the true Gospel, and make a stand in halls, or even in streets when the weather is favorable, where no denominational feelings and peculiarities can straiten the influences of the Spirit of God." Charles G. Finney's evangelical faith, which mediated Wesleyan and Calvinist beliefs, and his evangelistic campaigns, which had never been denominationally restricted, anticipated in this respect the citywide crusades of Dwight L. Moody and all who followed. His experience with international evangelicalism thus reinforced his conviction that evangelicalism was also interdenominational — and even, as Zinzendorf and Whitefield had known more than a century before, essentially *non*denominational. It was in reflecting on his English experience that Finney acknowledged that revivals were not just the "natural" or "philosophical result" of the right use of means, as he had said in his 1835 *Lectures on Revivals;* they were things to be "engineered."

After warm farewell receptions at Manchester and Bolton, Charles and Elizabeth Finney departed from Liverpool on August 4, 1860. The country to which they returned stood at the brink of civil war. Finney had foreseen even in the 1830s that the terrible crisis of slavery would be resolved only through bloodshed. As an evangelist, he had both rebuked that national sin and sought to avoid its detrimental effect on the revival spirit. The second tour of the British Isles was in some measure an effort by Finney to sidestep the antislavery conflict. In 1834 he suffered a breakdown and took a cruise to the Mediterranean when New York City was gripped in anti-abolition violence. In 1849-1850 his first English trip took him away from political conflict both in American society and on the Oberlin campus. And he was packing his trunk for the third trip across the Atlantic Ocean just as the national revival of 1857-1858 was giving way to renewed national preoccupation with the sectional crisis.

That crisis came to Oberlin in December 1858 in a way that rocked the community for almost a year. In defiance of the Fugitive Slave Law, a passionate group of Oberlin residents — including blacks and whites, students, church members, and professors — rescued a runaway slave from capture. They freed John Price from his captors at a hotel just south in Wellington and returned to Oberlin. Professor James Monroe, long active in the Underground Railroad, took Price to the home of another faculty member, James H. Fairchild, where he hid in a back room for three days before fleeing for Canada. Twenty of the "Rescuers" were jailed in Cleveland and stood trial for their crime. When they were finally released, Oberlin welcomed them home with torchlight parades and a public celebration with hymns, prayers, and festive hoopla. Finney left the country in December 1858 without commenting on this dramatic event, and he never mentioned it in his *Memoirs*. When the Oberlin faculty wrote Finney on July 21, 1860, to urge his return from Britain, they refuted his recently expressed view that ministers should avoid "active participation in politics." They contended that Oberlin should "labor to throw the power of an elevated and earnest Christianity into the domain of politics. Our past efforts to this end seem to have been not in vain." As president of the college, they argued, Charles Finney had to shoulder responsibility for Oberlin's leadership in the struggle against slavery.

Letters that Finney received before his return seemed to suggest that not only the nation but Oberlin itself was coming apart. A group from First Church, feeling that the congregation

Ordinary citizens, church members, students, and college professors banded together in December 1858 to hide runaway slave John Price and enable his escape to Canada. Twenty "Rescuers" were arrested on April 15, 1859, held in Cleveland's Cuyahoga County jail, and tried under the Fugitive Slave Law. This photograph, taken at the prison by J. M. Green, was widely reprinted. An engraved version appeared on the front page of *Frank Leslie's Illustrated Newspaper*. Although some of Finney's closest associates played a role in the episode, the evangelist avoided the controversy altogether. Photo courtesy of the Oberlin College Archives had grown too large, separated to form the Second Congregational Church in Oberlin. Finney had always opposed the idea of two churches, and it galled him that the split was made while he was away. Meanwhile, efforts had been made to secure a copastor for Finney, to enable Morgan finally to step down. These plans were frustrated when Michael Strieby of Syracuse first accepted and then backed away from the call. Most troubling of all, a member wrote Finney, a faction in the congregation led by the son of a deacon professed to have received "the gift of the Holy Ghost" and become more spiritual than the rest of the church. They were holding separate prayer meetings, and when they did attend meetings at the church "they prayed as though the church was all asleep." Some judged them insane and made plans to send the leader to "the assylum." But a deacon of the church who admitted he was mystified nonetheless believed that "with such a flow of language" he had undoubtedly "received a great blessing." Many Oberlin friends begged Finney to help resolve the situation. "We have felt if you knew what a division has arisen among the people you would soon come again, and it seems to us you would do better in guiding the troubled minds than any other one," wrote one. Another lamented, "It seems . . . we are like a great family and father gone." Charles Finney was not exaggerating when he wrote in his *Memoirs*, "It was thought by persons here [at Oberlin] that the state of things in our church demanded my presence."

Members of the Oberlin theology department added their voices in a letter signed by every student. "Your people here earnestly desire again to hear your voice," they implored. They had all enrolled at Oberlin in order "to enjoy the benefits of your instruction, and above all to learn of you, through the grace of God, the way to win souls," but this had not happened. Beckoning the missionary home, they echoed the Macedonian call of Acts 16:9, "Shall we beseech you then in vain to come over and help us?"

Charles and Elizabeth Finney landed in New York in the

middle of August. Finney suffered "a very painful attack of lumbago" during the voyage and could barely walk. After visits in Brooklyn and other cities along the way to Ohio, they arrived back in Oberlin to a joyous welcome on September 5. Finney was sixty-eight years old when he returned from his second British campaign. Unlike George Whitefield, who died and was buried in the United States after a lifetime of international travel, President Charles Finney of Oberlin College never again crossed the ocean.

10 President Finney's Evangelical Spirit

The graduating classes at Oberlin — students from the collegiate program, the theological department, and the female department — heard Charles G. Finney preach on the eve of his election to the presidency of the college at the end of August 1851. His text was 1 Kings 2:2-4, "Be thou strong therefore, and show thyself a man." He developed his career-long theme of personal responsibility to live up to God's call to righteousness. Each graduate was a free moral agent with the opportunity to live a Christian life committed to holiness and social reform. The evangelist-professor expounded the doctrine of "the higher law," for which Oberlin was becoming notorious: obedience to God's law required resistance to oppressive practices such as American slavery and disobedience of unjust human ordinances such as the Fugitive Slave Law. "Show yourselves to be men of principle," Finney exhorted, "in these trying times when the question is gravely raised whether the law of God is above the law of man, whether human institutions and law are to set aside the authority of God." He challenged the graduates to go into the world as missionaries of the gospel — "among the Indians of the forest, to the Islands of the great sea, among the slaves of the South, or the African tribes on their own soil." Charles Finney made a good start with students and faculty alike and signaled the moral tone of his presidency.

Finney was largely a figurehead as president of Oberlin College, but he was a symbol in the strongest sense of the term. He added a course on mental and moral philosophy to his existing teaching schedule of pastoral theology and systematic theology. This new course was an introduction to Christian life and thought traditionally taught by American college presidents in the nineteenth century. Oberlin attracted students for a variety of reasons, an important one being the presence of Charles Finney in the classroom and in the pulpit of First Church. In his *Memoirs*, Finney recorded his work at Oberlin each year during the 1850s as if it had become routine for him. One year, for example: "We came home and went on with our labors here as usual, with the almost uniform results of a great degree of religious influence among our students, and extending more or less generally to the inhabitants." Indeed, the meetinghouse was almost always full with upwards of two thousand worshipers. The Oberlin church became the largest in the Congregational denomination. Finney was also an effective fund-raiser, both personally and simply through the power of his name at the top of the masthead on college publications.

When President Finney chaired faculty and trustees meetings, his leadership contrasted markedly with that of Asa Mahan. Instead of directing decisions and events with an autocratic hand, he moderated meetings in a consensus-building style. His more collegial manner was perfectly in keeping with the so-called "Finney Compact" instituted when he came to the Oberlin — the agreement that the faculty would collectively govern the college. His method strengthened the faculty to the extent that, except in times of extreme crisis, they had little trouble functioning in his absence. Finney had made it clear to the trustees when he accepted the presidency that he must continue to be away during the winter for evangelistic work. They consented to this stipulation. He absented himself from the college for four or five months every year, and for a year and a half when he and Elizabeth made their second British tour in 1858-1860. Finney endured the presidency as a practical necessity, a spiritual inevitability, the natural consequence of his giant presence and influence on the college's national identity.

The letters Finney received from faculty and students when he was preaching elsewhere, often imploring him to return soon, indicate enormous affection for him on campus and in the church. Typical was correspondence from the faculty in April 1855, when the evangelist was in New York City after spending the winter preaching upstate. They were concerned with rumors that Finney was not planning to return at all. "We exceedingly desire your presence. We deem it essential to the best welfare of all the interests connected with our great work. . . . The Senior College Class, too, are inquiring anxiously when they are to expect the President's lectures on Moral Philosophy, or whether they are to have them at all. But we especially need your presence as our religious counsellor and guide." While admiration was by no means universal, it was overwhelmingly and generally shared. A composite daguerreotype of the Oberlin faculty from the early 1850s shows Charles Finney as a youthful sixty-year-old with piercing eyes, mutton-chop whiskers, and a distinctly pleasant smile. Willard Sears, writing from New England in 1853 in response to news of the summer revival at Oberlin, waxed poetic: "Brother Finney, I am glad to hear the Lord is with you. Without these seasons, and frequent too, Oberlin would not be Oberlin, as it now is in the hearts of God's people through the land that feel that the Kingdom of Christ is righteous progress over this lost world."

Many of the more radical reform-minded students, and especially female students who had joined the national struggle for women's rights and abolition, did not hold Finney — or the rest of the faculty — in such high esteem. Lucy Stone, who graduated from the collegiate course with a bachelor of arts degree in 1847, kept a picture of William Lloyd Garrison in her room and promoted *The Liberator* and other antislavery periodicals on campus. When the radical abolitionists Abby Kelley Foster and her husband Stephen S. Foster visited the campus in 1846, Stone helped with the arrangements. Charles Finney and a majority of the faculty determined that it was "undesirable and unadvisable" for the couple to make a return visit, but that did not deter them. Stone conveyed her opinion of the faculty in a letter to her parents: "They hate Garrison, and women's rights. . . . I love both, and often find myself at swords' points with them." Antoinette Brown, a contemporary of Stone, shocked many when she entered the theological course after graduating from the female department. Finney, to his credit, welcomed her full participation in his classes, but when she completed her studies in 1850 (while Finney was in England), she was not allowed to graduate. Brown was ordained by a Congregational church in upstate New York but soon became a Unitarian and left the ministry. In an 1853 letter to John Keep, Finney denounced all movements that elevated social reform above conversion and holiness, and he confided his feeling that Oberlin's two famous female activists had lost their religion.

Then there was the story of Arabella Phillips, who was known to be "somewhat contemptuous" of all the prayer meetings at Oberlin. When Finney met her on campus, he is supposed to have greeted her, "Good morning, Daughter of the Devil." And she is remembered to have responded, "I'm glad to see you, Father," at which Finney broke into friendly laughter and went on to speak to her of the need for salvation. Sometimes the story has been told with Lucy Stone as the protagonist. Actually, this was one version of an old joke that dogged Finney throughout his career. Back in April 1835, Lydia Finney's father, Nathaniel Andrews, wrote from Cleveland prior to the Oberlin move, advising the evangelist that Finney jokes from the Mohawk Valley had preceded him to the Western Reserve. "The devil is busy in propagating the old stories, such as [Finney] taking a boy by the hair of his head and telling him if you don't repent the devil will have you [and] the boy says I don't know but he will, I see he has got hold of me, and many others of the kind."

Some other students resented Finney because he embarrassed them in the classroom with his confrontational Socratic pedagogy. Finney's son-in-law J. Dolson Cox was possibly the most unfortunate example. In Cox's case, Finney pushed him too hard to accept his own resolution of the question of free will and divine sovereignty and lost patience when the student balked. "Dolson, you are not *honest*," Finney is remembered to have said. "You do not *want* to see the truth." John Morgan begged Finney to withdraw this accusation, but the damage was done. Cox left school; he and Helen moved to Warren, Ohio, where he practiced law and laid the groundwork for a political career. Charles Finney and Dolson Cox did salvage a relationship with one another, but they never again discussed theology. In another case, a female student whose face was scarred from smallpox carried inside her for the rest of her life a derogatory comment about her appearance from the professor of moral philosophy. There are other similar stories of Finney's occasionally harsh treatment of students in the lore of Oberlin's first three decades, some of them probably apocryphal. But more than a few students regarded President Finney with what one called "a wholesome fear."

Charles and Elizabeth Finney's family experienced both joy and sorrow during the years of his presidency. Finney's eight-year-old daughter Delia, cared for by Helen and Dolson during their extended stay in England, died at the end of the summer of 1852 just a few months after their return. His daughter Julia, who was born in 1837, matured from a teenager to a young adult in the decade of the 1850s. Finney's numerous letters to her display tender love, fatherly advice, and stern spiritual admonition. Plagued with eye problems, Julia had trouble studying but concentrated on music, especially piano.

271

She and her stepsister, Angie, often lived with Elizabeth's brother and sister-in-law in Brooklyn during her father's winter trips, but when she was seventeen she stayed alone at the house in Oberlin. Finney, preaching in Cincinnati, advised her in a letter to correct her "childish and affected habit . . . of lisping" and cautioned, "We expect . . . that you will be very guarded about gathering around you companions of either sex in our absence. The eyes of the people and of God are upon you, dear child." When she was twenty and her father was on his way to Boston, he wrote, "I saw you stand alone upon the platform after I entered the car and I felt sad to leave you. . . . I hope you will not be lonely." Finney was delighted to receive letters from her during the winter of 1858, the year of the national revival, indicating that her mind was occupied with spiritual matters. He wrote back, "Why should you not become a *Holy Ghost Christian?* Shall we not have one child wholly devoted to Christ?"

Finney had the pleasure of knowing that all his children married well and that the men excelled in their work. And he delighted in his grandchildren. Helen shared in the glory of Dolson's illustrious career in politics. After rising to the rank of major general during the Civil War, he served in the Grant administration as Secretary of the Interior and then was elected governor of Ohio. Charles married his stepsister Angelina and went into law and journalism. After serving in Washington during the war as an administrator in the Army, he and Angelina finally settled in California. After legal study, Norton moved with his wife, Jenny, to Oshkosh, Wisconsin, where he prospered in the railroad business. After the Civil War, Julia married Oberlin professor and state senator James Monroe. Monroe had been actively involved with the Underground Railroad and the 1858 Oberlin rescue incident, and, with Dolson Cox, he had recruited a company of men for the Union Army when war broke out. Julia accompanied James to Brazil, where he served a term as United States consul, and to Washington when he was elected to Congress. The offspring of

Charles Grandison Finney and their spouses certainly achieved the highest aspirations represented in his given names, but he was denied the satisfaction of seeing one of the next generation follow him into the ministry. That prayer did not prevail.

While Charles Finney loved Oberlin, his first love was his calling as an evangelist to the world. Each fall during the 1850s, he and Elizabeth traveled east for this broader work. From mid-October 1851 until early April 1852, he preached in New York City and Hartford, Connecticut; the winter of 1852-1853 found them in Syracuse; they stayed in Ohio for the 1853-1854 season, with two months each in Cleveland and Cincinnati; and at Christmastime 1854, the evangelist returned to the scene of his earliest work in the Mohawk Valley, the village of Western in Oneida County. The Finneys went to Rochester in December 1855 for his third revival there. And during the winters of 1856-1857 and 1857-1858, they committed themselves again to Boston, which Finney described to Julia in a January 1857 letter as "the hardest place to promote a revival that there is." But, he added with determination, "the Lord will prevail over it."

New York City was a disappointment to Charles Finney in October 1851, even though he was preaching at the Broadway Tabernacle. There were two problems. First, he required daily use of the facility, but the congregation relied on weekly rental income from many benevolent societies and agencies that met there. Although the church agreed to suspend these rentals during Finney's campaign and even raised enough money to offset the loss, the meetings were reinstated when the groups protested that unless they could continue they would find other locations and not be back. Second, the pastor, Joseph P. Thompson, was curiously unsupportive of Finney's efforts and refused to allow advertising in the city. In his *Memoirs* Finney wrote, "I told him that I had never known that to be objected to in any place where I had labored in this country or in Europe; and that the custom was universal in great cities to put up posters advertizing our meetings," but to no avail. Perhaps defensive on account of the evangelist's reputation, Thompson randomly switched preaching assignments, so people never knew whether he or Finney would be in the pulpit. Finally, after Finney was able to preach twice on a Sunday and "the congregation was very mellow," it "looked as if we were on the point of having a great outburst of religious interest." Just then he got sick and was unable to preach. Thompson went to the Tabernacle and simply told the crowd to go home. When he recovered, Finney decided to accept an invitation from the Rev. William Patton, representing a group of ministers in Hartford.

Finney scored a success at Hartford. From about New Year's Day through March 1852, he recalled, "a powerful revival influence was manifested among the people." Charles and Elizabeth Finney accomplished this — and Elizabeth's work with "prayer meetings for ladies" cannot be overestimated — despite the fact that the ministers blocked Finney's use of the anxious seat. Finney wrote, "They were afraid of any measures other than simply prayer-meetings, and preaching meetings, and meetings for inquiry." Since he could not invite penitents forward, the evangelist made do some nights by calling on "those that were willing then and there to give themselves up to God, to kneel down." And he made good use of the inquiry meetings, at which he offered "particular instruction" and prayer. "In this revival," he wrote, *"there was a great deal of praying,"* especially among "the young converts of both sexes," who "formed themselves into a kind of City Missionary Society" for evangelistic outreach. Perhaps Finney's most interesting experience at Hartford was working with the famous pastor-theologian Horace Bushnell and two ministers who had opposed the theological liberalism that Bushnell advanced in *God in Christ* (1849). Joel Hawes of Hartford's First Church was especially critical of Bushnell, but the cooperative effort of the revival brought them together at least temporarily. Finney preached in the Congregational churches of all three sponsoring pastors.

Bushnell, whose 1847 book *Christian Nurture* had presented a way to Christian faith at variance with revivalism, immediately welcomed Finney and admired him as a great preacher. "Pure gold," Bushnell called him. In their conversations they may have differed on how to balance revivalism and Christian nurture, but shared interest in Christian experience, sanctification, and holiness bonded the two men, as did Bushnell's growing support for coeducation. Bushnell stopped at Oberlin to visit the Finneys on a trip west the next year. "I do not know how it is," Bushnell reflected, "but I am drawn to this man, despite . . . the greatest dissimilarity of tastes and a method of soul . . . wholly unlike." He concluded, "It is because I find God with him." When Finney preached at Boston in 1857, Bushnell wrote, "I rejoice greatly to hear of your success and that God continues to put his seal upon you." And when Finney went to England the second time, he carried with him a letter of endorsement from Bushnell that described him as "apostolic" and "no fanatic." For his part, ever concerned for the souls of his children and grandchildren, ten years later Finney advised his daughters to read *Christian Nurture*. On their way back to Oberlin at the end of March, Charles Finney preached again in Brooklyn for another liberal-in-the-making, Henry Ward Beecher.

Syracuse, a city that never figured in the Finney revivals along the Erie Canal of the 1820s, finally received a visit from the evangelist in November 1852. Revivals among the Methodists the previous year, Finney wrote in his *Memoirs,* had stirred up resentment "on the part of professors of other denominations." Meanwhile, "the little Congregational church" that invited him to the city had been known more for its "very radical views in regard to all the great questions of reform" than for the members' evangelical piety. Finney began, as he always did in such an "unpleasant state of things," by preaching to church members, pressing for repentance, renewed salvation, and reconciliation. Although he said he originally intended to move to other cities in central New York, the fact that "interest continued to increase and to spread" convinced him to stay on, and soon the Presbyterian churches opened their pulpits to him. In February 1853 Charles Finney wrote Julia from Syracuse, "The revival here is progressing gloriously."

Elizabeth Finney's "ladies' meetings," conducted at the First Presbyterian Church, became huge ecumenical gatherings. In his *Memoirs* account of the Syracuse revival, Finney tells in detail of a devout woman's "fresh baptism of the Holy Spirit" and Elizabeth's role in her experience. The woman came to hear Finney preach, eager to hear about entire sanctification and "how she should obtain it." After a brief private conference with Finney, she went home to pray, soon returning "as full of the Holy Spirit, to all human appearance, as she could be." He wrote, "She seemed to be lifted up above herself, and her joy was so great that she could hardly refrain from shouting." A worried Finney tried to calm her. That evening at the "prayer and conference meeting," when she rose to testify "her face was literally radiant with religious joy," and everyone was "struck with the halo that seemed to fill her countenance." As she spoke, she soon became incoherent, however, and the evangelist feared she would slip into insanity. Elizabeth went home and stayed with her for several days. She counseled and "soothed and quieted her" until she regained emotional stability. Others received this "fresh experience" of the Holy Ghost at Elizabeth's meetings and rededicated themselves to lives of service. It was the women who most impressed Charles Finney at Syracuse.

After preaching in Cleveland and Cincinnati during the winter of 1853-1854, campaigns for which records are scant, Charles and Elizabeth Finney spent the next two winters again in upstate New York. Almost all of Finney's preaching since his earliest work had been done in cities, with the exception of his commitment to Potto Brown and Houghton, England. His decision to preach in the village of Western starting at Christmas 1854 was something of an anomaly. The village had always been special to him because of the Braytons, an extraordinary evangelical family, and perhaps he felt some nostalgia in retracing his early steps. But the Brayton family had all but died out, and, he wrote in the *Memoirs*, the feeble congregation was "composed principally of youngerly people who had grown up after the first revival" thirty years before. The revival took root, however, fed by several notable conversions. One involved a young man from a prominent family in the church who presented himself to Finney in despair, convinced that he had committed the unpardonable sin. In rebellion against his parents, he said, "I . . . set myself deliberately to blaspheme the Holy Ghost" by burning down the schoolhouse and allowing others to be suspected of the arson. When he confessed his crime and gave himself to God, "the people sobbed and wept all over the congregation."

The other case was a young schoolteacher who prided herself on being a skeptic. When she did not attend Finney's meetings, he called on her at the schoolhouse. "I took her very kindly by the hand and told her that I had dropped in to speak with her about her soul. 'My child,' I said, 'how is it with you? Have you given your heart to God?' . . . Her head fell, and she made no effort to withdraw her hand. I saw in a moment that a subduing influence came over her, and so deep and remarkable an influence that I felt almost assured that she would submit to God right on the spot." She agreed to have Finney pray for her and her students "in the presence of the school," and when he did "it was a very solemn, melting time." As was the case a generation before, news of the revival spread to Rome, and Finney preached in that city for almost two months until it was time to return to Oberlin in April. Conversions occurred, but, according to Finney at least, the prospect of a full revival was frustrated by disunity in the congregation over the pastor. He and Elizabeth returned to Oberlin with mixed emotions about the effectiveness of their winter's labors.

The Finneys' return to Rochester the following fall was a homecoming for them both. They found that they could go home again, and Finney demonstrated that at sixty-three he had still not lost his touch. After a slow start, the city responded to this third Finney revival with as much enthusiasm as in 1830 and 1842. The evangelist alternated among the pulpits of the Congregational church and two Presbyterian churches, though the conservative pastor of First Presbyterian Church refused to participate. Soon the city's two Baptist churches invited him to preach, and the faculty and students of the Baptist-related University of Rochester "engaged in the work with great cordiality." He wrote in the *Memoirs*, "the Methodist churches went to work in their own way to extend the work."

As in 1842, the legal community asked Finney to deliver "a course of lectures to lawyers on the Moral Government of God." Again, it was the business and professional leaders of the city who stood out among the converts and recommitted. Daily prayer meetings were established, and "it seemed as if the whole city would be converted." Efforts were made, reminiscent of the drive to stop the Sabbath-breaking stage lines in 1830, to convert the railroads to a six-day schedule. "Some men who had been open Sabbath breakers, others that had been openly profane, — indeed, all classes of persons, from the highest to the lowest, from the richest to the poorest, were visited by the power of this revival and brought to Christ." Elizabeth Finney, who had participated in the first two Rochester revivals as a community leader, now "labored as usual with great zeal and success" as the evangelist's wife and coworker. The numbers of conversions and new church members easily matched the statistics from previous campaigns. Charles Finney could say with complete honesty, "I never preached anywhere with more pleasure than in Rochester."

The third Rochester revival was a prelude to Finney's role in the great national revival of 1857 and 1858. This spasm of spiritual renewal occurred in the context of, and in reaction to, the national political and economic crisis. Sectional conflict threatened to tear the country apart. Boston convulsed in protest in 1854 when a runaway slave was captured and loaded on a Virginia-bound ship by federal troops. Passage of Stephen A. Douglas's Kansas-Nebraska Act that same year effectively shredded the old Missouri Compromise, which had contained slavery in the South. In the rush to determine whether Kansas would be a slave state or a free state when it was formally created, the territory became a bloody war zone. Charles G. Finney Jr. went there on a fact-finding mission and outraged Oberlin with his report of Southern aggression. "Beecher's Bibles" (rifles purchased with money raised by Henry Ward Beecher and shipped west packed in cases of Bibles) and John Brown's Liberty Guard private militia (which would attract Oberlin volunteers) symbolized the activism of some Northern evangelicals in the violent struggle. James Buchanan, a Pennsylvanian with Southern sympathies, defeated John C. Fremont, the candidate of the fledgling Republican party, in the presidential election of 1856. Then in 1857 the national economy, which had boomed through mid-decade, went bust in the first major financial panic in twenty years. Railroads, banks, merchants, and leading families collapsed into bankruptcy. Charles G. Finney and a cadre of preachers in every denomination exhorted the nation with the word of salvation by faith in Jesus Christ. With little hope to be found anywhere else, many people turned to religion with fresh enthusiasm.

Finney arrived in Boston early in December 1856 to a much warmer welcome than he had experienced during his previous visit, when few pastors opened their churches to him. The controversy surrounding Oberlin Perfectionism had faded, and Finney's prestige had risen with his England tour, his college presidency, and the recent Rochester revival. Willard Sears rallied the "the evangelical pastors," he wrote in a September 24 letter, and the city was eager for his message. Park Street Church, where Finney had preached in 1831, would again be the primary site of his evangelistic services. The pastor, Andrew Leete Stone, confessed to Finney after his first sermon that he felt himself in need of a new conversion. On his knees with Charles Finney, he "thoroughly [gave] his heart to God" and then made public testimony of his rededication. "The work was quite extensive that winter in Boston," Finney wrote. He left for Oberlin in the spring with the promise to return that fall.

The only sour note came from his old colleague at Albany Edward N. Kirk, who had fallen out with Finney over entire sanctification. He had served as pastor of Boston's Mount Vernon Congregational Church for fifteen years, and had been in France during Finney's 1856-1857 campaign. Kirk refused to endorse Finney's return to Boston. "I told you when you were about to embark for Europe," Kirk wrote in March 1858, "that I would not invite you to labor with me until you or I were changed. I have seen no reason to alter that decision. We may talk this over in heaven. In this world I am persuaded it would do no good. . . . May God abundantly bless you." He signed the letter "Your fellow-disciple," but his opposition saddened Finney.

The 1857-1858 awakening was larger than Edward Kirk and Charles Finney. When the evangelist returned to Boston in December, he found the city alive with religious interest. He wrote in his *Memoirs*, "It was at this time that a great revival prevailed throughout all the Northern states. It swept over the land in such a tremendous manner, that for some weeks it was estimated that not less than fifty thousand conversions occurred per week." The distinguishing characteristic of this national revival was that, as Finney put it, "it was carried on to a large extent through lay influence, so much so as almost to throw the ministers into the shade." The revival even had a theme song, written by the Presbyterian George Duffield:

> Stand up, stand up for Jesus,
>   The trumpet call obey;
> Forth to the mighty conflict,
>   In this His glorious day:
> Ye that are men now serve Him
>   Against unnumbered foes;
> Let courage rise with danger,
>   And strength to strength oppose.

Duffield, who had criticized Finney's theology a decade earlier, also opposed the abolition movement's sectional divisiveness. He was a staunch defender of what he termed "the national Union of these confederated States." His symbolically martial hymn sought to replace the armed conflict of "bleeding Kansas" and imminent civil war with the traditional "spiritual warfare" of evangelical piety. Charles Finney was less sanguine about the political usefulness of the 1857-1858 revival, believing that it never spread to the South because "slavery seemed to shut it out" and "the Spirit of God seemed to be grieved away from them."

This awakening has been called "the Businessmen's Revival" because much of the activity took place in cities during the workday. Organizers built on the practice of daily prayer meetings, as Finneyite revivals had for decades. In addition, churches in Boston and other cities had conducted daily meetings in the early morning or late afternoon for some time. At the time of the Panic of 1857, prominent Christian businessmen in New York City began to establish daily nondenominational meetings at noon in churches located in the commercial districts. The movement spread from New York to New England and through every state to the west. Before it was finished, hundreds of thousands of new members had been added to the churches. Charles Finney fully supported the "business men's prayer meeting" that convened at Boston's Old South Church every day at noon. Such crowds jammed the church that similar meetings were soon established around the city.

Elizabeth Finney, meanwhile, led her customary women's meeting at Park Street Church, where the vestry was filled daily to capacity under her leadership. Finney reported her work in glowing terms in a lecture in England the next year: "If the business men have had their daily meetings, so have the women; if the men have visited and conversed with individuals, so have the women. God has greatly honoured the instrumentality of woman." In the *Memoirs* he attributed the spread of the awakening to "the energetic efforts of the laity, male and female" in organizing their communities for "prayer meetings, personal visitation and conversation . . . [and] the distribution of tracts." Elizabeth enjoyed every minute of this work.

Charles and Elizabeth Finney's appearance in Boston by no means created the Businessmen's Revival, but they were at the center of it. A sample of the broadsides handed out in the streets indicates that his preaching schedule was essentially the same as the one he had adopted in every campaign of his career. "Rev. C. G. Finney, President of Oberlin College, will preach as follows," it announced for the week of January 24, 1858: "Sabbath A.M. In Chapel Corner Lowell and Causeway Streets. Sabbath Evening. 7 o'clock. In Park Street Church. Subject, 'Christ Seeking the Lost.'" On Tuesday evening at Pine Street Church, his subject was "Prejudice"; on Wednesday at Salem Street Church it was "Condition of Divine Teaching"; on Thursday at Park Street Church it was "Taking Pleasure in Sin"; and on Friday morning at Park Street it was "Shutting Up the Kingdom of God." The handbill also advertised three o'clock prayer meetings in the Park Street Church vestry daily from Tuesday through Friday and noted that the seats were free. In addition to weekly engagements in the city, Finney preached in Congregational churches of towns adjacent to Boston. After experiencing frustration there so often before, Finney at last sensed that "the Lord intended to make a general sweep in Boston." He wrote in his *Memoirs* that in the spring "when we left there the work was in its full strength, without any apparent abatement at all."

Neither the Panic of 1857 nor the awakening of 1857-1858 was of long duration, however. The economy quickly recovered, and the nation plunged again into political and ideological crisis. The Oberlin Rescuers were jailed and put on trial for aiding a runaway slave. In October 1859, John Brown and an armed band that included two black men from Oberlin raided the federal arsenal at Harper's Ferry, Virginia, with the intent of securing weapons to arm slaves for a massive uprising. The eulogy for John Brown in *The Oberlin Evangelist* called him "the Wise Man of our times" and "the true representative of the American idea." The presidential election campaign of 1860 — there were torchlight parades for Abraham Lincoln at Oberlin — convinced Northerners and Southerners alike that their differences were irreconcilable. During these events, Charles and Elizabeth Finney were in Great Britain, having left the country in the middle of December 1858. In a letter to Professor Henry Cowles commenting on Oberlin's preoccupation with the trial of the Rescuers, Finney expressed his "painful convictions of the danger of spiritual declension." Another Oberlin colleague acknowledged in a February 1860 letter to Finney that this local episode and "the invasion of Virginia by John Brown . . . seemed to turn a majority of minds from the subject of salvation." Oberlin residents had concluded "that Slavery can only be purged from our land through torrents of blood." The Finneys would not be back in Oberlin until September 1860, two months before Lincoln was elected president. The Businessmen's Revival had abated soon after the Finneys left the country, and the Civil War dominated the national life after their return. The Boston campaign, so wondrously successful from the viewpoint of conversions and church membership growth, was Charles Finney's last major urban revival in the United States.

When shots were fired on Fort Sumter, Oberlin College president Charles Finney was approaching his sixty-ninth birthday. His health had been fragile since returning from England. Letters urging him to return had rather testily reminded him, "Your name as President, as the head of our Theological department, goes out on our Catalogue. The public of course assume that your personal services will be found *here*. But *here*, when persons arrive, you are not." Friends at the college and in the church pleaded, "I hope you will spend your last days with us." During the 1860s, Charles Finney was physically incapable of traveling, and he preached nowhere else but at Oberlin. He devoted himself to evangelistic preaching and theological instruction at home.

Upon his return, President Finney stated that the purpose of the college was to provide a Christian education. "The spiritual culture of our pupils," he insisted, was "more important than all other culture." He had to compromise on his wish that social gatherings and clubs be discontinued, but he still complained, as he did in his *Memoirs,* that "College Societies have increased in number, and the class exhibitions and everything that is exciting have been multiplied a good deal for several years; so that it has become more and more difficult to secure a powerful revival during the Summer term." Still, religious exercises at the start of each class session, prayer services every evening, a weekly prayer meeting and religious lecture, and required English Bible class were all part of the academic program. James Fairchild had taught Finney's courses while he was away, but the president eagerly took up his responsibilities in the classroom again.

With Charles Finney in the pulpit at the First Church, the revival spirit was renewed at Oberlin in the fall of 1860. It was the best time of year for religious activity, as new students arrived and enthusiasm was high. Finney observed, "Our fall term is properly our harvest here." Despite the fact that Oberlin now had a Second Congregational Church and an Episcopal parish and a group of Methodists that would begin meeting in 1861, "the revival became very general throughout the place, and seemed to bid fair to make a clean sweep of the unconverted." Finney recalled that, "besides preaching twice on Sabbath, and holding a meeting of inquiry in the evening of every Sabbath, I preached several times on week evenings each week" and also spent many hours "conversing with inquirers." When the fall semester ended, he began dictating sermons for *The Oberlin Evangelist.* Elizabeth Finney wrote in a letter to England, "His labors here have been beyond everything I have ever known him to do. . . . The whole town seems moved at the presence of God and such breaking down and humbling of the church I have never seen in Oberlin." Hundreds were converted. It was said that Oberlin again was Oberlin.

But Finney had overtaxed himself. After a full Sabbath in mid-December 1860, he came down with a chill. Then a December 21 letter came from his son Charles, who was visiting Norton's family in Oshkosh, that "our dear Jenny . . . is failing very rapidly." Norton "much desired to have Father come and see Jenny before she died," for "a cloud seems to have come over her spirit," and "her faith appears gone." Jenny recovered, but Finney made it only as far as Chicago before he was so ill that he had to turn back. On January 11, 1861, Elizabeth's son James wrote his mother from New York, "I am very sorry that you and Father are sick." Finney lay in bed for three months. With Morgan and other professors in the pulpit, he wrote, "the conversions grew less frequent." On May 15 Finney wrote Julia that he "went to meeting a part of the forenoon last Sabbath for the first time since I have been ill." The Civil War had begun. He worried about Dolson, who had immediately enlisted as an officer, and he prayed, "I hope this war has no worldly ambition in it."

Just as Finney was recovering, in September 1861 he contracted a case of shingles and was confined to home. Not until February and March of 1862 was he able to resume preaching and teaching on a limited schedule, and then only for a few weeks before his health again failed. Finally, as he turned seventy in August 1862, Finney regained his strength and resumed his work as pastor, professor, and president. But his days of travel and evening prayer meetings were finished. He wrote in his *Memoirs*, "Although continually pressed by churches, east and west, to come and labor as an Evangelist, I have not dared to comply with their request. With home comforts and nursing I can still perform a good deal of ministerial labor; but I find that I cannot bear excitement in the evening without preventing my sleep." Finney replied to one letter, "To decline accepting such invitations causes me to groan in spirit, but I must submit." Maybe "by another winter" he would be able to travel. But then Elizabeth became seriously ill. Finney wrote Julia, who was living with Helen while Dolson was in the Army, "Your mother is not at all well any of the time." He found comfort in small things; "our raspberries are now ripe and we have abundance of them."

On November 27, 1863, Elizabeth Finney died in Syracuse after spending time at an upstate New York spa for her health. She was with several relatives on her way to Rochester to visit her son when the end came. "I think I have never known her superior as a wife, mother, a neighbor, a Christian female, a laborer for Christ," Charles Finney said of her. "I am left to make the rest of my journey home without my sweet companion and helpmate." She had been more than a helpmate for Finney. Elizabeth was an emancipated woman who labored alongside her husband and often pushed him farther than he would have gone alone, both geographically and intellectually. The second England trip might not have happened without her determination, and many of the converts of Finney's later campaigns were women who attended her meetings. Moreover, Elizabeth Finney voiced a more radical feminism than her husband ever publicly espoused. She announced in her lectures that "a new era has dawned upon woman's history, and . . . she is now beginning to understand her power, position, and mission in this world." She believed God created women "to be the equal of man, and with him forming a united head for the family." She asserted that Jesus Christ elevated women and gave them an equal partnership with men in proclaiming the gospel. Moreover, in several face-to-face meetings she mediated between Finney and leading feminists Susan B. Anthony, Elizabeth Cady Stanton, and Antoinette Brown. Finney was deeply grateful both for her energetic leadership of prayer meetings and for her progressive influence on his life and thought.

Charles Finney engaged in a lively relationship by mail with Mary A. Parker of New York City. Starting almost immediately after Elizabeth's death, it was Mrs. Parker, a relative of Finney's late wife and an active Christian feminist, who initiated the almost weekly correspondence. She was a married woman, her husband a noted physician, and she occasionally added as a postscript to her long letters, "Dr. Parker sends greetings." But her customary salutation — "My dear Friend" — and her intimate confiding of personal feelings, political opinions, and religious beliefs suggested something like infatuation on her part. She was also obsessed with the Catholic threat to the Protestant American way of life. New York was "quite governed by Catholics," she wrote. "They vote away our money to their own institutions [and] divide the spoils." Finney also indulged in some anti-Semitic correspondence with his financial agent in New York City for several years when his Catherine Street house was rented to a Jew who failed to make his payments and allegedly abused the property. Finney was no nativist, but it was a rare evangelical Protestant who thought it worthwhile to rebuke such prejudice. He did not argue when Mary Parker wrote, "I know you say we are in no danger, but I do not believe you see as much of it as I do."

Mary Parker's regular correspondence abruptly halted when Charles Finney married his third wife, Rebecca Allen Rayl, a widow and assistant principal of the Oberlin College female department. He was seventy-eight, and she was forty-one. His old colleague Asa Mahan, now president of Adrian College in Michigan, performed the ceremony on October 9, 1865. Rebecca Rayl had had a fine teaching career at Oberlin, and in her new capacity as Mrs. Finney was named to the Ladies' Board of the College. She became a loving friend, nurse, and, with her keen intellect, a stimulating companion. She also became Finney's scribe for several writing projects he undertook in the second half of the decade and wrote some of his letters as he dictated. Finney said to a friend a few weeks after the wedding, "I have taken to myself another wife and am well pleased and happy with her and my people are greatly pleased with the arrangement."

Charles Finney ignored the Civil War in his *Memoirs*. Lee's surrender at Appomattox and the assassination of Abraham Lincoln five days later, on April 14, 1865, passed with no mention. It is not that he was uninformed. Commenting in a letter to Dolson and Helen on the presidential election of 1868, he asked if they read *The Nation*, a New York weekly. "It is of more value than any ten of our newspapers." In more than a few of his sermons during the war years, he denounced the South for its sinfulness in defending slavery and the North for its lack of will to put a quick end to the evil institution. Indeed, Finney had spoken out and written against the presidential candidacy of Abraham Lincoln in both 1860 and 1864 because he considered Lincoln too slow and compromising on emancipation. None of this is in the *Memoirs*. True to the purpose of his narrative, Finney skipped directly to the revival of 1866.

In addition to omitting mention of his third marriage and the end of the war, Finney also failed to note that in 1865 he retired from the presidency of Oberlin College. On August 21 the trustees accepted his resignation and expressed "their deep sense of the value of [his] influence and labors in the Institution." Finney had been "the main earthly source of its popular power and spiritual influence." Although he was giving up "the nominal Presidency," they hoped he would "continue his Services in the Theological Department in such measure as may be consistent with his health." Indeed, he continued to teach pastoral theology, when he was well enough to go to class, until the week before he died.

Finney did comment on the end of the Civil War in a letter dated November 1, 1865. Among other observations, he noted the beneficial impact it had on enrollment at Oberlin. Not only did old students return, but new ones with war experience arrived. They were "more serious [and] earnest" than ordinary students, he wrote. "The war has been an excellent school for them." Charles Finney seemed renewed in the pulpit as he set to work to convert these students and rejoiced that in 1866 and 1867 "the revival was more powerful among the inhabitants than it had been since 1860." Although his strength failed periodically, he retained his position as pastor of First Church for another seven years and preached once a Sabbath whenever he was able.

Many times in the 1850s observers offered the opinion that Charles G. Finney's revival preaching was a relic from a bygone era, that the evangelist had somehow been frozen in the style of the 1820s and 1830s. Such criticism failed to recognize the ways in which his thinking had developed. There was his endorsement of entire sanctification, for example, a development that had alienated old friends in the 1840s. Few failed to recognized that Finney had polished his manner and softened his tone over the decades, however. For all his limitations, Charles Finney was a remarkably open-minded and progressive evangelical Christian. In his November 1, 1865, letter on the effects of the war, he reflected on the new era that lay ahead for the nation: "Indeed, this war has wrought almost a miraculous change in the view and character of the great mass of the people. 'Young America' has in four short years grown to be old America. We have emerged from this sea of blood a sobered and thoughtful people. We are not all right politically yet. We are progressing with the settlement of many grave questions in the reorganization of the rebel States. We want now to make all men, white and black, equal before the law." For Finney, maturity — having "grown to be old America" — brought a renewed if cautious optimism.

Finney believed the only hope for the new "old America" of the post–Civil War era was the same spiritual power that had fueled "Young America" during the revivals of the early national period. It would not be possible simply to replicate the "new measures" employed at Utica and Rochester, but an understanding of them might provide an inspiration and a model for late nineteenth-century revivals. Finney foresaw a problem in this regard, because he believed that some of the participants in the events of those early days had published accounts that gave a false impression. He felt it necessary, for example, to write a rebuttal to Bennett Tyler's edition of the *Memoir of the Life and Character of Asahel Nettleton, D.D.* (Hartford, 1844), published in Scotland in 1859. At the urging of some friends and church leaders, in 1861 Charles Finney announced in *The Oberlin Evangelist*, "If my health will allow, I hope to write some account of the revivals that have occurred under my observation, and since I have been in this ministry, for the purpose, if possible, of disabusing the minds of those who have been prejudiced against those revivals by false reports."

Elizabeth Finney asked those to whom she had written long letters describing their first campaign in England to send them back to her. It is altogether possible that she also worked to collect in one place other materials that would constitute the Finney papers in preparation for this project. When the two-volume *Autobiography, Correspondence, etc. of Lyman Beecher, D.D.*, was published (New York, 1864, 1865), Charles Finney realized it was time to busy himself with his own narrative. He was reluctant because he feared the effort might be perceived as egotistical — "I dislike Auto Biographies . . . [and] at any rate, I cannot bear to write my own." But he decided to undertake a story of the revivals to set the record straight. "The truth of history demands it," he resolved in July 1866. "The cause of revivals demands the substantial facts in regard to what was called in New England the western revivals and which were stigmatized as being promoted by 'New Measures.'"

Finney probably began dictating his narrative in the fall of 1866, but he was unhappy with both the first stenographer and the apparent self-centeredness of the task, and so he dismissed the woman and destroyed the work. Henry Matson, a Congregational minister with stenographic experience, was hired, and the project resumed in August 1867. By the middle of January 1868, a first draft was complete, and Finney began working on revisions. Lewis Tappan, Finney's old patron whose friendship with him had endured disagreements over abolitionism, heard of the project and was eager to help with editing and financing. Finney sent Tappan the manuscript in the spring. In New York, the aging philanthropist and his wife enthusiastically read the manuscript, made a copy for safekeeping, and wrote out many suggestions for improvement. In July the manuscript was back in Finney's hands, and he set about

incorporating some of Tappan's suggestions. In further correspondence, Tappan encouraged him to be bolder "to set the
world right with respect to the misstatements of Dr. Beecher
and Mr. Nettleton." Finney did rewrite the sections dealing
with the New Lebanon Convention and his two old antago-
nists, but then the project stalled. Finney's friends wanted to
rush into print, but he remained uncertain about whether the
narrative should be published at all.

While Finney was turning down offers to publish his large
manuscript, in 1871 the New York *Independent* requested from
him "a rousing article . . . of a religious character." The editor
wrote, "What do you say to a brief account of the revivals of
thirty and forty years ago in which you took part, with the
natural 'application' to the needs of the church at the present
time." Rebecca Finney transcribed her husband's dictation of
several sermonic articles, one of which incorporated a story of
early Jefferson County revivals. These pieces appeared in *The
Independent* in 1872. Then the couple began work on a new
series entitled "Revival Memories." They completed three articles on the revivals at Gouverneur and Philadelphia, which
were published in early 1873. Several Baptist readers challenged Finney's accuracy, noting some discrepancies between
his account and the way they remembered events at Gouverneur, and this prompted him to write a number of letters to
old friends seeking corroboration of his information. He
wanted his narrative to be accurate, but the incident increased
his concern that if the larger work were published, his frank
portrayal of colleagues and contemporaries might produce hurt
feelings. The narrative remained in manuscript until the end of
his life. Indeed, the day before he died, he told Rebecca he
wanted her to burn it along with all the rest of his papers. She
did not do this. The fact that the New York *Independent* ran his
articles after he was eighty and publishers hounded him for his
autobiography indicated that there was still a market, and a
spiritual hunger, for Charles G. Finney.

James H. Fairchild finally edited and published Finney's

manuscript the year after his death, with the approval of his family and under the auspices of Oberlin College, as *Memoirs of Rev. Charles G. Finney, Written by Himself* (New York, 1876). Finney's narrative was certainly flawed by occasional factual errors, confusion about details, and his repetitive style, but it was a prodigious feat of memory and a magnificent interpretation of God's gracious activity in human history. The *Memoirs* achieved their chief purpose: the book helped to shape the new revivalism of the late nineteenth century, and it continued to influence evangelicals and evangelists well into the twentieth century.

Charles Finney's other major project after 1865 was less felicitous but every bit as revelatory of American evangelicalism. He and others, including the president of Wheaton College, Jonathan Blanchard, launched a renewed attack on the Masonic Order as a dire threat to evangelical religion and American democracy. As we have already noted, Finney had joined the lodge as a student in Connecticut and attended meetings as a young lawyer in Adams but resigned before his ordination to the ministry. He opposed the order at that time but did not take much of an active role in denouncing it during the period of the first national anti-Masonic movement in the late 1820s. But, following the Civil War, a new generation of men began joining the order, and Finney's concern was rekindled along with that of a number of other church leaders. In 1862 he published letters on the danger of Freemasonry in the New York *Independent*. He immediately received letters endorsing the effort, including one from an elderly upstate New York physician who wrote, "I was rejoiced to see one man who had the moral courage to step forward and expose the accursed institution."

Masons living in the Oberlin area formed a lodge in 1867, and the question of how Christians should view the secret order came before First and Second Churches when some of them applied for church membership. Finney said in his *Memoirs* — though the entire section was removed by editor James H. Fairchild as needlessly divisive — that he "dreaded to have the subject brought into the church, or anything said about it." Finney hoped that simply having the applicants read David Bernard's standard exposé, *Light on Masonry* (Utica, 1829), would convince them to renounce their affiliation, but he was disappointed to find them persisting both with lodge membership and their bid for membership in the church. A joint committee from the two churches issued proposals, and the congregations debated whether simply to condemn Freemasonry or to take the next step and bar Masons from membership. Finney was on his sickbed during much of the discussion, but he roused himself to preach in October and again in December on the subject. Although he attempted to approach the topic "in a Christian spirit" with some gentleness, he unequivocally branded the order as "immoral in its nature and tendency, and dangerous to government and to society." He was satisfied that "Christian people here, with very few exceptions, are entirely opposed to Masonry as a vile and evil institution." The two Congregational churches passed resolutions expressing this conviction, but in the end they did not take the next step and disqualify Masons from membership. Finney hoped that in practice they would be excluded on principle even without an explicit policy.

Finney entered the national movement against the Masonic Order by writing a series of articles for *The Independent* in 1868 which he then revised as a book, *Freemasonry: Its Character, Claims, and Practical Workings,* published the next year by the Western Tract and Book Society. He wrote the book "to arrest the spread of this great evil" and as a warning to the young men of America. "Forty years ago, we supposed that it was dead," he recalled, "and had no idea that it could ever revive. But, strange to tell, while we were busy getting rid of slavery, Freemasonry has revived, and extended its bounds most alarmingly." He told of his own experience in the lodge, reviewed the story of William Morgan, and recited the evidence for a Masonic conspiracy to control the United States. The main body of Finney's book was a detailed analysis of Masonic literature in which he argued that the order was antithetical to Christianity for a number of reasons: it involved "blasphemous oaths of loyalty," approval of bloody vengeance, the "perverse and profane use of the Bible," the propagation of "false historic claims," the financial "swindle" of members, and a "spurious and selfish morality." It amounted to a substitute church with "sacerdotal robes" and "pompous" rites, and promoted the "fatal delusion" of salvation by works rather than by faith in God's grace in Jesus Christ.

At first blush *Freemasonry* appears to be the retrograde product of an old man's bile, or at best a fanciful return to the battleground of young adulthood. Some of Finney's friends were embarrassed by the book. But Finney was not alone in his hostility toward secret societies. He was especially convinced that "there is nothing morally good in Freemasonry" by the fact that it diverted a man's attention and income from his wife and family. "It is really an insult to a wife for a husband to go and pledge himself to conceal from his wife that which he freely communicates to strangers." The flood of letters Finney received from women in appreciation of his book suggests that his crusade was at least partly an expression of his support for the movement for women's rights. One wrote in desperation, "They have my husband in their power!" At the same time, correspondence from evangelical leaders informed Finney of the founding of new anti-Masonic periodicals and organizations such as the National Christian Association, in which Oberlin College and church leaders participated. The fact that *Freemasonry* went through several printings in its first year and that Finney received more fan mail from it than from any of his other books indicates that here he touched a very sensitive nerve in American evangelicalism.

Charles Finney enjoyed an active correspondence in his late seventies. Invitations to preach continued unabated from the east and the west, though he could respond positively to none of them. When a convention devoted to opposition to secret societies was planned for Syracuse in 1870, Finney was invited to speak. The planners wrote, "You have an influence no other man who takes your position can have." Andover Seminary invited him to present a short series of lectures. A Hartford Seminary student praised God that, after praying for "a full salvation" and reading Finney's *Lectures on Revivals* and *Systematic Theology*, "the Pentecostal glory descended." Finney debated about contemporary preaching with the editor of *The Independent*, who argued, "You are utterly wrong in saying as you do that no minister will convert souls who preaches sermons only half an hour long." Letters arrived regularly from former Oberlin students expressing their love and admiration.

The National Council of Congregational Churches chose Oberlin's Second Church as the site for its first real meeting as a denomination, in November 1871. It was a notable event in the history of American Congregationalism, all the more remarkable for occurring at the college that had long been held in suspicion by many. Charles G. Finney, who had never cared for Presbyterian assemblies, remained aloof from the proceedings. Near the end of the gathering, however, the National Council turned its attention to President Finney. He spoke for an hour on the gift of the Holy Spirit, "Power from on High." Though it was a theme that had separated many of them from Finney in the past, the delegates were deeply moved by the sermon, and the reporter from *The Independent* raved. The following day Finney offered the prayer at the dedication of the new building for the theological seminary, named Council Hall in honor of the event. He rose to the occasion with a witty comment: "I have felt somewhat embarrassed with regard to performing this part of the service, because the house is not entirely finished. I have several times refused to take part in dedicating a house of worship that was not paid for; but this is neither finished nor paid for, and hence I have had some hesitation about offering it to God in this state. But I remember that I have often offered myself to God, and I am far from being finished yet, and why should I not offer this house just as it is?

Charles G. Finney in old age.
Photo courtesy of the Oberlin College Archives

I will do so, relying upon the determination of those having it in charge to finish it as soon as possible." At the end of the Council meeting, the moderator thanked God that prejudice against Oberlin had been buried.

Charles Finney was indeed not yet finished. He retired as pastor of First Church in May 1872, a few months short of his eightieth birthday, but he still preached from time to time as health permitted. He continued to publish sermons regularly in the New York *Independent*. He criticized the new liberalism of Washington Gladden and Henry Ward Beecher as an ineffectual, diluted version of the gospel and shook his head at Beecher's adultery scandal. At the age of eighty-two, Finney explored the possibility of writing an article condemning "the policy of our government in its treatment of the Indians." Also in 1874, in addition to answering scores of other letters, he engaged in an extended and serious correspondence with retired Williams College president Mark Hopkins on moral philosophy after reading his book "on doing the good." When the National Council of Congregational Churches reconvened at Oberlin that same year, the delegates rose to their feet in respect as Finney approached the pulpit once more. He taught his beloved pastoral theology course during the summer term, completing his last lectures in July 1875. That same month he preached once at each of Oberlin's Congregational churches. James H. Fairchild wrote in his conclusion to Finney's *Memoirs*, "He still stood erect, as a young man, retained his faculties to a remarkable degree, and exhibited to the end the quickness of thought, and feeling, and imagination, which always characterized him."

Even so, Charles Finney was preparing for the end of his earthly life. He wrote Lewis Tappan, "I pray you to forgive whatever in your judgment may have been amiss in my treatment of you, at any period of my life." Tappan replied, "I can truly say I heartily do, and ask the same of you in my own behalf. It would give me great pleasure to meet you again in this world, but if that be not the will of God, may we enjoy each other's society through a blissful eternity." He and Edward N. Kirk in Boston wrote one another with the simple request "Pray for me." Horace Bushnell — "coughing out my life" — thanked Finney for writing "with so much heart and Christian sweetness" on the comfort of faith. Finney also exchanged letters with Jacob Helffenstein in Philadelphia, who recalled "those precious seasons of refreshing we were permitted to witness in our early ministry" and added, "You and I are drawing near our eternal home. Let us be thankful for the past and hopeful for the future. . . . Our consolation is that God reigns and will plead his own cause."

Charles G. Finney died on August 16, 1875. James H. Fairchild wrote, "His last day on earth was a quiet Sabbath, which he enjoyed in the midst of his family, walking out with his wife at sunset, to listen to the music, at the opening of the evening service in the church near by." Rebecca, Julia and James, and Norton and Jenny sat with him. He suffered chest pains through the night, and by the morning he was gone.

The following summer, a host of former colleagues, students, and friends gathered at Oberlin to honor his memory. Speeches were given extolling Finney's power in the pulpit, the magnitude of his revivals, and his influence on the theological thought of many believers. In a fine memorial sermon, President Fairchild celebrated Finney's career-long theme of the life of obedience and benevolence. "It is impossible to fall within the range of such a life, without coming under higher obligations to God and to mankind." It was Professor John Morgan, for thirty-five years Finney's copastor and friend, who identified the essence of Charles G. Finney's evangelical spirit: "I think that all of us felt that his spiritual power was that in which he most excelled. . . . There was in him, in prayer, the most remarkable power that I have ever seen in any human being."

A Note on the Sources

The study of Charles G. Finney received new life in 1989 with the publication of the masterly Garth M. Rosell and Richard A. G. Dupuis edition of *The Memoirs of Charles G. Finney: The Complete Restored Text* (Grand Rapids: Zondervan, 1989). Scholars and general readers previously relied on the version edited by James H. Fairchild, Finney's successor as president of Oberlin College (New York: A. S. Barnes, 1876). Although this volume achieved wide readership and influence, Fairchild excised many details and, in places, substantial amounts of material from the manuscript. Often this was simply good editing, but at times Fairchild's efforts obscured an accurate picture of Finney and his relationship with people. The Rosell and Dupuis edition not only restores the text of the *Memoirs* as Finney left it but, with the use of different typefaces and extensive footnotes, provides a fascinating editorial history of the book itself. Rosell and Dupuis also provide full annotations on every person, place, and event mentioned in the text and a thirty-page bibliography of primary and secondary sources.

This is one of the finest modern critical editions available of a text by any historical figure and is both the alpha and omega of scholarly work on Finney.

The second source for understanding the life of Charles G. Finney is, of course, the body of his other published works. Finney's first publication was a pamphlet, *A Sermon Preached in the Presbyterian Church at Troy, March 4, 1827* (Troy, N.Y.: Tuttle & Richards, 1827). His first books were *Sermons on Various Subjects* (New York: John S. Taylor, 1835), which included the Troy sermon and which subsequently came out in an enlarged edition as *Sermons on Important Subjects* (New York: John S. Taylor, 1836), and *Lectures on Revivals of Religion* (New York: Leavitt, Lord, 1835). A modern critical edition of *Lectures* was edited by William G. McLoughlin (Cambridge: Harvard University Press, 1960). These works were followed with *Lectures to Professing Christians* (New York: John S. Taylor, 1837), which, like the revival lectures, first appeared as articles in *The New York Evangelist.* In 1838, Finney and his colleagues at Oberlin Collegiate Institute founded a periodical, *The Oberlin Evangelist,* in which he published numerous sermons, lectures, and letters over the years; it was here that he first put forth his teaching on entire sanctification. A series of Finney's articles in *The Oberlin Evangelist* from 1839 and 1840 have been reprinted in *The Promise of the Spirit,* ed. Timothy L. Smith (Minneapolis: Bethany House, 1980). Individual sermons were occasionally published in booklet form, as in the case of *The Sinner's Excuses Condemn God* (Oberlin, Ohio: James M. Steele, 1840; 3d ed., 1858). Finney's 1840 lectures in *The Oberlin Evangelist* were quickly gathered into book form as *Views of Sanctification* (Oberlin, Ohio: James Steele, 1840); this material was edited for modern devotional reading by Louis Gifford Parkhurst Jr. and published as *Principles of Sanctification* (Minneapolis: Bethany House Publishers, 1986). The first fruit of Finney's lectures to theological students at Oberlin in book form was *Skeletons of a Course of Theological Lectures,* vol. 1 (Oberlin, Ohio: James Steele, 1840).

Finney wrote an important series entitled "Letters on Revivals" for *The Oberlin Evangelist* from January 1845 through June 1846 that is now available in a modern edition, *Reflections on Revival,* ed. Donald Dayton (Minneapolis: Bethany House, 1979). Other Finney sermons and lectures from *The Oberlin Evangelist* from the 1840s, and some from the 1850s, have been published in an ambitious, extensive, and handsome paperback series incorporating the word *Principles* in the title by Bethany House of Minneapolis, but these have been rather heavily edited for devotional reading and in places are not true to the original versions. Finney published another collection of sermons on the theme of entire sanctification, *Guide to the Savior; or, Conditions of Attaining to and Abiding in Entire Holiness of Heart and Life* (Oberlin, Ohio: James M. Fitch, 1848).

Charles Finney's most formal presentation of his thought is in *Lectures on Systematic Theology,* vols. 2 and 3 (Oberlin, Ohio: James M. Fitch, 1846, 1847). Volume 1 never appeared, but it exists in outline form in the earlier *Skeletons.* Finney published responses to Charles Hodge and George Duffield, two conservative Presbyterian critics, in *The Reviewer Reviewed; or, Finney's Theology and the Princeton Review* (Oberlin, Ohio: James M. Fitch, 1847) and *A Reply to Dr. Duffield's "Warning against Error"* (Oberlin, Ohio: James M. Fitch, 1848). Finney revised his *Systematic Theology* while in England, and this edition (London: William Tegg, 1851) included these responses to Hodge and Duffield. James H. Fairchild edited and published an abridged version of the *Systematic Theology* (New York: George H. Doran, 1878), which was further abridged in a modern edition, *Finney's Systematic Theology* (Minneapolis: Bethany House Publishers, 1976).

During his second visit to the British Isles, Finney gave a lecture in Glasgow on the history of American revivals which was transcribed and published as *The Prevailing Prayer-Meeting* (London: Ward, 1859). The last book Charles Finney published in his lifetime was *Freemasonry: Its Character, Claims, and Practical Workings* (Cincinnati: Western Tract & Book Society, 1869).

Following his death, several collections of sermons were published: *Sermons on Gospel Themes* (Oberlin, Ohio: Goodrich, 1876); *Sermons on the Way of Salvation* (Oberlin, Ohio: Goodrich, 1891); and *An Earnest Appeal to Christians: Be Filled with the Spirit* (Boston, n.d.).

The third important source for Finney studies is the "Charles Grandison Finney Papers," collected in the Oberlin College Archives and on microfilm. Most of the items in the collection are letters to Finney and his wives, but there are also letters written by Finney and his wives as well as hundreds of sermon outlines and lecture notes. Also available in the Oberlin Archives are collections of letters received by Oberlin College (1832-1866), minutes of the Board of Trustees of the Oberlin Collegiate Institute (March 10, 1834–August 22, 1866), minutes of faculty meetings, and the records of the First Church at Oberlin. For a complete listing of extant primary source materials on Finney, see Rosell and Dupuis, *The Memoirs of Charles G. Finney,* pp. 671-78.

Several biographies of Charles G. Finney have been written since the evangelist's death in 1875. Biographical information is included in *Reminiscenses of Rev. Charles G. Finney: Speeches and Sketches at the Gathering of His Friends and Pupils, in Oberlin, July 28th, 1876, together with President Fairchild's Memorial Sermon, Delivered before the Graduating Classes, July 30, 1876* (Oberlin: E. J. Goodrich, 1876). See also Hiram Mead, "Charles Grandison Finney," *Congregational Quarterly,* January 1877, pp. 1-28; Helen Finney Cox, "Charles Finney," in *Lives of the Leaders of Our Church Universal* (Philadelphia: Presbyterian Board of Publication, 1879); James Brand and John M. Ellis, *Memorial Addresses on the Occasion of the One Hundredth Anniversary of the Birth of President Charles G. Finney* (Oberlin, Ohio: E. J. Goodrich, 1893); and William Cleaver Wilkinson, "Charles Grandison Finney," in *Modern Masters of Pulpit Discourse* (New York: Funk & Wagnalls, 1905). The first full biography appeared in the American Religious Leaders series, by Oberlin professor George Frederick Wright, *Charles Grandison Finney*

(Boston: Houghton, Mifflin, 1891). Most other published biographies are written in a devotional style bordering on hagiography. These include Frank G. Beardsley's *Mighty Winner of Souls: Charles Grandison Finney* (New York: American Tract Society, 1937); Basil W. Miller's *Charles Grandison Finney: He Prayed Down Revivals* (Grand Rapids: Zondervan, 1942); V. Raymond Edman's *Finney Lives On: The Man, His Revival Methods, and His Message* (New York: Fleming H. Revell, 1952); and Lewis A. Drummond's *Charles Grandison Finney and the Birth of Modern Evangelism* (London: Hodder & Stoughton, 1983). The first scholarly biography published since Wright's is Keith J. Hardman's *Charles Grandison Finney, 1792-1875: Revivalist and Reformer* (Syracuse, N.Y.: Syracuse University Press, 1987; reprint, Grand Rapids: Baker Book House, 1990). Hardman's study is extremely useful, though the careful reader will find countless instances where I differ from his portrayal of Finney — both in the description of events and the interpretation of his thought. The popularly written magazine *Christian History* published an issue entitled *Charles G. Finney: Nineteenth Century Giant of American Revivalism* (1988) that contains a number of insightful articles.

Leonard I. Sweet devotes two excellent chapters to Lydia and Elizabeth Finney in *The Minister's Wife: Her Role in Nineteenth-Century American Evangelicalism* (Philadelphia: Temple University Press, 1983). Sweet also wrote a seminal article entitled "The View of Man Inherent in New Measures Revivalism," *Church History,* June 1976, pp. 206-21. Other recent studies that deal with Finney's theology and influence include Nancy A. Hardesty's *Your Daughters Shall Prophesy: Revivalism and Feminism in the Age of Finney* (Brooklyn: Carlson, 1991); Glenn A. Hewitt's *Regeneration and Morality: A Study of Charles Finney, Charles Hodge, John W. Nevin, and Horace Bushnell* (Brooklyn: Carlson, 1991); and David L. Weddle's *Law as Gospel: Revival and Reform in the Theology of Charles G. Finney* (Metuchen, N.J.: Scarecrow Press, 1985). Among the doctoral dissertations written on Finney, see especially Marianne Perciaccante's "Calling Down Fire: Charles Grandison Finney and Revivalism in Jefferson County, New York, 1800-1840" (University of Virginia, 1992).

Indispensable to the study of Finney is Robert Samuel Fletcher's monumental work *A History of Oberlin College: From Its Foundation through the Civil War*, 2 vols. (Oberlin, Ohio: Oberlin College, 1943). An older history is Delavan L. Leonard's *Story of Oberlin: The Institution, the Community, the Idea, the Movement* (Boston: Pilgrim Press, 1898). See also John Barnard's *From Evangelicalism to Progressivism at Oberlin College, 1866-1917* (Columbus: Ohio State University Press, 1969). Interesting pieces of information that must be viewed with care can be found in early issues of the *Oberlin Alumni Magazine* and a small book by A. L. Shumway and C. DeW. Brower entitled *Oberliniana: A Jubilee Volume of Semi-Historical Anecdotes Connected with the Past and Present of Oberlin College, 1833-1883* (1883; reprint, Oberlin, Ohio: Oberlin College, 1983).

On the settlement of Ohio, see Harlan Hatcher, *The Western Reserve: The Story of New Connecticut in Ohio* (Indianapolis: Bobbs-Merrill, 1949), and George W. Knepper, *Ohio and Its People* (Kent, Ohio: Kent State University Press, 1989). For a fine book on the Oberlin "Rescuers," see Nat Brandt, *The Town That Started the Civil War* (New York: Laurel/Dell, 1990). On American education in general during the era of Finney, see Lawrence A. Cremin, *American Education: The National Experience, 1783-1876* (New York: Harper & Row, 1980).

The writings of a number of nineteenth-century religious leaders relate to the work and thought of Charles Finney. Among the most important (in chronological order) are *A Narrative of the Revival of Religion, in the County of Oneida, Particularly in the Bounds of the Presbytery of Oneida, in the Year 1826* (Utica, N.Y.: Hastings & Tracy, 1826); Ephraim Perkins, *A "Bunker Hill" Contest, A.D. 1826* (Utica, 1826); [William R. Weeks], *Pastoral Letter of the Ministers of the Oneida Association, to the Churches under Their Care, on the Subject of Revivals of Religion* (Utica, N.Y.: Ariel, 1827); Joseph Brockway, *A Delineation of the*

Characteristic Features of a Revival of Religion in Troy, in 1826 and 1827 (Troy, N.Y.: Adancourt, 1827); *A Brief Account of the Origin and Progress of the Divisions of the First Presbyterian Church in the City of Troy; Containing, also, Strictures upon the New Doctrines Preached by the Rev. C. G. Finney and N. S. S. Beman* (Troy, N.Y.: Tuttle & Richards, 1827); "Honestus," *Revivals of Religion, Considered as Means of Grace* (Ithaca, N.Y., 1827); "Philalethes," *The Importance of Revivals as Exhibited in the Late Convention at New-Lebanon, Considered in a Brief Review of the Proceedings of that Body* (Ithaca, N.Y.: n.p., 1827); Asa Rand, *The New Divinity Tried: Being an Examination of a Sermon Delivered by the Rev. C. G. Finney, on Making a New Heart* (Boston: Lyceum, 1832); [Benjamin Wisner], *Review of "The New Divinity Tried"* (Boston: Pierce & Parker, 1832); William R. Weeks, *A Letter on Protracted Meeings* (Utica, N.Y.: n.p., 1832); [Albert Dod], "Review of Finney's *Lectures on Revivals of Religion* and *Sermons on Various Subjects*," *Biblical Repertory and Theological Review,* July 1835, pp. 482-527 and October 1835, pp. 626-74; Samuel J. Baird, *A History of the New School, and of the Questions Involved in the Disruption of the Presbyterian Church in 1838* (Philadelphia: Claxton, Remsen & Hoffelfinger, 1868); Calvin Colton, *History and Character of American Revivals of Religion* (London: Westley & Davis, 1832); *Autobiography (to 1834) of George Washington Gale* (New York: privately printed, 1964); John W. Nevin, *The Anxious Bench* (Cambersburg, Pa.: Publication Office of the German Reformed Church, 1844), reprinted in *Catholic and Reformed: Selected Theological Writings of John Williamson Nevin,* ed. Charles Yrigoyen Jr. and George H. Bricker (Pittsburgh: Pickwick Press, 1978); [Charles Hodge], "Review of *Lectures on Systematic Theology,*" *Biblical Repertory and Theological Review,* April 1847, pp. 237-77; [George Duffield], *A Warning against Error, Being the Report of a Committee, Adopted by the Presbytery of Detroit* (Detroit: Willcox, 1847); *The Autobiography of Lyman Beecher,* ed. Barbara M. Cross, 2 vols. (Cambridge: Harvard University Press, 1961); *Autobiography of Peter Cartwright, the Backwoods Preacher,* ed. W. P. Strickland (New York: Carlton & Porter, 1856). On Horace

Bushnell and Finney, see Robert L. Edwards, *Of Singular Genius, of Singular Grace: A Biography of Horace Bushnell* (Cleveland: Pilgrim Press, 1992).

Scholarly studies of the Great Awakening of the early and middle eighteenth century form an important background for an understanding of nineteenth-century American revivalism. Most recent studies, in contrast to earlier works, treat the Awakening in the context of the international evangelical movement in America, Great Britain, and the Continent. The significant books include Patricia U. Bonomi's *Under the Cope of Heaven: Religion, Society, and Politics in Colonial America* (New York: Oxford University Press, 1986); Michael J. Crawford's *Seasons of Grace: Colonial New England's Revival Tradition in Its British Context* (New York: Oxford University Press, 1991); Leigh Eric Schmidt's *Holy Fairs: Scottish Communions and American Revivals in the Early Modern Period* (Princeton: Princeton University Press, 1989); W. R. Ward's *Protestant Evangelical Awakening* (Cambridge: Cambridge University Press, 1992); and Marilyn J. Westerkamp's *Triumph of the Laity: Scots-Irish Piety and the Great Awakening, 1625-1760* (New York: Oxford University Press, 1988). See also the volumes in the Yale edition of *The Works of Jonathan Edwards*, especially *Religious Affections*, ed. John E. Smith (New Haven: Yale University Press, 1959); *The Great Awakening*, ed. C. C. Goen (New Haven: Yale University Press, 1972); and *The Life of David Brainerd*, ed. Norman Pettit (New Haven: Yale University Press, 1985).

Two of my own articles address the continuities from Puritanism to the Great Awakening: "The Spiritual Pilgrimage of Sarah Osborn (1714-1796)," *Church History*, December 1992, pp. 408-21; and "The Spirit of the Old Writers: Print Media, the Great Awakening, and Continuity in New England," in *Communication and Change in American Religious History*, ed. Leonard I. Sweet (Grand Rapids: William B. Eerdmans, 1993), pp. 126-40.

Theological developments within the Congregational and Presbyterian churches from the time of the Great Awakening through the mid-nineteenth century are analyzed in several key books: Joseph A. Conforti's *Samuel Hopkins and the New Divinity Movement: Calvinism, the Congregational Ministry, and Reform in New England between the Great Awakenings* (Grand Rapids: William B. Eerdmans, 1981); Allen C. Guelzo's *Edwards on the Will: A Century of American Theological Debate* (Middletown, Conn.: Wesleyan University Press, 1989); Joseph Haroutunian's *Piety versus Moralism: The Passing of the New England Theology* (New York: Henry Holt, 1932); George M. Marsden's *The Evangelical Mind and the New School Presbyterian Experience: A Case Study of Thought and Theology in Nineteenth-Century America* (New Haven: Yale University Press, 1970); and Perry Miller's *The Life of the Mind in America: From the Revolution to the Civil War* (New York: Harcourt, Brace & World, 1965).

Revivalism as a distinctive feature of American religion has been the focus of a number of scholars for several generations. Classic works, in chronological order, include William Warren Sweet's *Revivalism in America: Its Origin, Growth and Decline* (New York: Scribner's, 1944); Bernard A. Weisberger's *They Gathered at the River: The Story of the Great Revivalists and Their Impact upon Religion in America* (Boston: Little, Brown, 1958); Timothy L. Smith's *Revivalism and Social Reform: American Protestantism on the Eve of the Civil War* (1957; reprint, Baltimore: The Johns Hopkins University Press, 1980); William G. McLoughlin's *Revivals, Awakenings, and Reform: An Essay on Religion and Social Change in America, 1607-1977* (Chicago: University of Chicago Press, 1978); and Iain H. Murray's *Revival and Revivalism: The Making and Marring of American Evangelicalism, 1750-1858* (Edinburgh: Banner of Truth Trust, 1994). For a good study of the music of evangelical revivalism, see Sandra S. Sizer, *Gospel Hymns and Social Religion* (Philadelphia: Temple University Press, 1978). See also Jay P. Dolan, *Catholic Revivalism: The American Experience, 1830-1900* (Notre Dame, Ind.: University of Notre Dame Press, 1978).

Historians, many of them evangelicals themselves, have recently undertaken the task of understanding the movement that has been so influential throughout American history and that, by the end of the nineteenth century, had come to include holiness, fundamentalist, and Pentecostal as well as broadly evangelical groups. Important studies include: *The Variety of American Evangelicalism*, ed. Donald W. Dayton and Robert K. Johnston (Downers Grove, Ill.: InterVarsity Press, 1991); George M. Marsden's *Understanding Fundamentalism and Evangelicalism* (Grand Rapids: William B. Eerdmans, 1991); *Evangelicalism: Comparative Studies of Popular Protestantism in North America, the British Isles, and Beyond, 1700-1990*, ed. Mark A. Noll et al. (New York: Oxford University Press, 1994); and *The Evangelical Tradition in America*, ed. Leonard I. Sweet (Macon, Ga.: Mercer University Press, 1984).

One can also fruitfully approach Finney and his era by exploring the relationship between religion and society in the early Republic and antebellum periods of the United States. The classic early works in this area are Whitney R. Cross's *Burned-Over District: The Social and Intellectual History of Enthusiastic Religion in Western New York, 1800-1850* (Ithaca, N.Y.: Cornell University Press, 1950); and Alice Felt Tyler's *Freedom's Ferment: Phases of American Social History from the Colonial Period to the Outbreak of the Civil War* (1944; reprint, New York: Harper & Row, 1962). Recent works include Jon Butler's *Awash in a Sea of Faith: Christianizing the American People* (Cambridge: Harvard University Press, 1990); Richard J. Carwardine's *Transatlantic Revivalism: Popular Evangelicalism in Britain and America, 1790-1865* (Westport, Conn.: Greenwood Press, 1978) and *Evangelicals and Politics in Antebellum America* (New Haven: Yale University Press, 1993); Mark Y. Hanley's *Beyond a Christian Commonwealth: The Protestant Quarrel with the American Republic, 1830-1860* (Chapel Hill, N.C.: University of North Carolina Press, 1994); Nathan O. Hatch's *Democratization of American Christianity* (New Haven: Yale University Press, 1989); Victor B. Howard's *Religion and the Radical Republican Movement, 1860-1870* (Lexington, Ky.: University Press of Kentucky, 1990); Curtis D. Johnson's *Islands of Holiness: Rural Religion in Upstate New York, 1790-1860* (Ithaca,

N.Y.: Cornell University Press, 1989); Paul E. Johnson's *Shop-keeper's Millennium: Society and Revivals in Rochester, New York, 1815-1837* (New York: Hill & Wang, 1978); Paul E. Johnson and Sean Wilentz's *Kingdom of Matthias: A Story of Sex and Salvation in Nineteenth-Century America* (New York: Oxford University Press, 1994); R. Laurence Moore's *Selling God: American Religion in the Marketplace Culture* (New York: Oxford University Press, 1994); Julius H. Rubin's *Religious Melancholy and Protestant Experience in America* (New York: Oxford University Press, 1994); and George M. Thomas's *Revivalism and Cultural Change: Christianity, Nation Building, and the Market in the Nineteenth-Century United States* (Chicago: University of Chicago Press, 1989).

On abolitionism and other reform movements, see Charles C. Cole Jr., *The Social Ideas of the Northern Evangelists, 1826-1860* (New York: Columbia University Press, 1954); Lori D. Ginzberg, *Women and the Work of Benevolence: Morality, Politics, and Class in the Nineteenth-Century United States* (New Haven: Yale University Press, 1990); John R. McKivigan, *The War against Proslavery Religion: Abolitionism and the Northern Churches, 1830-1865* (Ithaca, N.Y.: Cornell University Press, 1984); Leonard L. Richards, *"Gentlemen of Property and Standing": Anti-Abolition Mobs in Jacksonian America* (New York: Oxford University Press, 1970); Dorothy Sterling, *Ahead of Her Time: Abby Kelley and the Politics of Anti-Slavery* (New York: W. W. Norton, 1991); Ronald G. Walters, *American Reformers, 1815-1860* (New York: Hill & Wang, 1978); and Bertram Wyatt-Brown, *Lewis Tappan and the Evangelical War against Slavery* (New York: Atheneum, 1970).

Many books reconstruct for us a portrait of American society in the first half of the nineteenth century. Among the most helpful are Elizabeth Blackmar's *Manhattan for Rent, 1785-1850* (Ithaca, N.Y.: Cornell University Press, 1989); Paul Boyer's *Urban Masses and Moral Order in America, 1820-1920* (Cambridge: Harvard University Press, 1978); James MacGregor Burns's *Vineyard of Liberty* (New York: Alfred A. Knopf, 1982); Richard L. Bushman's *Refinement of America: Persons, Houses, Cities* (New York: Alfred A. Knopf, 1992); *Ante-Bellum Reform,* ed. David Brion Davis (New York: Harper & Row, 1967); Samuel Haber's *The Quest for Authority and Honor in the American Professions, 1750-1900* (Chicago: University of Chicago Press, 1991); Jack Larkin's *Reshaping of Everyday Life, 1790-1840* (New York: Harper & Row, 1988); Anne Norton's *Alternative Americas: A Reading of Antebellum Political Culture* (Chicago: University of Chicago Press, 1986); Lewis Perry's *Boats against the Current: American Culture between Revolution and Modernity, 1820-1860* (New York: Oxford University Press, 1993); Robert V. Remini's *Jacksonian Era* (Arlington Heights, Ill.: Harlan Davidson, 1989); Anne C. Rose's *Voices of the Marketplace: American Thought and Culture, 1830-1860* (New York: Twayne, 1995); Charles Sellers's *Market Revolution: Jacksonian America, 1815-1846* (New York: Oxford University Press, 1991); and Robert H. Wiebe's *Opening of American Society: From the Adoption of the Constitution to the Eve of Disunion* (New York: Alfred A. Knopf, 1984).

The political movements and elections of the antebellum period form another piece of the backdrop for the career of Charles Finney. Books that help illuminate this aspect of American life (in addition to Carwardine's *Evangelicals and Politics*, noted above) include Frederick J. Blue's *Free Soilers: Third Party Politics, 1848-54* (Urbana, Ill.: University of Illinois Press, 1973); Thomas Brown's *Politics and Statesmanship: Essays on the American Whig Party* (New York: Columbia University Press, 1985); Paul Goodman's *Towards a Christian Republic: Antimasonry and the Great Transition in New England, 1826-1836* (New York: Oxford University Press, 1988); Daniel Walker Howe's *Political Culture of the American Whigs* (Chicago: University of Chicago Press, 1979); Lawrence Frederick Kohl's *Politics of Individualism: Parties and the American Character in the Jacksonian Era* (New York: Oxford University Press, 1989); Arthur M. Schlesinger Jr.'s *Age of Jackson* (Boston: Little, Brown, 1945); William Preston Vaughn's *Antimasonic Party in the United States, 1826-1843* (Lexington, Ky.: University Press of Kentucky, 1983); and Harry L. Watson's *Liberty and Power: The Politics of Jacksonian America* (New York: Hill & Wang, 1990).

310

Index

THERE'S A ROAD TO EVERYWHERE EXCEPT WHERE YOU CAME FROM